Yale Publications in Religion, 17

AGAPE

An Ethical Analysis

by Gene Outka

New Haven and London, Yale University Press

1972

Copyright © 1972 by Yale University.
All rights reserved. This book may not be
reproduced, in whole or in part, in any form
(except by reviewers for the public press),
without written permission from the publishers.
Library of Congress catalog card number: 72–88070
International standard book number: 0–300–01384–1

Designed by John O. C. McCrillis
and set in Granjon type.
Printed in the United States of America by
The Colonial Press Inc., Clinton, Massachusetts.

Published in Great Britain, Europe, and Africa by
Yale University Press, Ltd., London.
Distributed in Canada by McGill-Queen's University
Press, Montreal; in Latin America by Kaiman & Polon,
Inc., New York City; in Australasia and Southeast
Asia by John Wiley & Sons Australasia Pty. Ltd.,
Sydney; in India by UBS Publishers' Distributors Pvt.,
Ltd., Delhi; in Japan by John Weatherhill, Inc., Tokyo.

To my mother,
Gertrude Elliott Outka,
and in memory of my father,
Harold Irvin Outka, 1902–1966

Contents

Acknowledgments

I was the fortunate recipient of a Rockefeller Doctoral Fellowship which permitted me to do basic research in theological literature during 1964–65. I am also extremely grateful to the American Council of Learned Societies for a Study Fellowship, to the Society for Religion in Higher Education for a supplemental grant as a Cross-Disciplinary Fellow, and to Princeton University for allowing me a leave during the academic year 1968–69, all of which made possible my spending that year in Oxford, England studying recent Anglo-American moral philosophy. The general stimulation afforded by lectures and discussions during that year is reflected in the following pages in ways too plentiful to mention and many of which I am doubtless unaware.

I owe a particular debt to five persons. Paul Ramsey gave many hours to an assessment of each chapter. John P. Reeder, Jr. also read and commented on the entire manuscript. James M. Gustafson supervised my dissertation on this general subject which was presented to the faculty of Yale University in candidacy for the Ph.D. degree in 1967. Basil Mitchell of Oxford discussed most of the ample revisions of the dissertation written during 1968–69. Carole, my wife, worked with me on a wide assortment of drafts. I would also like to thank a number of friends, colleagues, and graduate students in the Department of Religion, Princeton University, who read parts of the manuscript at one stage or another, including Anthony Battaglia, David Cain, Myron McClellan, O. M. T. O'Donovan, Theodore Ryan, and George F. Thomas. Finally, I am grateful to Jenny Alkire of the Press for her careful copyediting. The help received from all, named and unnamed, improved the final result to a sobering extent, for which I am deeply appreciative. Mistakes of substance and organization, and inelegancies of style were reduced considerably due to their counsel.

G. O.

Princeton, N.J.
March 1972

Introduction

Thou shalt love the Lord thy God with all thy heart, and
with all thy soul, and with all thy mind. This is the first and
great commandment. And the second is like unto it, Thou
shalt love thy neighbour as thyself. On these two commandments hang all the law and the prophets.

Matthew 22: 37–40

These verses have had an incalculable influence on Western culture.
They are perhaps still of serious interest to skeptics as well as to
believers. For whatever doctrines and ritual practices may be rejected, a certain general fascination and respect persists for the subject
of love in the sense of other-regarding care rather than personal acquisitiveness. Of course the second great commandment has not always been construed as a principle necessarily dependent on religious
belief or unique to religious ethics. Yet there does seem to be at least
a tenacious historical association with religious belief and ethics, and,
as is well known, a vast corpus within the Judeo-Christian tradition
on the entire subject of love has accumulated over the centuries.

I propose to submit a portion of this literature to analysis. The
literature I shall examine is a body of Christian theological writing
which dates roughly from 1930 to the present. It was in that year
that Anders Nygren first distinguished what he took to be two
radically different kinds of love. He so effectively posed issues about
love that they have had a prominence in theology and ethics they
never had before. His critics have been legion, but few have ignored
or been unaffected by his thesis. Thus, whatever the reader may think
of it, one may justifiably regard his work as the beginning of the
modern treatment of the subject. A vast amount of attention has
subsequently been given the problem by thinkers who have brought
to their task the most varied preoccupations and equipment. If one
is therefore to avoid becoming hopelessly lost in a very tangled discussion, it is necessary to apply restrictions to the number of writers
whose works can be examined in detail and to the method for such
examination. My own restrictions are as follows.

1. In chapters 1 through 6, I consider some of the major claims by a representative group of thinkers, both Roman Catholic and Protestant, selected roughly on the basis of importance and influence, representativeness, and cogency. Some of the figures (e.g. M. C. D'Arcy, Gérard Gilleman, Søren Kierkegaard,[1] Reinhold Niebuhr, Anders Nygren, and Paul Ramsey) receive more detailed attention than others (e.g. John Burnaby, Emil Brunner, Denis de Rougemont, Joseph Fletcher, Bernard Häring, Robert Johann, Paul Tillich, George F. Thomas, and Dietrich von Hildebrand). But in every instance this analysis is a sketch only, and I focus on the claims themselves rather than attempting to do full justice to any single thinker. Though such a sketch seems to me an indispensable preliminary, it must prove to some extent selective and arbitrary. Thus in chapter 7 I examine in much more detail one thinker, Karl Barth, having in mind the claims sorted out previously. Lastly, in chapter 8, I try to assess my findings.

2. My governing interest is in the ethical features of the literature under scrutiny. "Ethics," of course, is hardly an unambiguous restriction, even when we agree that generally it is concerned with the guidance of life. But it is more sharply defined when one adds: ethics primarily as treated in contemporary Anglo-American analytic philosophy. My objective is to bring badly-needed clarity to a theological literature which is confused as well as rich. I am convinced that the issues considered in such literature could properly benefit from studies which take more cognizance of recent work in Anglo-American moral philosophy. The benefit here envisaged is roughly of two kinds: overall organization of topics in ethical theory and comparison of certain more specific questions of substance. Concerning overall organization, philosophers broadly speaking have engaged in *normative* inquiries (about *what* is "right" and "good," as a general principle and/or in a particular case) and in *metaethical* ones (about the

---

1. Kierkegaard is the one exception to the twentieth-century confines of the study. He is included because his *Works of Love* has had influence largely in this century and, while the work has obvious affinities to Nygren's, it is more oriented toward specifically ethical matters and can therefore in part serve as a substitute for Nygren.

meaning and justification of normative judgments). For my purposes, the organization is as follows: an inquiry into love as a normative ethical principle or standard with perhaps unvarying meaning or
content (chapter 1); the relation of this standard to the two with
which it is most often compared and contrasted, namely, self-love and
justice (chapters 2 and 3); the application of the standard to judgments about conduct and character (chapters 4 and 5); the justification of the principle or standard (chapter 6). The latter metaethical
consideration, in the case of the literature in question, involves discussion of explicitly theological grounds for holding the principle.
I shall also offer points of specific comparison where this seems appropriate and possibly illuminating. Examples include the relation of
agape to utilitarianism and of eros to psychological egoism.

Nonetheless, to take cognizance of recent moral philosophy is not
to abandon the theological center of gravity. My attempt to focus on
the concerns actually present in the literature involved selection from
among the topics discussed by philosophers. Not all of the formulations and problems were equally applicable or illuminative. I have
tried to take the theological literature seriously, not approaching it
with a prearranged list of possible alternatives and then casting
around for illustrations. I wanted to allow the various writers to
speak for themselves as much as practicable. Finally, another sort of
selection was unavoidable: I have extracted the "ethical portions"
from works which are often more comprehensively theological — a
practice, it should be acknowledged in advance, that may lead to some
oversimplification.

I should also indicate further what I mean by analysis. To some
extent it involves simple description of actual usage of terms in the
literature. This description cannot be a matter of straightforward
tabulation, since the uses themselves are diverse and the meanings
often frustratingly obscure. But I have tried to elucidate some of the
major existent meanings.

Yet the literature is not sufficiently unified to allow an organization consisting purely of literal adherence to self-conscious and explicit usage. If only for the sake of coherence, the description has to
be systematized so that many of the headings and issues adduced go

beyond what is immediately apparent; thus at certain places I have employed new formulations. But their final purpose is still to clarify actual usage and to trace implications of such usage.

The determinative formal purpose of the study from beginning to end, then, is to examine existent material, not to construct my own theory of love, religious or otherwise. It seems to me no small matter to contribute in even a modest way to our understanding of what love has been taken ethically to be, rather than what it must be. (In any case, when a normative principle already set in a tradition is being considered, one may follow out implications or simply abandon the principle, but not just stipulate whatever meaning he pleases.) Nevertheless, I should emphasize one difference between the first seven chapters on the one hand, and the last chapter on the other. In the former, the focus remains almost exclusively on the major claims actually present in the literature. They are there to be discovered and are not imported. The final chapter is more exploratory and less reportive, in three interrelated ways. (1) I have tried to locate some of the most critical and unresolved issues. (2) Sometimes I have not only exhibited the features put forward but also followed out implications and consequently considered modifications. This is true, for example, in the case of both self-sacrifice and self-love. (3) I have identified and discussed further what seems to be the fundamental content of human agape or Christian love and some characteristic problems of such content. All of this is an exploration only; but I hope it may serve to tie some of the threads together, since unavoidably the earlier chapters introduce more problems than they discuss. For instance, the question of the connection between neighbor-love and self-love, sketched in chapter 2, is considered more fully in the concluding chapter.

In examining even a portion of literature on love we may find that the only thing certain authors have in common is the employment of the same word; and that such employment may obscure important conceptual differences. This need not disturb us unduly, but certainly it should serve to put us on our guard. Sometimes words like eros and "self-love" drift uncertainly between different concepts. Yet I have not assumed at the outset that all of the treatments I examine are like variations in a spectrum. There may be value in showing that in some instances the meanings are incompatible or simply un-related, however widespread the assumptions to the contrary because the same word is used. If the literature abounds in conceptual differences, these should be made clear and some of the reasons for them considered. It would be a mistake to suppose, however, that all of the authors examined only talk past each other or that major points at issue are not in fact isolable. Many of the disagreements are genuine; moreover, some of those which are not seem worth sorting out in their own right.

The current state of the discussion seems to me to require a study which is rather catholic in its range. Thus, I consider a number of traditional questions in ethics as these apply to the literature. One doubtless pays a price for this in that no individual subtopic can be explored as minutely as it deserves. But I think in this case it is better initially to walk with some deliberation around the whole territory. At a later date perhaps there may be opportunity for more localized and detailed examination. But in either case, I am convinced that many of the historic ethical concerns of the Judeo-Christian tradition have been encapsulated in the "love-language," and one ought to try to understand more clearly just what has been meant within that language.

1

The Content of Human Agape

Erotic love is determined by the object; friendship is determined by the object; only love to one's neighbour is determined by love. Since one's neighbour is every man, unconditionally every man, all distinctions are indeed removed from the object.

Søren Kierkegaard

What are the features most important for ethics which have been held to constitute Christian love or human agape as such? I shall begin with this question about basic normative content.[1] I am concerned about agape in its utmost generality, about the kinds of "material" or substantive content which it has been said to possess irrespective of circumstances. Such an inquiry is formally similar to the one philosophers have pursued in discussing, e.g., utilitarianism as an ultimate normative standard, criterion, or principle for judgments of value and obligation. Thus I shall defer consideration of some of the other major inquiries in ethics, such as the more specific applications of love to judgments of conduct and character (chapters 4 and 5) and the status and justification of the standard itself (chapter 6). In the literature under scrutiny a number of such proposed unvarying features may be distinguished, some of them heterogeneous; however, often the reader may find them compounded by a given author. I hope to locate the most recurrent ones, though there are too many complexities to make possible a full characterization.

The starting-point is obvious (given simply the two great commandments): agape identifies *for whom* someone is to have regard. Yet even here one immediately encounters difficulties, since it matters

---

1. I shall use the Greek word agape, because it is conspicuously prevalent in the New Testament and in current usage is almost uniformly the referent for any alleged distinctiveness in Christian love.

enormously whether the someone for whom I am to have regard is God or my neighbor. The distinctions are so clearly pronounced, and the subject matter falling under each so complex, that a restriction for the volume as a whole is required. The restriction is a practical one only. I shall concentrate on the claims about neighbor-love. A large price will be paid: some of the profoundest themes will remain unexplored. I shall, however, consider several of the ways love for God has been understood in relation to neighbor-love, both toward the end of this chapter and in the one on Barth.[2]

In the most minimal and platitudinous interpretation of neighbor-love, a man is to consider the interests of others and not simply his own. Others are to be regarded for their own sakes, for what *they* may want or need, and not finally because they bring benefits to the agent. Disputes arise around the nature and extent of such regard, especially in comparison with the self's own interests. Is it anything like enough to say that I ought to consider the interests of others and not simply my own? Instead of not simply, should I say equally? Or should I have a bias toward the interests of others? Or more strongly still, should I regard the interests of others rather than my own? This may in turn raise questions about self-giving and self-sacrifice. Is it here that one finds the quintessence of agape? If so, are there any limits, without recourse to another principle? Should I not merely attend to another's needs but also submit to his exploitation of me? Should I not only rejoice in his successes and suffer

---

2. Two additional reasons stand behind this practical restriction, though neither is free of objections. First, much Protestant literature reflects misgivings about direct love for God and transposes it altogether to neighbor-love. God is the basis more than the object of creaturely agape. Religious warrants for neighbor-love will be examined in the chapter on justification. For many, in the Catholic tradition in particular of course, such transposition will not do. I shall discuss this disagreement later. Second, it is sometimes suggested that the first great commandment asserts a *religious* obligation; the second a *moral* one. (See, e.g., William K. Frankena, *Ethics* [Englewood Cliffs, N.J.: Prentice-Hall, Inc., 1963], pp. 44–45.) Since my concern here is with ethical questions, concentration on the second clause is appropriate. There is something in this suggestion so far as ordinary language is concerned. Yet it raises difficulties, and many in the literature are not satisfied to limit the scope of morality in this way. I shall also indicate later some of the grounds for their dissatisfaction.

in his tragedies, but also be willing to surrender my own commitments and, if need be, my integrity and my life?

These are well-worn but notoriously difficult questions whose almost obstinate longevity among sophisticated and unsophisticated alike suggests how deeply they are felt and how inescapable they are in ethical reflection. The literature exhibits distinguishable and sometimes conflicting answers to them. In this first chapter I shall attempt mainly to identify those features most commonly said to characterize agape as an other-regarding principle; I shall then undertake to relate these more specifically to what is said about self-love and justice.

Equal Regard

The normative content most often accorded to agape as neighbor-love may be stated in summary fashion as follows. Agape is a regard for the neighbor which in crucial respects is independent and un-alterable. To these features there is a corollary: the regard is for every person qua human existent, to be distinguished from those special traits, actions, etc., which distinguish particular personalities from each other. I shall introduce each of the points separately, while recognizing that they are typically (and I think cogently) assumed to be correlative.

One may start with "regard." Minimally, as we have seen, the neighbor ought to be cared about for his own sake; there ought to be active concern for what *he* may want or need, and not for the sake of benefits to the self. The richness of the meaning of neighbor-regard is nicely exemplified in H. Richard Niebuhr's statement:

> Love is *rejoicing* over the existence of the beloved one; it is the desire that he be rather than not be; it is longing for his presence when he is absent; it is happiness in the thought of him; it is profound satisfaction over everything that makes him great and glorious. Love is *gratitude*: it is thankfulness for the existence of the beloved; it is the happy acceptance of everything that he gives without the jealous feeling that the self ought to be able to do as much; it is a gratitude that does not seek equality; it is

wonder over the other's gift of himself in companionship. Love is
reverence: it keeps its distance even as it draws near; it does not
seek to absorb the other in the self or want to be absorbed by
it; it rejoices in the otherness of the other; it desires the beloved
to be what he is and does not seek to refashion him into a replica
of the self or to make him a means to the self's advancement.
As reverence love is and seeks knowledge of the other, not by
way of curiosity nor for the sake of gaining power but in rejoicing and in wonder. In all such love there is an element of
that "holy fear" which is not a form of flight but rather deep
respect for the otherness of the beloved and the profound unwillingness to violate his integrity. Love is *loyalty;* it is the
willingness to let the self be destroyed rather than that the other
cease to be; it is the commitment of the self by self-binding will
to make the other great.[3]

For the present, as an introductory sketch, I wish to locate those
features depicted in Niebuhr's statement and in the literature generally
which give to "regard" its most distinctive and recurrent meaning.
Niebuhr's statement is representative in part because it accords to
love both a declaration of policy by the lover and a viewpoint about
the neighbor; both an agent-commitment and a recipient-evaluation.
The commitment concerns the agent's energies as directed toward the
other; the evaluation concerns the other toward whom the energies
are directed. In short, one ought to be committed to the other's well-
being independently and unalterably; and to view the other as irreducibly valuable prior to his doing anything in particular.

I do not mean that no restrictions of any kind are permitted, as if
the agent were conditioned neither by the limited number of neighbors with whom he has even remotely to do nor by the different interests of different persons. On the latter point, as I shall try to show,
some distinction is normally made between equal consideration and
identical treatment. I mean rather that agape enjoins an equal consideration that is independent of changes in the particular states of

3. H. Richard Niebuhr, *The Purpose of the Church and Its Ministry* (New
York: Harper, 1956), p. 35. Italics mine.

the other, and unalterable in that some attitudes toward the other are never set aside; on no conceivable occasion are they out of place. In Barth's words, agape means "identification with his interests in utter independence of the question of his attractiveness." [4] Independence connotes that the love in question does not arise from and is not proportioned to anything a given neighbor individually possesses or has acquired. It is based neither on favoritism nor instinctive aversion. Its presence is somehow not determined by the other's actions; it is independent both in its genesis (he need not know who I am) and continuation (he may remain my enemy). One ought to be "for" another, whatever the particular changes in him for better or for worse.

Similarly, agape involves permanent stability. The loyalty enjoined is indefectible; neither partial nor fluctuating. No conditional demand for compensation is licit. To regard someone as a neighbor, on this usage, is to preclude from the outset any specific judgment which signifies that he himself is expendable. No assessment of (say) his weakness or wickedness can ever lead one to ignore him as if he were some mere thing. Whatever a person does in particular never in itself qualifies or disqualifies him from such attention and care. Even when the agent does not approve of the other's behavior it still makes sense to talk of regarding him as worthwhile and caring about what happens to him. However, it is probably also the case that the agent will be disposed to stress the importance of the good things about the other's behavior rather than the bad. Yet a certain "cost" may sometimes follow such permanence. For example, among the effects of permanence talk about a "forgiving disposition" may properly come in. Forgiveness may be the cost of permanence in a situation of injury.[5] Whenever an injury threatens to sever the relation altogether, restoration may require forgiveness. More generally, permanence involves persistence in the face of obstacles and continued concern for another's welfare despite lack of personal benefit. Regard must not fall victim to certain kinds of injury, anxiety, and envy

4. Karl Barth, *Church Dogmatics*, IV/2, trans. G. W. Bromiley (Edinburgh: T. & T. Clark, 1958), p. 745.

5. Cf. R. S. Downie, "Forgiveness," *Philosophical Quarterly* 15 (April, 1965): 133–34.

when these revolve around a concern for one's own welfare. In these various ways then, some element of the agent's attitudes and actions is unalterable.

The corollary to such independent and unalterable regard is that the other is held to be irreducibly valuable. This typically means that (1) he is valued as, or in that he is, a person qua human existent and not because he is such-and-such a kind of person distinguishing him from others; and (2) a basic equality obtains whereby one neighbor's well-being is as valuable as another's. One way to formulate the distinction in (1) is to call those characteristics of a person qua human existent his generic endowments and those which constitute his being such-and-such a kind of person his idiosyncratic qualities and attainments.[6] One values the human being prior to his doing anything in particular which differentiates him from other men. At the most basic level there ought to be no exclusiveness, no partiality, no elitism. To admire one man and be outraged by another is to say nothing different about the first as human existent than about the second: the regard for each logically must extend to both in that, again, it does not arise from anything either of them individually possesses or has acquired. It is universal in that not a single person is to be excluded, though of course de facto not all come into range.[7] The "other" to

6. Cf. R. S. Downie and Elizabeth Telfer, *Respect for Persons* (London: George Allen & Unwin Ltd., 1969), esp. pp. 19–23, 74, 84–92. In the theological literature attention is largely confined to this kind of distinction. The relation between valuing human beings in a generic sense and valuing non-human things, for example, is rarely treated in detail. Generally the ancient Augustinian affirmation seems to be assumed: persons are to be loved or enjoyed as ends in themselves (*frui*) and things are to be used (*uti*).

7. Two modifications are sometimes placed on "universal." The first appears infrequently in the literature we are considering, but it does arise in the case of Barth and I shall consider it in that chapter. Occasionally Barth restricts the full expression of agape to the community of believers. The second modification is far more common. While the agent ought to regard all other persons affected by his actions, many hold that he ought not to regard *himself* as one of those whose well-being *he* is to value equally. And some philosophers distinguish altruism (I have a moral obligation to promote the interests of others but not my own) from universalism or ethical neutralism (I have a moral obligation to

be regarded in this generic sense therefore appears to mean anyone and everyone affected by the agent's actions. The evaluation of the other as of irreducible worth and dignity extends to everyone alike. Comparisons at the most basic level are also ruled out. One ought not, strictly speaking, to talk of superior and inferior neighbors, or of preferring one neighbor to another. Whatever differences obtain in the needs persons have in the realization of their well-being, the relative and appropriate satisfaction of such needs is equally valued. Hence in any moral judgment one starts off from a baseline of equality. One does not discriminate at the beginning among those affected by the action in question. Discriminatory judgments normally relate to actions involving the interests of several parties, where each neighbor is considered not just in himself but as a part of the "moral landscape" [8] of others.

It is necessary to choose a shorthand referent for the recurrent features described above. Naturally not all of the nuances will be adequately caught by a single phrase. I shall use "equal regard" to refer to the agent-commitment and neighbor-evaluation already noted. Whenever I use the phrase, then, I shall mean the regard which is independent and unalterable; and which applies to each neighbor qua human existent.

Naturally too there are characteristic and formidable difficulties with this normative content, some of which I shall discuss in detail in the last chapter. But for now let me try to put the above account in the language of Kierkegaard and see where he takes us. At one point he calls love "a characteristic by which or in virtue of which you exist for others." [9] As such it is both independent of changes in

promote the interests of all, including my own). For the time being, I shall take the universalism enjoined to refer at least to everyone else and leave open the question whether the self is likewise to be included. See W. G. Maclagan, "Self and Others: A Defence of Altruism," *Philosophical Quarterly* 4 (April, 1954): 109–27.

8. The phrase is Austin Farrer's in "Examination of Theological Belief," *Faith and Logic,* ed. Basil Mitchell (London: George Allen and Unwin, 1958), p. 16.

9. Søren Kierkegaard, *Works of Love,* trans. Howard and Edna Hong (New York: Harper and Brothers, 1962), p. 211.

the particular states of others and unalterable in that some other-regarding attitudes are never set aside. To show this, Kierkegaard contrasts neighbor-love with all those human relations (e.g., friendship and erotic love) which, he claims, are incurably susceptible to change not only in expression but also in fundamental character.

> You can also continue to love your beloved and your friend no matter how they treat you, but you cannot truthfully continue to call them beloved and friend when they, sorry to say, have really changed. No change, however, can take your neighbour from you, for it is not your neighbour who holds you fast . . . it is your love which holds your neighbour fast.[10]

What agape is minimally independent of, then, are particular attitudes and actions which constitute a *condition* for one's actively regarding him at all. So we are likewise told that love "abides," that it is limitless and unchanged, even if and when the object becomes changed. Its independence is unassailable precisely because it does not require reciprocity.[11] Its unalterability sometimes involves the hiding of a multiplicity of sins "in silence, in a mitigating explanation, in forgiveness." [12] It seeks a "victory of reconciliation" even when this means that the one who does not need the forgiveness offers the reconciliation.[13]

Kierkegaard's designation for the person as human existent is the *neighbor* and here no distinctions of any kind are permitted. Each

10. Ibid., p. 76.
11. Ibid., p. 228.
12. Ibid., p. 268.
13. Ibid., p. 310. References to such points could be multiplied, but I am concerned now only to note some basic moves. In any case, I cannot do justice here to the nuances of Kierkegaard's discussion. For further examples of his insight into moral perplexity, see "Has a Man the Right to Let Himself be put to Death for the Truth?" *The Present Age and Two Minor Ethico-Religious Treatises,* trans. Alexander Dru and Walter Lowrie (London: Oxford University Press, 1949); *Meditations from Kiergegaard,* trans. and ed. T. H. Croxall (London: James Nisbet and Company, Ltd., 1955), esp. pp. 49, 83, 135–36.

is like every other and when one has proper regard for any, one can be said to be regarding all.

> The category *neighbour* is just like the category human being. Every one of us is a human being and at the same time the heterogeneous individual which he is by particularity; but being a human being is the fundamental qualification. . . . No one should be preoccupied with the differences so that he cowardly or presumptuously forgets that he is a human being; no man is an exception to being a human being by virtue of his particularising differences. He is rather a human being and then a particular human being.[14]

Such a statement nicely illustrates the difference between generic sameness and idiosyncratic difference. Comparisons between neighbors are also ruled out whenever these threaten the independence of love from all particularizing differences. Kierkegaard attacks especially those sublime comparisons the agent may make between his love and that of someone else or when the agent compares his love with the particular deeds he himself has performed. Such comparisons undermine not only the essential equality between men[15] but also the unalterable character of the agent's own commitment.

> In comparison everything is lost; love is made finite and the debt something to repay just like any other debt, instead of love's debt having its own characteristic of infinitude. . . . The moment of comparison is a selfish moment, a moment which wants to be *for* itself; precisely this is the break, the fall — just as concentrating on itself means the fall of the arrow.
>
> In comparison everything is lost; love is made finite, the debt something to repay. Regardless of position, whether or not it

14. Kierkegaard, *Works of Love,* p. 142. Cf. p. 70.

15. Kierkegaard's understanding of the essential equality among persons will be considered further in chapter 6.

be the highest, love expects *by way of comparison* to get status in relationship to others' love or in relationship to its own achievements.[16]

So far Kierkegaard's formulations are widely representative of some major themes in the Christian tradition.[17] His further moves are in-

16. Kierkegaard, *Works of Love,* p. 178.

17. The summary offered here prior to considering Kierkegaard directly is mainly my own formulation. But I would argue that it summarizes the content most recurrent in a literature replete with substantive differences. Kierkegaard then, for our purposes, is considered because he sets out with exceptional clarity and force a content found repeatedly elsewhere. For other examples of those who accept various parts of this content (whatever their important differences in other respects, some of which will be examined), see Emil Brunner, *The Divine Imperative,* trans. Olive Wyon (Philadelphia: The Westminster Press, 1947), e.g., p. 115; Albert Dondeyne, *Contemporary European Thought and Christian Faith,* trans. Erran McMullin and John Burnheim (Pittsburgh: Duquesne University Press, 1963); E. Clinton Gardner, *Biblical Faith and Social Ethics* (New York: Harper and Row, 1960), esp. pp. 174–86; Bernard Häring, *The Law of Christ,* trans. Edwin C. Kaiser, 3 vols. (Westminster, Md.: The Newman Press, 1963), 2: esp. 351–88; Karl Hörmann, *An Introduction to Moral Theology,* trans. Edward Quinn (London: Burns & Oates, 1961), pp. 239–71; John McIntyre, *On the Love of God* (London: Collins, 1962); Anders Nygren, *Agape and Eros,* trans. Philip S. Watson (London: S.P.C.K., 1957); Paul Ramsey, *Basic Christian Ethics* (New York: Charles Scribner's Sons, 1950); Helmut Thielicke, *The Ethics of Sex,* trans. John W. Doberstein (New York: Harper and Row, 1964), pp. 20–98; Paul Tillich, *Systematic Theology,* 3 vols. (Chicago: University of Chicago Press, 1951–63), 1:280–82 and 3 passim, *Love, Power, and Justice* (New York: Oxford University Press, 1954), and *Morality and Beyond* (New York: Harper and Row, 1963); George F. Thomas, *Christian Ethics and Moral Philosophy* (New York: Charles Scribner's Sons, 1955). A representative Catholic statement is the following by Dondeyne: "There is, at the origin of Christian moral choice, a stable and unchanging vision. This is the constant and effective recognition of the great dignity of every human person, taken not only as an end in himself existing for himself, but also as a child of God, loved by God and called to possess Him. Christianity demands of Christians that this effective recognition, this constant and active preoccupation with the person and with everything that is necessary for his development, be the very breadth of their life, the unwavering inspiration of all their actions, the rule of their conduct everywhere and at all times" (p. 196).

I think it is also significant that several philosophical writings which explicitly characterize agape do so in accordance with much of this same content. See

creasingly subject to controversy, due in part to an uncertainty about just how exhaustive he intends them to be. I shall try to isolate at least the principal moves which he eloquently discusses, leaving open the question of the degree of his commitment to them. I think these moves taken together reflect one very persistent view in the tradition and this, above all, is what I wish to introduce here. I shall then be in a better position to locate lesser and greater departures.

Kierkegaard sometimes seems to attempt what might be called both a religious assessment and a psychological explanation of the human relations which are subject to change. Alterable relations involve dependence upon the other being such-and-such a kind of person rather than simple acceptance that he is a person qua human existent. And preference and partiality invariably express such dependence. I admit some persons to the inner counsels of my own mind and heart and exclude others, because they are insufficiently sensitive or do not share certain values, etc. Or I hope myself to be included in the counsels of those I esteem and am commensurately pleased or hurt when I am or am not. For Kierkegaard preferential relations such as friendship and erotic love are from the standpoint of agape inherently flawed, a state of affairs disclosed in the self's constant suspicion that the relation is not all it seems or ought to be, and that anything offered may not be requited.

> In this suspicion . . . lies hidden the anxiety which makes erotic love and friendship dependent upon their objects, the anxiety which can kindle jealousy, the anxiety which can bring one to despair.[18]

---

for instance W. G. Maclagan, "Respect for Persons as a Moral Principle," *Philosophy* 35 (July and October, 1960): 193–217, 289–305; Downie and Telfer, *Respect for Persons*. In the preface to the latter volume the authors claim that "we provide an analysis of the Judaeo-Christian concept of *agape*, and in general present in secular or humanistic terms a view of morality which is characteristically expounded by Judaeo-Christian thinkers" (p. 10). It is open to someone to question this claim at a number of points, while recognizing that the overlap whenever it occurs has largely to do with such content. Cf. also H. H. Price's account of unconditional love in Christian ethics in *Belief* (London: George Allen & Unwin, 1969), pp. 391–92.

18. *Works of Love*, p. 78.

The intractableness of suspicion is one of the psychological indications Kierkegaard cites to illustrate what is finally dominant in preferential relations: instead of regarding the other for his own sake, the self is moved by a secretly controlling interest in receiving affection in return, in acquiring some private benefit. This is why at times Kierkegaard can explicitly treat preferential love as reducible to self-love.[19]

This account of the dominant motive in preferential relations is significant in at least two ways for the content of neighbor-regard or agape. First, such regard appears to be a sufficient as well as necessary condition in the sense that *agape* only has reference to each person taken individually. It is altogether separate from the question of reciprocity (where, that is, some degree of mutual consciousness obtains). Kierkegaard suspects immediately that even an interest in a response reflects self-interested dependence upon the particular qualities of the object; nothing essential is lost if neighbor-regard is totally inconspicuous or meets with unrelieved ingratitude and hostility. A reciprocal relation such as friendship is not, say, the optimal internal fruition of neighbor-regard. Kierkegaard does more than distinguish the latter from the former, while allowing for at least some sort of concordat between them. He sees them as incompatible.[20] Incom-

19. "Christianity has misgivings about erotic love and friendship because preference in passion or passionate preference is really another form of self-love" (ibid., p. 65). I say "at times" because it is hard to determine how unqualifiedly Kierkegaard holds that (1) all preferential relations are always and without remainder reducible to self-love and (2) such relations furnish an exhaustive account of what finally governs every human relation other than neighbor-love. Thus it is difficult to be certain how far Kierkegaard propounds a version of psychological egoism to be discussed in chapter 2. Though there may be legitimate uncertainty, I think that Robert G. Hazo in his massive and often helpful study, *The Idea of Love* (New York: Frederick A. Praeger, 1967), has nonetheless gone wrong in *stressing* the possibility for Kierkegaard of a "natural" and "authentic benevolence" and contrasting the views of Kierkegaard and Nygren on this point (e.g., pp. 128, 268). Kierkegaard's preponderant emphasis appears to be on the *difference* between the most elevated "natural" love (even one involving sacrifice) and love "Christianly understood." See *Works of Love*, pp. 133–34.

20. "Confusion and bewilderment . . . develops when the defence amounts to this . . . that Christianity certainly teaches a higher love but *in addition*

patibility would seem to follow whenever one holds that there is one isolable and fixed dominant interest in preferential relations, that this interest is "self-love," and that such "self-love" is wholly and not just potentially or partly nefarious. Second, just as "self-love" effectively governs preferential relations, so its opposite, "self-renunciation," is taken as the quintessence of neighbor-regard.[21] Perhaps it is more accurate to say that self-renunciation or self-sacrifice is the only fully appropriate "temporal" embodiment or the inevitable "historical" manifestation of agape. To the extent that the preferential relations characterizing earthly life are governed by self-interest, it is the fate of agape to find an expression which is not accommodated to such governance. Speaking very cursorily, in the crucifixion of the one who was the paradigm of agape Kierkegaard believes we see depicted the final character of "earthly existence" as well as the quintessence of agape and the unceasing conflict between them. Every follower must expect a similar collision.

In the second part of this chapter I shall examine more closely the feature of self-sacrifice. Before doing so, however, I shall say something more about the content we have so far considered, and Kierkegaard's treatment of it. I want simply to introduce two questions which arise with great frequency.

The first question concerns the repeated distinction between regard for each neighbor qua human existent and the special traits, actions, etc., which distinguish particular personalities from each other. Does agape as equal regard allow one to distinguish between indiscriminate acceptance of and indentification with each neighbor and discriminate response to special traits and actions? The answer varies, as it turns out, depending on the sort of discriminatory judgment in question. Under discriminatory judgments about special traits and actions one has to distinguish at least between judgments determining the *character* of the relation as such and those pertaining to fitting *expressions*. Agape prohibits discriminatory judgments where these de-

---

praises friendship and erotic love. To talk thus is a double betrayal — inasmuch as the speaker has neither the spirit of the poet nor the spirit of Christianity" (ibid., p. 59).

21. "Wherever Christianity is, there is also self-renunciation, which is Christianity's essential form" (ibid., p. 68).

termine whether the other is to be cared about at all, but it allows
and perhaps requires that he be cared about appropriately. In the
latter case diverse assessments and actions may be in order or are
in any case unavoidable. I observed earlier that such diverse assessments normally also relate to the interests of several parties, where
someone is considered not just in himself but as part of the moral
landscape of others. In short, equal consideration is not the same as
identical treatment. Agape requires the former, but not always the
latter.

To grant such a distinction means that not all judgments about
special traits and actions can be lumped under preferential relations
as these are treated by Kierkegaard (whether or not one accepts entirely Kierkegaard's account of what governs such relations). There
is nothing like equivalence. Kierkegaard's own awareness of a difference is indicated in the following statement:

> This love is not proudly independent of its object. Its equality
> does not appear in love's proudly turning back into itself, in-
> different towards the object. No, its equality appears in love's
> humbly turning itself outwards, embracing all, yet loving every-
> one in particular but no one in partiality.[22]

"Loving everyone in particular" presumably involves acting in diverse
ways appropriate to the individual needs of each object. There is then
for Kierkegaard a way to distinguish legitimately between indiscriminate acceptance and identification, and discriminate response.
He insists, moreover, on concreteness: the task is to remain in the
"world of actuality," to love particular individuals and thereby attend
to their distinctive strengths and corruptions.[23] "No one in partiality"
signifies that my actions toward another must not be arbitrarily
restricted in scope or governed finally by his importance for my own
interests — by, that is, the features constituting preferential relations
as Kierkegaard treats them. So far, so good. Yet the connections between agape and various special relations are, I think, more com-

22. Ibid., p. 10.
23. Ibid., pp. 159–61.

plicated than his view about preference suggests, and obviously are not all accommodated by allowing in general for differential treatment. One of the characteristic problems for agape as equal regard is its connection to special *moral* relations, a subject to be discussed in chapter 8.

The second question has somewhat more to do with the nature of agent-commitment as well as neighbor-evaluation and especially with the agent's response to moral evil. Does agape as equal regard in itself allow for any way to differentiate between attention to another's needs and submission to his exploitation, and any warrant for resisting the latter? Let us call this the question about the blank check.

I alluded earlier to the lesser and more extreme ways in which self-interest can be contrasted to a regard of the neighbor for his own sake. One can find references in the literature, particularly among those who stress self-sacrifice, to something approaching indiscriminate self-abnegation.[24] All judgments which involve self-interest, or even attempt a distinction between, e.g., acceptance and permissiveness, are consigned to some non-agapeistic realm (which can, of course, be variously characterized). Most writers, however, do not go this far, and among those who do not is, a little surprisingly and perhaps not always consistently (in the light of his stress on self-renunciation), Kierkegaard himself. Though they are often run together, I think one can identify three different reasons which recur in the literature for drawing back in the name of agape from the issuing of a blank check. The first reason is explicitly proposed by Kierkegaard, the second he virtually ignores, the third he considers in part.

However difficult to apply in practice, *for the sake of the neighbor* one may have to resist his exploitation as well as attend to his needs. It is one thing to say I ought to regard the interests of another more than or even rather than my own. It is another to say that such

24. Nygren, for instance, approvingly describes Luther's passion to eliminate any interest in "success in the end," rational calculation, hesitancy, or reservation. Agape is "a lost love," *eine verlorene Liebe*. It does not cease even when there is clearly impending betrayal and failure, when nine out of ten lepers fail to return to give thanks, when it is thrown away and forgotten. No attempt is made to distinguish between real and spurious need (*Agape and Eros*, pp. 731–33).

regard is tantamount to a wholesale surrender to whatever the other's interests happen to be. Kierkegaard speaks of a "misplaced caressing indulgence" and contrasts it with the "earnestness" of neighbor-regard which, while never terminating the relationship, can seek the neighbor's good only by actively striving against particular weakness and turpitude.[25] Otherwise the other is not being loved appropriately. How one executes such a policy in practice obviously depends on the sorts of things in which one estimates his good consists. One may, for instance, stress the importance of the other's need for psychological stability and security and withhold certain truths from him when one has good reason to suppose they might seriously threaten such security. Or alternatively, one may think that his dignity as a responsible agent involves a policy of non-deception, even in the hardest cases, and it is preferable to risk an unwanted diminution in security (for at least the matter will not be decided for him) than be condescendingly protective. Such perplexities need not be pursued now. The point is simply that one very general way in which the principle of equal regard has been understood to allow for a distinction between attention to needs and submission to exploitation has involved a reference to the good of the neighbor himself.

The second reason is a complication of the first. Many (including Kierkegaard) are inclined to neglect the distinction between the treatment of someone else in relation to the self, and the treatment of someone else in relation to still another (or others) than the self. As a consequence, they often fail to give sufficient attention to the moral dilemmas peculiar to the latter case, precisely where many of the most difficult moral problems arise.[26] And if the "good of the

25. "One does not become alien to the other person because of his weakness or his error, but the union regards the weakness as alien, and to both it is equally important that this be conquered and removed. . . . As soon as the relationship is made ambiguous, you do not love the person you see; it is indeed as if you demanded something else in order to be able to love. On the other hand, when the fault or weakness makes the relationship more inward, not to entrench the fault but to conquer it, then you love the person you see" (*Works of Love*, p. 164).

26. W. G. Maclagan, "Respect for Persons," pp. 196–97; Farrer, "Examination of Theological Belief," pp. 15–16.

neighbor" justifies certain kinds of resistance in a self-other relation, this is more obviously and yet complexly the case in "other-other" relations. Indeed, some have held that while agape may not permit resistance to, say, an act of aggression against the self, it does lead to such resistance on behalf of others; to, for instance, a "preferential ethics of protection" for innocent third parties.[27]

A third reason concerns the self rather than others. Despite Kierkegaard's usual concentration on self-love as altogether nefarious, occasionally one comes across passages in which he does speak of a proper or justified self-love.

> When the frivolous person throws himself, almost like a nonentity, into the folly of the moment, is it not because he does not understand how to love himself rightly? When the melancholic dejectedly desires to be rid of life, of himself, is this not because he will not learn earnestly and rigorously to love himself?[28]

Just as the neighbor must be regarded as a human being prior to a particular human being, so even the self must value itself in the same way. "The law is, therefore: you shall love yourself in the same way as you love your neighbour when you love him as yourself." [29] At a minimum, then, whatever pertains to a person's "thatness" and not his "suchness" applies to the self as well. This point is treated in cryptic and somewhat obscure fashion by Kierkegaard (and I shall not be directly concerned about self-love until chapter 2), but even the occasional references reflect a persistent effort in the literature to distinguish some sense of "self-identity," "self-respect," and so on, from "selfishness." In Kierkegaard's case, for instance, it has been argued that he refers to self-love in two senses: "false self-love" as egocentric possessiveness to be condemned, and "true self-love" as

---

27. See, e.g., Paul Ramsey, *Basic Christian Ethics,* esp. pp. 165–84, 326–66; also *War and the Christian Conscience* (Durham, N.C.: Duke University Press, 1961); *The Just War Force and Political Responsibility* (New York: Charles Scribner's Sons, 1968).
28. Kierkegaard, *Works of Love,* p. 39.
29. Ibid.

one's own theocentrically-determined task to be pursued whatever the consequences.[30] Hence frequently "self-love" has several meanings which have to be clarified before one can determine the nature and extent of substantive as contrasted with verbal disagreements. My immediate concern, however, is only with the way a "proper" sense of self-regard sometimes provides a third general agapeistic reason for distinguishing attention to needs from submission to exploitation. Kierkegaard seems to confine "loving one-self rightly" to an internal assessment where the self struggles against hypocrisy and superficiality, and toward obedience to providential guidance in his own case; and he does not expressly link it to responses to others. But one possible extrapolation is that if whatever characterizes my being a human person as such falls under equal regard, this may justify resistance to certain kinds of demands and encroachments.

I shall return to these areas *inter alia*. But first some other features must be introduced.

Self-Sacrifice

Earlier, when considering Kierkegaard's treatment of self-renunciation or self-sacrifice, I said that often this feature appeared as the inevitable historical manifestation of agape insofar as agape was not accommodated to self-interest. Perhaps the figure who has taken up most explicitly and influentially self-sacrifice as the quintessence of agape is Reinhold Niebuhr.

In the following passage Niebuhr states a contention, which he often reiterates, that "disinterested" love will inevitably end in self-sacrifice in this life.

The perfect disinterestedness of the divine love can have a counterpart in history only in a life which ends tragically, because it refuses to participate in the claims and counter-claims of historical existence. It portrays a love "which seeketh not its own." But

---

30. Valter Lindström, "A Contribution to the Interpretation of *The Works of Love,*" *Studia Theologica* 6 (1952): 3–6. See also N. H. Søe, *Christliche Ethik,* 3d ed. (München: Chr. Kaiser Verlag, 1965), pp. 136–40.

a love which seeketh not its own is not able to maintain itself in historical society. Not only may it fall victim to excessive forms of the self-assertion of others; but even the most perfectly balanced system of justice in history is a balance of competing wills and interests, and must therefore worst anyone who does not participate in the balance.[31]

It should be observed at once that this passage reflects a central characteristic common to many treatments of self-sacrifice, which will determine my initial inquiry here, namely: as a concept, self-sacrifice is not as isolable as equal regard. Its meaning and point, the sense in which it is historically inevitable, are located by reference to that (e.g., "competing wills and interests") with which it is compared and usually contrasted. At the same time, it often constitutes the effective criterion for appraising these same wills and interests. The term "self-sacrifice" possesses a welter of possible meanings which, unfortunately, are not very precisely considered in and of themselves by Niebuhr or in the literature at large. Thus it seems wisest to begin inductively and attempt to locate in a rough way the meaning he appears to assign it. I shall sketch the context in which his meaning is almost invariably discussed, i.e., the comparison between self-sacrifice on the one hand and self-love, self-assertion, and the like on the other, together with all the accompanying references to contending wills and interests. Later on I shall inquire whether the comparative lack of isolability reveals something problematical about the feature of self-sacrifice. But for the moment I must turn directly to his own formulations.

A view of disinterested love as utterly independent of the claims and counterclaims of historical existence implies first, that the normative content has a necessarily ideal, i.e., in this case eschatological, reference; and second, that a certain appraisal follows concerning the moral judgments which take into account the claims and counterclaims. I shall consider both implications of such independence be-

31. Reinhold Niebuhr, *The Nature and Destiny of Man,* 2 vols. (New York: Charles Scribner's Sons, 1949), 2:72.

fore examining how agape is likewise positively related to historical existence.

Niebuhr's characterization of the ideal content is curiously fragmentary, almost as if he assumes its self-evidence. On occasion he does affirm that "ultimately" it involves a state of "frictionless harmony," and at such points he shifts the center of gravity somewhat, placing greater emphasis on a concordant relation between selves and less on sacrifice as a property or quality of the self's own attitudes and actions.[32] Yet he never dwells on such affirmations. For he is preoccupied with what occurs in the confrontation between the ideal and the multiple claims and interests of this life (in both personal and especially socio-political relations). The problem of how to specify the ideal content of, roughly, frictionless harmony does not seem a difficult one to Niebuhr. In addition to citing scripture, he appeals — rather sweepingly and vaguely — to the requirement of our intellects for order and consistency, and to a more elemental and diffuse sense of what he considers our deepest and most worthy aspirations. For instance, "Man knows both by experience and by the demand for coherence in his rational nature, that life ought not to be lived at cross purposes, that conflict within the self, and between the self and others, is an evil." [33] The task he does find exceedingly difficult is to relate such content to all the moral judgments which must attend to claims and interests that are manifestly seeking their own and endlessly resulting in conflict. One thing seems clear to Niebuhr: we cannot attempt straightforwardly to apply the ideal to these judgments. "It is impossible to construct a social ethic out of the ideal of love in its pure form, because the ideal presupposes the resolution of the conflict of life with life." [34] The closer one comes to such

32. See, e.g., ibid., pp. 78, 81, 95–97.

33. Ibid., pp. 81–82. Cf. the following statement: "The sense of harmony belongs to all the communications of love. In their moments of greatest passion men and women feel this oneness with each other. . . . A single rhythm . . . creates a unity between their bodies, their senses, their instincts, and their emotions" (Irving Singer, *The Nature of Love: Plato to Luther* [New York: Random House, 1966], p. 237).

34. Harry R. Davis and Robert C. Good, eds., *Reinhold Niebuhr on Politics* (New York: Charles Scribner's Sons, 1960), p. 136.

judgments, therefore, the more the ideal is placed in jeopardy. But if there cannot be frictionless harmony then friction may at any rate be mitigated by self-sacrifice, and the latter accordingly appears as the purest expression possible in a world of vying interests.

It is essential to observe how in this way the feature of self-sacrifice frequently becomes the effective criterion for appraising the character of claims and interests. Niebuhr's very terms for such appraisal follow naturally and perhaps inevitably. Claims and interests are *tainted* by self-seeking and attending to them is a *compromise* of the ideal. Even the personal relations of mutual love, when they are not replenished by a heedlessness about self-interest, involve a *calculation* of reciprocal advantages threatening always to degenerate "first to the cool calculation of such advantages and finally to resentment over the inevitable lack of such advantages in all actual relations." [35] The ideal places the calculation of interests in a kind of shadow-realm enclosed by final resignation, where there are importantly different variations of gray shading toward black, but where all is nonetheless restricted to something less than the content of ideal agape.

If, then, the ideal is to remain the ideal, one must accept that it cannot be straightforwardly applied to the world of contending interests and claims. Hence other ethical principles may be necessary, which, while compromises with sacrificial love, are more directly applicable, e.g., justice. Let us now say something more about that world itself, its moral possibilities and requirements. Niebuhr speaks repeatedly but usually imprecisely about the greater "historical justification" or "historical validation" of the ethical principles which in themselves are compromises of the ideal. He seems to refer to consequences assessed by this-worldly criteria. Perhaps he has in mind results intelligible from every angle and point of view, for the sake of societal viability and the fostering of a "tolerable peace" and a "tolerable justice." Behind his contention that the ideal itself cannot be fully justified historically (as this pertains to clarifying the content), one can detect two distinguishable but closely related points.

(1) The world of contending interests and claims is always only

35. Reinhold Niebuhr, *Faith and History* (New York: Charles Scribner's Sons, 1949), p. 185.

partly corrigible to the "strategy of the Cross"; the effects of that strategy involve no guarantee that the forces acted upon will be brought into complete congruency with the ideal. If one is not to relinquish the ideal content, therefore, one must allow for the permanent possibility that the harmony sought is unrealized, and that any attendant suffering and forgiveness in this life may, from the point of view of discernible effects upon others, simply fail.

My point . . . is that the whole of modern culture tries too desperately to contain the ultimate within the fragmentary tasks and possibilities of history. I have never criticized a statesman for responsibly seeking to maintain a tolerable peace or establish a tolerable justice. I have criticized the Christian perfectionist who either claimed that these tasks could be accomplished more perfectly by the "love method" or who have sought to prove that their love was "perfect," even if they had to disavow responsibilities to preserve its perfection. I have never insisted on a sharp distinction between sacrificial and mutual love, that is, between the love which is, and which is not, reciprocated and historically justified. I have only criticized the tendency to identify these two facets of love completely, so that the New Testament ethic is reduced to the limits of a prudential ethics, according to which we are counselled to forgive our foe because he will then cease to be our foe; and are promised that if suffering love becomes sufficiently general it will cease to be "suffering" and change society into a harmony of life in which no one need suffer.[36]

(2) The world of contending interests and claims requires its own body of moral principles and judgments which (often in addition to reflecting in some measure the inordinate self-interest of groups in power) are legitimately designed to foster a "tolerable peace" and "tolerable justice"; and from the standpoint of such principles and

36. Reinhold Niebuhr, "Reply to Interpretation and Criticism," *Reinhold Niebuhr,* eds. Charles W. Kegley and Robert W. Bretall (New York: The Macmillan Company, 1961), p. 442.

judgments the ideal is not entirely intelligible or explicable. This is not all there is to say, for Niebuhr does argue that sacrificial love furnishes a perhaps indispensable "support" for "historical ethics" in a way I shall examine presently. Moreover, the principles and judgments themselves, "the nicely calculated more and less," cannot responsibly be avoided, and he nowhere argues that the believer or anyone else ought to try. For the sake of survival and tolerable social conditions, ethical principles such as justice quite properly serve to adjudicate between conflicts of interest which are an inevitable part of communal existence. Presumably he would see moral language itself as an essential tool for societal viability. It is also urgently important to recognize that there are significant relative differences in the kind and amount of historical good appropriate and attainable and that clarity about ideal content ought not to obscure the need for moral judgments weighing these differences. In his debate with certain pacifists prior to America's entry into World War II, for instance, Niebuhr protested what he took to be a perfectionism that waxed hot and cold, beginning with inappropriately rigorous demands and ending in indiscriminate moral cynicism.[37] But after serious allowance is made for the legitimacy of principles like justice and the vital importance of the relative degrees of good historically achievable, none of this exhausts the meaning of agape. For if the business of an ethical principle such as justice is to adjudicate between conflicting interests, then an ideal which "presupposes" the resolution of conflict can hardly be made fully intelligible in terms of the work of adjudication.

Standing behind Niebuhr's general account of agape and its relation to contending interests and claims is a complex set of doctrines about the self. I cannot do more here than make the barest allusion to them. At the beginning of this section I said that the normative content had a necessarily ideal, in the sense of eschatological (or "otherworldly"), reference. This reference is due in part, in Niebuhr's view, to the self's ability to rise in "indefinite transcendence" over its natural and historical conditions — an ability which points toward

37. An eloquent example is Reinhold Niebuhr, "An Open Letter (To Richard Roberts)," *Love and Justice,* ed. D. B. Robertson (Philadelphia: The Westminster Press, 1957), pp. 267–71.

its final longing for God. The self cannot "complete" itself in history; it can conceive of an "integrity of spirit which has validity in 'eternity'" and thus of devotions and gains which cannot be contained within the usual canons of historical success but which are finally specifiable only eschatologically.[38] Without stopping to ask about the cogency of this view of the self or its intellectual antecedents (which do, however, most emphatically include Kierkegaard), I shall only observe that for Niebuhr it provides the matrix within which agape is made applicable to the sublimest levels of human experience: not exhausted, as justice, etc., seem to be, by "the fragmentary tasks and possibilities of history." Niebuhr is especially unyielding on the fragmentariness; horrendous mistakes have been made in the twentieth century, he thinks, by expecting too much of our socio-political life and minimizing the worth of what is actually achievable. Life in "historical society" has its limits to which men must be returned repeatedly, and the limits determine our workaday moral principles. Apart from religious belief,

> the ethical life of man is always haunted by the skeptical reflection that "a living dog is better than a dead lion," which is to say that all moral imperatives are limited by the survival impulse which lies at the foundation of historical existence.[39]

It would be misleading to suppose that historically sacrificial love is altogether supererogatory. Once one recognizes that agape will never be progressively realized to the point where all contradiction between it and "competing wills and interests" is removed, one can then go on to state the historical role it does play. What has previously been said about the important relative degrees of historical good appropriate and attainable would imply (correctly) a denial that men in their personal or social life are thoroughgoing egoists. Their self-seeking is typically inconsistent and incomplete, hardly the product of a deliberate and carefully-considered policy.

38. Niebuhr, *Nature and Destiny of Man*, 2:75; *Faith and History*, pp. 174–75.
    39. Niebuhr, *Nature and Destiny of Man*, 2:76.

Yet it might become a consistent policy, except for the ameliorative effects of sacrificial love. Niebuhr contends that all the highest personal relations of mutual love and social conditions which may be called just tend — under the pressures of egoism, without the "pull" of sacrificial love upon them — to degenerate into something less than themselves.[40] While this is a favorite theme of his, it must be said that he asserts the significance of such a "pull" far more often than he demonstrates it. I think his most convincing attempt at the latter is to refer to sacrificial love as a kind of psychological requirement for the de facto *capacity* to identify seriously and continuously with the interests of others. It is simply the case, he thinks, that the vast majority of men are disinclined to give equal weight to the interests of all parties in various situations of moral choice. In order that such natural self-seeking may not degenerate into settled egoism, Niebuhr believes some sacrifice or at any rate suspension of one's own interests is required. For only then is one able *imaginatively to identify* with the needs of other persons or groups. A person with this ability is far more disposed to recognize the inordinately self-interested character of most human claims, including his own. Such awareness fosters humility and a sense of contrition, which in turn liberates him from the need to rationalize his own interests and permits him to acknowledge the partial justice and legitimate needs of even those whose claims are directly antithetical to his own.[41] Agape then apparently enables man not only to counter inordinate self-seeking, but also to identify with others so as to acknowledge their just claims.

On occasion we also confront here one of the historical ironies of which Niebuhr is so fond. Those agents who most effectively achieve the greatest amount of good possible in a situation may be the ones who do more than simply identify with others, who believe in the illusion of a perfect realization of agape in this life. The uninitiated or spontaneous movements of sacrificial love, in their radical and utopian proponents, may overcome obstacles that seem hopeless to more cautious and "realistic" spirits. Eschatological visions and aspirations

40. Niebuhr, *Faith and History*, p. 185.
41. Ibid., pp. 186–87.

are in this way of enormous benefit to historical society. But the "sublime madness in the soul" which they generate, while sometimes effecting more good than its prosaic detractors think possible, is nonetheless potentially pernicious and destined always to achieve less than it hopes.

> Nothing but such madness will do battle with malignant power and "spiritual wickedness in high places." The illusion is dangerous because it encourages terrible fanaticisms. It must therefore be brought under the control of reason. One can only hope that reason will not destroy it before its work is done.[42]

Anyone who attempts, as Niebuhr does, to hold together dialectically an ideal of heedless self-sacrifice (or at least an ideal leading to such heedlessness) and a viable, "realistic" social ethic must be prepared for some arduous moments. For he will be attacked on his left flank by those who think he is right about the ideal but wrong about the realism, that he must drop the connection altogether (and perhaps withdraw into a gathered community, leaving the "world" to its own devices) or hold out for some hope of general progressive realization of the ideal.[43] And he will be attacked on his right by those who reject an ideal which perennially reveals deficiencies as practically irrelevant and theoretically confused.[44] It is held to be confused because the "greatest good possible," in a situation of moral choice, is invariably characterized as the "lesser evil." An atmosphere of habitual hand-wringing obscures the sense in which an action may

42. Reinhold Niebuhr, *Moral Man and Immoral Society* (New York: Charles Scribner's Sons, 1960), p. 277.

43. See, e.g., G. H. C. Macgregor, *The Relevance of the Impossible, A Reply to Reinhold Niebuhr* (London: The Fellowship of Reconciliation, 1941).

44. See, e.g., Joseph Fletcher, *Situation Ethics* (Philadelphia: The Westminster Press, 1966), pp. 61–62; Paul Ramsey, *Deeds and Rules in Christian Ethics* (New York: Charles Scribner's Sons, 1967), pp. 187–88. Long ago one of his critics complained that sacrificial disinterested love "if it existed, would be a nuisance. But he [Niebuhr] thinks it sublime, and therefore regards as inescapable tragedy the fact that it won't work" (George A. Coe, "Letter to the Editor," *The Christian Century* 50 [March 15, 1933]: 362).

be *right* (and therefore, so far as such critics are concerned, what *love* — and not some lesser principle — finally requires), even when it includes doing evil.

Much has been written about and by Niebuhr which need not be recounted now on the success of his program.[45] My present interest is in the feature of self-sacrifice and the way Niebuhr has depicted this additional major theme in the tradition. Later on I shall consider some major difficulties with the feature when it is given the prominence Niebuhr accords it. For the moment I shall simply note one further example of the connection between a particular feature, such as self-sacrifice, and wider views. It is not accidental that those who stress self-sacrifice usually offer a correspondingly dour appraisal of self-love. In Niebuhr's case, such a correlation has already been pointed out. I would only add that the dour appraisal connects more generally with a decided preoccupation with the theological doctrine of sin where "self-love" and "pride" are often used interchangeably, and "pride" more often than "unbelief" or "sloth" is the primal character of sin.[46] Niebuhr seems to assume, for instance, that the dangers of active arrogance are much greater than those of drift, apathy, and resignation. This accounts in part for the virtually exclusive interest in "self-love" as not only not praiseworthy but also always blameworthy. It is likewise not adventitious that by and large

45. See esp. *Reinhold Niebuhr*, ed. Kegley and Bretall, and also Gordon Harland, *The Thought of Reinhold Niebuhr* (New York: Oxford University Press, 1960).
46. Perhaps the best indication is found in *Nature and Destiny of Man*, 1:178–264. Cf. Dan Rhoades, "The Prophetic Insight and Theoretical-Analytical Inadequacy of 'Christian Realism,' " *Ethics* 75 (October, 1964): 1–15. Cf. also Barth: "[S]in has not merely the heroic form of pride but also, in complete antithesis yet profound correspondence, the quite unheroic and trivial form of sloth. In other words, it has the form, not only of evil action, but also of evil inaction; not only of the rash arrogance which is forbidden and reprehensible, but also of the tardiness and failure which are equally forbidden and reprehensible" (*Dogmatics*, IV/2:403). And within another theological scheme, "the sin which most profoundly threatens the believer . . . is not the evil he does, but the good he does not do, not his misdeeds but his omissions, that accuse him" (Jürgen Moltmann, *Theology of Hope*, trans. James W. Leitch [New York: Harper and Row, 1967], p. 23).

those who stress the feature I shall next consider refuse to take sin
in this sense as seriously as Niebuhr.

Mutuality

For a number of writers the features so far treated possess a common defect. The criterion for agapeistic actions appears to be only
what *exemplifies* or *expresses* something resident in a person, irrespective of all questions of response and reciprocity. Whether the enemy
remains my enemy or whether the beloved is aware of my devotion
are considerations for which the criterion itself appears to authorize
no interest. According to these critics, it is preferable to introduce
some feature of mutuality into the content of agape, though in what
sense and how far are matters of disagreement and confusion.

The critics begin by disagreeing with Kierkegaard and Niebuhr
about their accounts of what is going on and their estimates of what
is possible in personal and social relations. Clearly, if there is only
one isolable and fixed dominant interest in a personal relation such
as friendship, namely nefarious self-love, then friendship may be incompatible with neighbor-regard in the way Kierkegaard maintains.
And if apart from self-sacrifice, mutuality simply involves a calculation of reciprocal advantages, then as Niebuhr supposes it may require replenishment by draughts of heedlessness more than anything
else.[47] But the alternatives in both cases are held to be mistakenly
conceived and the choices unnecessarily constrained; relations of
mutual love actually include other elements suppressed by these
alternatives so that the alternatives themselves falsify the character
of such relations.

In the first place, it is argued, one should distinguish self-love
as usually construed by Kierkegaard and Niebuhr from another sense
which they either ignore or confusedly attempt to reduce to their
own construction. Approximately, what they describe is an interest

---

47. For a criticism of Niebuhr's account of mutuality, see Daniel Day Williams,
The Spirit and the Forms of Love (Digswell Place: James Nisbet and Co., Ltd.,
1968), p. 299. See also Williams, "Niebuhr and Liberalism," *Reinhold Niebuhr,*
pp. 210–11.

in exalting the self to the point where the other is only the means
for aggrandizement, perhaps the audience before whom the self
poses or gains status.[48] But there is another sense in which self-love
is both a requirement and an existential possibility in relations of
mutual love. Self-love here refers roughly to the agent's regard for
his own integrity, his endeavor to stay with his own considered insights and commitments. One must be wary of pandering or of any
sociability which risks capitulation to the expectations or wishes of
any person or group. The point at the moment is only that without
such personal integrity, without the self being conscious and affirmative of itself in this way, a relation such as friendship is impossible.
For friendship involves mutual action and influence between distinctive persons where neither side consumes or abnegates. And the
achievement of a requisite degree of this integrity is possible. It is not
simply self-deceptive to speak of "continuous mutual encounter of
centered self with centered self." [49] Such centeredness is not a covert
and dishonest referent for that self-aggrandizement in the pursuit of
which the other is merely a means, though admittedly in any de facto
friendship there may be a mixture of both senses of self-love.

In the second place, those who follow Kierkegaard and Niebuhr are
said to err in their preoccupation with the thanklessness which may
attend neighbor-regard. I noted how Niebuhr for example insists that
from the point of view of discernible effects upon others in this
life agape may fail. The critics are far less concerned about such
insistence. If one must be cautious in making claims about triumphant
love, one must not then be satisfied to speak only of suffering love.
The personal relations and perhaps also (or sometimes instead) the
social order in which one finds oneself may be more amenable to a
progressive realization of harmony and brotherhood than Kierkegaard
and Niebuhr believe. While there is no strict guarantee that the
appropriate response will be elicited, there should be no systematic
refusal to hope, if not for perfection, then at least for continuous
progress.

48. M. C. D'Arcy, S.J., *The Mind and Heart of Love* (New York: Meridian
Books, 1959), p. 132; cf. Martin Buber, *Between Man and Man,* trans. Ronald
Gregor Smith (Boston: Beacon Press, 1959), esp. pp. 29–30.
49. Tillich, *Systematic Theology,* 3:41.

It is easier to state these general disagreements than it is to clarify the more precise nature of the critics' constructive proposals. I shall distinguish two broad ways in which some feature of mutuality is introduced into the content of agape. Crudely, the first way concerns love as a characteristic of personal relations; the second concerns love as a characteristic of social relations. In both, some notion of communication and sharing is involved. Love refers, in part or altogether, to a quality of relation *between* persons and/or groups. Those actions are loving which *establish* or *enhance* some sort of exchange between the parties, developing a sense of community and perhaps friendship.

One major ambiguity ought to be identified at the outset, since we shall encounter it particularly in the consideration of personal relations. It is often unclear whether mutuality supplements or supplants equal regard. Sometimes a writer may hold that a state of sharing is simply the most appropriate fruition of such regard. At other times he may hold that agape unrequited is not fully agape, that some mutuality is a necessary condition. In the latter case, one might say for example of a man who remained one's enemy not "I loved him," but rather "I *tried* to love him." For love is absent when one party does all the giving and the other all the taking.

I shall begin with personal relations. I have in mind one-to-one or small group relations where human beings have the opportunity to know and understand each other intimately. Overriding value is often attached to such relations so that inevitably the quintessence of agape is altered. The purest and most perfect manifestation is not in self-sacrifice, but in those instances of personal devotion where a response in kind is forthcoming. Statements such as the following, by M. C. D'Arcy and John Burnaby, illustrate the change.

> The *perfection* of love . . . is to be found in personal friendship, whether between a man and a woman, between man and man, or between man and God.[50]

50. D'Arcy, *Mind and Heart of Love,* p. 31 (italics mine). Such a view of the perfection of love is of course not restricted to believers, however different the way it is taken and the respective reasons for holding it. "To converse with other

It is indeed the *test* of a love which would be like God's, that it is all-embracing; but we may be certain that Christ did not mean either that it is better to have enemies than friends, or that any outward act of beneficence can be a substitute for the inward disposition of heart which would make a friend out of the enemy.[51]

It is fitting then for the agent, in adherence to the principle of agape, to have an interest in a response from the other. At the pinnacle, devotion exists and is shared on both sides. "Charity . . . is the measure of an active conviction that unity in love is the greatest of all good things, expressing itself in the effort to overcome all hindrance to that unity." [52]

So far it would seem that mutuality supplements equal regard. For at its origin and during its continuation, the regard for another may still be held to remain independent of a response. If mutuality is understood only as the final ideal fruition of neighbor-regard, the estimated likelihood or even the possibility of a response in a particular case need not necessarily constitute a condition for the agent's actively regarding another at all. One may seek a response without thereby being dependent on that response for one's regard as such. Moreover, the notion of being interested in a response can be quite restrictedly conceived. In itself it need not mean what Kierkegaard, for example, seems to take it to mean: I have regard for the other *in order to* achieve a response in the sense that I always have an ulterior, acquisitive motive, a secretly *controlling* interest in being

---

living things in amiable and pleasant association — that is the end and essence of right love. The converse may be conversation, or silent being together, or stroking the dog, or working or playing together, or writing letters, or other. Love is primarily conversation. The loving man teaches himself to converse. That is not necessarily to talk and display himself, though some do this too little, and some wrongly despise it; but it is to be with others in understood and amiable communion" (Richard Robinson, *An Atheist's Values* [Oxford: Clarendon Press, 1964], pp. 105–06).

51. John Burnaby, *Amor Dei* (London: Hodder and Stoughton, 1947), pp. 307–08. See also Burnaby, "Love," *A Dictionary of Christian Ethics,* ed. John Macquarrie (London: SCM Press, Ltd., 1967), esp. pp. 199–200.

52. Burnaby, *Amor Dei,* p. 310.

cared about in return, in deriving some benefit for myself. As I have already observed, this meaning assumes an account of the entire nature of a personal relation such as friendship the accuracy and exhaustiveness of which D'Arcy and Burnaby would deny. Clearly my friend and I each derive individual happiness from the relation. But that is not all, nor is it controlling. For the friendship is also an end in itself and the friend is valued for his own sake. It would still be a good thing that he is alive, even if his being alive did not contribute to my happiness.[53] Likewise, being interested in a response need not mean that I *anticipate* a response. We have also seen that a D'Arcy and a Burnaby are not as struck by thanklessness and failure as are Kierkegaard and Niebuhr. Yet the greater optimism this implies about the likelihood of response need not lead to the conclusion that one is *assured* of a response in every case, provided only that he is devoted in the right way. Suffering and sacrifice may remain, though no longer specially valued.

Let us now consider a proposal of a more sweeping kind. Robert Johann offers one example.[54] He does so in the context of a general attempt to formulate a "metaphysics of intersubjectivity," most of the details of which we may ignore. Following Aquinas, Johann distinguishes two kinds of love, "desire" (for which on occasion he substitutes the word eros) and "direct love" (for which on occasion he substitutes agape).[55] It is the exigencies of direct love which mainly concern us.

For him, the possibility of a response *is* a requirement for my loving another directly. This is because in direct love the other must be *accessible* to me as a *thou*. Such accessibility involves two conditions.

53. Cf. Price, *Belief*, pp. 447–50.

54. Robert Johann, S.J., *The Meaning of Love* (Westminster, Md.: Newman Press, 1955). Some may object to including this work with more explicitly theological writings, since it purports to be wholly a philosophical undertaking. I do so nevertheless because it is informed throughout, I would argue, by a theological perspective which comes out of Thomist circles; it involves criticism of theologians such as Nygren; and the position it defends, which I am concerned to identify above, may be found as well in many writings ostensibly more theological.

55. Ibid., e.g., pp. 48, 65–66.

First, "it is not sufficient that the value loved in myself be somehow present *in the other*. If I am to love him as myself, it must also be present *to me*." [56] Being present "to me" in this way means that he must come into range and somehow turn toward me. Thus direct love does not include "a merely abstract recognition of another's subjectivity." Johann explicitly sets aside the passive kind of sympathy involved, for instance, in contemplating mass suffering in wartime. This sympathy may be called pity and even benevolence of a sort, but not really love. So too in all those cases where I refer to someone in the third person: however concrete my action toward him, I do not love him directly so long as I regard him as a *he*. Johann refuses simply to disparage the notion of "he"; to reduce it, say, to the status of an *I-It* relation in which I regard the other merely as an instrument for my purposes or an object of my detached curiosity. The designation "personal" should not be altogether withheld. "To treat another formally as a *he* is still to respect his rights, his liberty, the obligations of justice." [57] Nonetheless, a *he* is never the object of direct love.

> For, while I recognize him as a nucleus of liberty and initiative, that initiative is turned, as it were, in another direction. His interests are exclusive of me, and I am in a real sense out of contact with that deep and profound center which is himself and which I see only from the outside.[58]

Second, the neighbor's presence to me must be such that I communicate with that "profound center." He must be accessible as a kind of "second self"; i.e., I have to be in touch with those basic motives and interests really constitutive of his self-awareness, the same elements that determine my own identity. The opportunity for such communication is what distinguishes a "second self" from a personal "he."

The conclusion about such accessibility may be succinctly put. "Now

56. Ibid., p. 31; see also p. 97.
57. Ibid., pp. 34–35.
58. Ibid., p. 35.

the only presence that meets these exigencies . . . is that of the *thou*. This is nothing more or less than to say that direct love implies between two persons a state of reciprocal consciousness." [59] A "maximum of reciprocity," where mutuality is fully conscious, Johann calls friendship. Here, then, agape unrequited appears not to be fully agape, and some mutuality is a necessary condition. However, I think it is still unclear exactly how the feature of mutuality supplants equal regard. Two possibilities seem most likely.

(1) The exigencies of personal relations are restrictive only in the sense that they are time-consuming and so cannot be sustained with very many people. It is not that regard for the other is conditioned by certain qualifications possessed by some and not by others (where those in the latter group would be otherwise accessible because sufficiently near-at-hand). No, the sole condition for agape is accessibility to anyone who de facto comes into the necessary intimate range. Here any neighbor possesses the essential capacity for communion with any other. The restrictions on agape's full manifestation concern only the peculiar requirements of one-to-one relations, not the special traits, actions, etc., which distinguish particular personalities from each other. At times Johann seems to affirm a metaphysical equality between "subsistent selves" in a fashion which lends support to such an interpretation.[60] We have to do more with "thatness"

59. Ibid., p. 36. An obvious objection, which Johann considers, is that at the inception of an *I-Thou* relation such implied reciprocity may be absent, since the parties may not be individually conscious of each other and therefore cannot *explicitly* reciprocate. His reply, so far as I understand it, is that even if the other has not initially and expressly turned toward me by any special volitional act, he has given himself to the "world" in which I move as well. The latter giving makes itself evident in self-authenticating fashion. This reply seems to me elusive. Any line appears tenuous in the extreme between a personal *he* whose initiative happens to be turned in another direction and a *thou* who has turned specifically not toward me, but rather toward the "world" in which I move. See also his discussion of the relation between his own account and that of Aquinas (following Aristotle) on the love of benevolence and friendship, pp. 37–38. See likewise Maurice Nédoncelle, *Vers une Philosophie de L'Amour et de la Personne* (Paris: Aubier Editions Montaigne, 1957).

60. Cf. Jacques Maritain, *The Person and the Common Good*, trans. John J. Fitzgerald (Notre Dame, Indiana: University of Notre Dame Press, 1966), p. 39: "Love is not concerned with qualities. They are not the object of our love.

than "suchness." Still, equal regard is supplanted in a sense because there is for Johann one sort of love — benevolence — for those to whom I can refer only in the third person, and another sort — direct love or agape — for those whom I may address as "you" or "thou." Perhaps the difference in this instance is verbal rather than substantive. Johann distinguishes between benevolence and direct love and reserves agape for the latter, whereas in most of the literature agape includes benevolence in his sense as well. But at least we should be clear that such a restriction has occurred. For equal regard often cuts across this division and is applicable in both kinds of relations. If the neighbor is anyone affected by my actions, then the interests of those whom I do not know directly may nevertheless have to be weighed. Everyone affected by my actions is not reducible to anyone with whom I have an *I-Thou* relation. Suppose a man is trying to decide between giving his wife an expensive anniversary gift and giving part of the same money to a special educational program for underprivileged children in urban ghettos. He ought to weigh the latter alternative seriously, even though he can refer to the interests of the affected parties only in the third person. He could argue for morally relevant differences between the two kinds of relations and some scale of priorities, but not that third person references in such a case fall outside the principle of equal regard.

(2) The exigencies of personal relations are restrictive not just because they are time-consuming, but also because they do involve special qualifications. Only certain persons are *willing* to be open to me in the appropriately self-disclosing way. And so friendship has special requirements attached which not everyone meets, even where the opportunity for closeness exists. Or perhaps only certain persons realize what all persons are capable of realizing. The claims here are obscure and revolve in part around different conceptions of friendship, a subject to which I shall return.

To hold that mutuality supplants equal regard in the sense of either

We love the deepest, most substantial and hidden, the most *existing* reality of the beloved being. This is a metaphysical center deeper than all the qualities and essences which we can find and enumerate in the beloved." Such a statement could be taken as an explication of that which is irreducibly valuable, and shared equally by everyone. But the exigencies of direct love take us beyond this.

(1) or (2) raises a major difficulty in any event. For usually agape is taken as a principle applicable to other-other as well as self-other relations, and to all the moral relations between men, whether these are between colleagues, spouses, acquaintances, friends, or others.

Not everyone who stresses mutuality attaches supreme and overriding value to personal relations. Men are reciprocally connected with larger groups as well and attention must be given to collective welfare. Love has to do with social community and not only personal communion. Indeed, the former may be stressed even if the latter is not, even if one believes that the effort to understand each other in relations of intimacy is doomed to frustration.

Love, then, has been taken to furnish a comprehensive ideal of social cooperativeness. Actions are loving when they create and sustain community.[61] Certain groups, and most notably the Church, are often regarded as peculiarly appropriate for the realization of harmony and brotherhood. Sometimes, however, the ideal is applied straightforwardly to the whole society, and to relations between societies. Once again the claims are frequently obscure, but the following generalizations seem warranted. I shall contrast them with Niebuhr's views, because they often involve explicit repudiation of such views. One can begin by distinguishing two claims about the process of adjudicating interests among groups. First, one may advance (as Niebuhr does on occasion) an essentially empirical claim that sacrificial love is the most effective way to realize the aim of balancing interests and fostering cooperativeness. Second, one may advance the evaluative judgment that there is something wrong with the aim itself. I noted earlier that from the standpoint of sacrificial love, the social world of contending interests is for Niebuhr only partly amenable to the strategy of the Cross. Our workaday moral principles are always something of a compromise with agape. This latter judgment is the one most in dispute.

Groups are not as incorrigible as Niebuhr supposes. He selects with tiresome regularity the elements of conflict in group relations

<hr/>

61. Such a case has been made by Williams, *Spirit and Forms of Love*. See also his *God's Grace and Man's Hope* (New York: Harper and Row, 1965).

and neglects both actual and possible areas of cooperation. It may be more difficult for groups to suspend their own interests to the extent desirable than it is for individuals, but Niebuhr appears to deny even the possibility of such suspension.

> In our own era, Reinhold Niebuhr has stressed the great difficulty men have as members of social groups to achieve the information, the imaginative grasp of how members of other groups are affected by their actions, and the detachment from their own vested interests and passions necessary for loving as they ought. The difficulty of this we acknowledge; the impossibility of it is what we deny.[62]

The aim ought to be construed more in terms of fostering cooperativeness and less in terms of simply balancing interests. However much Niebuhr may dislike the "political cynicism" of a Hobbes, he too makes the situation of incompatible interests the paradigm of moral reflection within "historical society." But this is a mistake. For the interests of men are by and large more complementary than conflicting. In addition to an interest in survival, and often outweighing it, men want to communicate culturally. Love as "voluntary cooperativeness" [63] at once expresses the dominant interests men have in their social organization and is the criterion for judging particular arrangements.

Finally, even if one granted for the sake of argument that Niebuhr has described with penetration some major characteristics of collective life to the present hour, one could not conclude that institutional life for all time will involve very important and yet finally limited variations on well-established themes. Instead, one should consider not only what interests men have possessed but also what interests they might acquire. Conflict may be increasingly channeled in non-violent

62. Arthur J. Dyck, "Referent-Models of Loving: A Philosophical and Theological Analysis of Love in Ethical Theory and Moral Practice," *Harvard Theological Review* 61 (October, 1968): 540.

63. See, e.g., David Little, "Calvin and the Prospects for a Christian Theory of Natural Law," *Norm and Context in Christian Ethics,* ed. Gene H. Outka and Paul Ramsey (New York: Charles Scribner's Sons, 1968), p. 191.

directions, for example, and in any case is not as much of a fixed datum as Niebuhr appears to believe. If one accepts, then, a more expansive estimate than Niebuhr's of man's potential for the acquirement of different, more other-regarding interests, the content of agape in this life may be turned from self-sacrifice toward harmony.

Much more might be said about social cooperativeness. I shall take up some connected issues when justice is considered in detail. I shall also in the last chapter say something about the relation of equal regard and social cooperativeness, which seems to me to be misconceived by many of the disputants. The debate between Niebuhr and his critics involves perhaps more than anything else differing estimates of what is realizable in man's collective life. The normative content given to agape, and the relation of agape to other principles such as justice, is affected accordingly.

Love for God and Neighbor-Love

I come now to the first term in the God-neighbor-self triad. Let us first locate one point of substantive overlap between neighbor-love and love for God on which virtually everyone formally agrees but around which many of the ethical disputes arise nonetheless. Whatever else loving God with heart, soul, and mind may mean, one criterion is neighbor-love itself. Jesus links permanently together the two great commandments, the second being "like unto" the first. And the author of I John declares flatly: "If a man say, I love God and hateth his brother, he is a liar" (4:20). Neighbor-love involves substantive overlap with love for God, as a test and mark of its genuineness. By "substantive overlap" here I mean, first, that neighbor-love is a *necessary* test in that it shares in the seriousness of a *divine* command. If one loves God one is not free to decide whether to love the neighbor or not. Moreover, normally beliefs concerning God's action in creation and redemption are invoked to emphasize that the neighbor is the object of divine love. Love for God thus implies conformity in loving what He loves. To quote Austin Farrer:

> The regard we owe him is unqualified, because it is owed to God through him. And yet he is no mere channel through which

regard is paid to God, for God is regarded by regard for what He regards, and what He regards is the man.[64]

Second, neighbor-love is an *appropriate* test in a way that reflects on both the majesty of God and the limitations of human existence. There is for example a natural reticence, though how thoroughgoing it ought to be is disputed, to say very much about direct giving to God. Indeed, such talk strikes many as anomalous and quickly presumptuous. The following statement by Kierkegaard is representative.

If you want to show that your life is intended as service to God, then let it serve man, yet continually with the thought of God. God is not a part of existence in such a way that he demands his share for himself; he demands everything, but as you bring it you immediately receive, if I may put it this way, an endorsement designating where it should be forwarded, for God demands nothing for himself, although he demands everything from you.[65]

So far all of the above may seem the most serious sort of religious commonplace, with controversy restricted largely to questions of inducement. Where then do theoretical disputes arise? They have to do with the correctness of an inference sometimes drawn from affirmations about substantive overlap. Why not explicitly conclude, it is argued, that the principle of neighbor-love is *all* the content that "love for God" possesses? So far at least as normative ethics is concerned, what more is there to be said? Agape as an other-regarding principle has only the neighbor for its object, but not God in a way substantively applicable to the making of moral judgments. On occasion it is even held that little more need be said about religious belief itself. To love the neighbor agapeistically *is* to know and believe in God, or at least is the self-authenticating way for coming to

64. Farrer, "Examination of Theological Belief," p. 20.
65. Kierkegaard, *Works of Love*, p. 159.

know and believe in Him.[66] One might say that only as a person actually loves his neighbor is he in a position to understand what it means to believe in God or to be capable of noticing and interpreting correctly providential action. For us to consider here this latter identification with all its ambiguities would require an unwarranted digression. And the claim that neighbor-love exhausts the material content of agape as an ethical principle is itself sufficiently ambiguous to make sketchiness unavoidable. I must begin by examining how more exactly this conclusion is drawn in the literature.

Two arguments urged on its behalf may be distinguished, though they are frequently confused: one about linguistic usage and the other more about theological substance.

First, everyone agrees that the meaning of "love" in love for God and neighbor-love cannot be altogether univocal. The fitting attitudes and actions toward the two objects may often differ patently. One is free to worship and obey God; but to worship the neighbor is an act of idolatry. And one may suffer and forgive the neighbor, but to presume to "forgive" God would constitute blasphemy.

A man should love God in unconditional *obedience* and love him in *adoration*. It would be ungodliness if any man dared love himself in this way, or dared love another person in this way, or dared to let another person love him in this way.[67]

66. Cf. Graeme de Graaff, "God and Morality," *Christian Ethics and Contemporary Philosophy,* ed. Ian T. Ramsey (London: SCM Press Ltd., 1966), pp. 31–52; F. Gerald Downing, *Has Christianity a Revelation?* (London: SCM Press Ltd., 1964), p. 101; Price, *Belief,* pp. 472–73. See also the following statement (however pillaged from context) of Father Zossima in Dostoyevsky's *The Brothers Karamazov* (trans. Constance Garnett [New York: Modern Library, n.d.], p. 55): "Strive to love your neighbour actively and indefatigably. In as far as you advance in love you will grow surer of the reality of God and of the immortality of your soul. If you attain to perfect self-forgetfulness in the love of your neighbour, then you will believe without doubt, and no doubt can possibly enter your soul. This has been tried. This is certain."

67. Kierkegaard, *Works of Love,* p. 36. See also H. Richard Niebuhr, *Christ and Culture* (New York: Harper and Brothers, 1951), pp. 18–19: "His [Jesus'] love of God and his love of neighbor are two distinct virtues that have no common quality but only a common source. Love of God is adoration of the only

One must then acknowledge and live with two very different meanings of the same word. Some query the wisdom of leaving it at that. The confusions which accompany the use of the same word in such different senses seem so intractable that clarity would be served if two different words were consistently employed. Anders Nygren proposes that in place of "love for God" one susbstitute "faith."

> Faith includes in itself the whole devotion of love, while emphasising that it has the character of response, that it is reciprocated love. Faith is love towards God, but a love of which the keynote is receptivity, not spontaneity.[68]

Nygren is of course careful to say that this proposal is not merely his own stipulation. It has, he maintains, decisive scriptural warrant. He admits that some obscurity exists in the case of the writers of the synoptic gospels. So far as the first great commandment is concerned, Nygren is forced to equate it with "possession by God, . . . belonging absolutely to Him." [69] But it is Paul who really clarifies the issue. Augustine's familiar observation is entirely correct: when Paul speaks of Christian love, he almost always means neighbor-love rather than love for God.[70] This usage is in no way accidental, for at least two reasons. Paul is chary of talk about love for God because he wishes to underscore the *strictly responsive* character of all such human devotion. This emphasis reflects to some extent his doctrine of grace (and/or Nygren's), a subject to which I shall return. In addition, the material continuity is far greater between divine love

---

true good; it is gratitude to the bestower of all gifts; it is joy in Holiness; it is 'consent to Being.' But the love of man is pitiful rather than adoring; it is giving and forgiving rather than grateful; it suffers for and in their viciousness and profaneness; it does not consent to accept them as they are, but calls them to repentance. The love of God is nonpossessive *Eros*; the love of man pure *Agape*; the love of God is passion; the love of man, compassion."

68. Nygren, *Agape and Eros,* p. 127; see also Gustaf Aulén, *The Faith of the Christian Church,* trans. Eric H. Wahlstrom and G. Everett Arden (Philadelphia: The Muhlenberg Press, 1948), p. 16.

69. Nygren, *Agape and Eros,* p. 94.

70. Ibid., pp. 123–24.

and neighbor-love than between love for God and neighbor-love. To confine agape to the former makes such continuity more manifest.

How shall we understand Nygren's proposal? Given the fact that crucial differences in meaning are admitted by everyone, the proposal to use "faith" for love of God and to restrict human agape to neighbor-love may be what is sometimes known as a "precising definition." [71] In the face of vagueness in the use of a term where serious misunderstandings may and do occur, one proposes to modify ordinary literal usage (including in this case some, but by no means all, biblical usage) for the sake of greater clarity. Such a proposal is different from a purely stipulative definition, since the *definiendum* is not a matter of individual choice. One must appeal to established usage and do justice to the supposed "intentions" of the various users. One simply goes beyond established usage and so partly stipulates, in an effort to avoid recurrent misunderstandings. The issue involved is one more of verbal convenience than conceptual faithfulness. Certainly the quest for a precising definition should make the reader wary of many of the claims about substantive disagreement present in the literature. As one Roman Catholic has concluded, for instance, Protestants such as Nygren often subsume under "faith" precisely what the Catholic holds in his treatment of both faith and charity.[72]

Yet suppose for the moment that one grants the cogency of the case for more precision in linguistic usage, perhaps systematically substituting faith for love for God. In this sense the conclusion that neighbor-love exhausts the content of agape as an ethical principle becomes true by definition. But then presumably we should still like to know why that devotion to God now included under "faith" is not part of normative ethics as such. Whether it is a part or not is a question independent of the advisability of a precising definition. And here the argument solely about linguistic usage, while perhaps important in its own right, is left hanging in the air.

71. See, e.g., Irving M. Copi, *Introduction to Logic* (New York: The Macmillan Company, 1961), pp. 104–05.

72. This is the contention, for example, of W. H. van de Pol, *The Christian Dilemma,* trans. G. van Hall (New York: Philosophical Library, 1952), esp. p. 23.

But this is not the whole story, for a second argument put forward is, as I mentioned, more substantive. Its general character is nicely indicated in Nygren's contrast between receptivity and spontaneity. Nygren shares what might fairly be called a characteristic Protestant suspicion of all claims about human spontaneity in relation to God. Through all such talk runs a dominant strain of presumption. Even in the case of Jesus' teachings, where Nygren does admit to finding assumed a certain "relative spontaneity," one must take care to restrict its meaning to internal liberation from desiring to *gain* anything, even God or God's agape. Such implacable suspicion carries over into everything Nygren says about self-love and sanctification as well.[73] And often the substantive issue of receptivity and spontaneity seems to reduce itself to historic Roman Catholic and Protestant disputes filtered through the language of agape and eros. The issues thus pertain, for example, to infused virtues, operative and cooperative grace, and merit.[74]

The general character of such historic disputes is sufficiently well-known and so need not detain us here. Thus I shall mention only one illustration of the way Nygren proceeds. He distinguishes what he calls an ethics of causality and teleology.[75] Though not in every respect conforming to current usage, it nicely represents the conflict between spontaneity and receptivity as seen through Nygren's eyes. Nygren thinks teleological schemes accommodate more readily an element of spontaneity. He focuses on a teleological ethic largely along Augustinian lines, where he believes everything is acquisitively subordinated to the vision of God and thereby to the self's ultimate fulfillment and rest. Everything which equips the agent to aspire more ardently and ascend more successfully is construed on a means-end pattern; even a revelatory act uniquely authoritative has instrumental rather than intrinsic value.

Causal schemes, on the other hand, allow only for receptivity. Crudely put, God's love invades the human sphere, but never in

73. As I shall demonstrate in chapter 2.
74. For a Thomist statement on grace and its divisions see Reginald Garrigou-Lagrange, O.P., *Grace*, trans. the Dominican Nuns, Corpus Christi Monastery (St. Louis: B. Herder Book Co., 1952).
75. Nygren, *Agape and Eros*, e.g., pp. 539, 737.

such fashion that there is any gradual accretion of power at the agent's own disposal, proper to him as such. The choice of the word "causal" is a problematical one at best. It may imply for instance a form of irresistible grace. The classic example supporting such an interpretation is his depiction of the Christian as "merely the tube, the channel, through which God's love flows." [76] It is one thing to affirm that creaturely agape has its source in God, another that it is identical with His agape. To say that God's love is the source of man's love may simply mean that the basis is outside man's own power of initiation and sustenance; it can also mean that the subject is actually God in all genuine neighbor-love. Nygren appears to mean both.

I have now strayed into matters having more to do with the source of human agape than with its content. But I hope I have said enough to give some sense of the general character of the discussion. For Nygren and his followers, the devotion to God under "faith" cannot be more or other than pure reception. Thus, love for God cannot be part of the content of agape as an ethical principle, since in relation to God the agent has nothing whatever to do. This then is the substantive argument which seems to be offered.

One could find of course any number of reasons for rejecting Nygren's program. It might be contended, for instance, that the depiction of the Christian as a tube or channel makes nonsense of every part of ethics, neighbor-love included. Or to go further: for ethics to be intelligible at all may require the view that the movement of the will is "self-wrought," even purely self-wrought. Any doctrine of grace will be tolerated only insofar as it is consistent with such a view.[77] However, it is possible now to attend only to the more intramural discussion in which everyone agrees ostensibly if not always clearly that the love for God in question is a purely responsive one. What is denied is that response and passive receptivity should be identified.

76. Ibid., p. 735. This is the point at which Nygren has been most consistently criticized. See e.g., D'Arcy, *Mind and Heart of Love*, p. 82; Thomas, *Christian Ethics and Moral Philosophy*, p. 54.

77. For a powerful defense of this view of morality in relation to certain theological doctrines, see W. G. Maclagan, *The Theological Frontier of Ethics* (London: George Allen and Unwin Ltd., 1961).

In the first place, the price paid for a precising definition is in this case too high. While love for God does fall outside the "strict correlation" between the content of divine love and neighbor-love, its use need not be given up altogether. A systematic substitution of faith misleads more rather than less. For justice must be done to an active as well as a passive element in response, which the normal sense of "faith" is ill-prepared to include. The content of active response shares with neighbor-love the feature of self-giving to an extent that legitimates the use of the same word. For while it may be true that the agent cannot give any*thing* to God, he can meaningfully withhold *himself*. And if he can be said to withhold himself, or if you like his final loyalty, his heart, soul, and mind, he can also plausibly be said to give them.[78] In short, the keynote of faith is indeed receptivity but this does not exhaust the meaning of response. Love for God refers to the active element in this response, the placing of the self at God's disposal. Faith is being grasped by God and love is adhering to Him.[79]

I mentioned earlier that much of the substantive argument involving spontaneity versus receptivity seems in effect a restatement of historic doctrinal alternatives. While these are tolerably familiar and so need not be rehearsed, one should note in addition that Nygren's critics find his own account a far too crude dichotomy even of these alternatives. His characterization of teleological ethical schemes, for instance, is held to be simplistic and little more than a straw man.

I said Nygren construes a teleological ethic on a simple means-end pattern: thus, doing x for the sake of A always signifies that x is a means and A an end or "ulterior motive." For example, in the case of loving the neighbor for the sake of God it seems to Nygren that the neighbor is then a mere means to a further and more lofty end and cannot in any intelligible sense be regarded for his own sake. This misleadingly narrows the options. One may distinguish (1) I ought to do x (i.e., serve men) for the sake of A (i.e., as service to God) where x is simply a means and A is the "ulterior motive," from (2) I ought to do x for the sake of A where x is its internal and

---

78. C. S. Lewis, *The Four Loves* (London: Geoffrey Bles, 1960), p. 146.
79. Tillich, *Systematic Theology*, 3:138.

indispensable accompaniment.[80] In (2), "for the sake of A" involves
no further objective or consequence (of, say, obtaining benefit for
God or reward for myself) beyond doing x. One might, perhaps,
call "for the sake of A" an originative and justificatory reason. One
is distinguishing why-one-did-it from what-one-did, but not identifying some forward-looking objective which reduces the action itself
to an instrumental status. In fact I think much of the talk about love
for God is really based on this second assumption, a rich and complex
notion which I cannot undertake to unravel now. It involves an
array of issues about reasons-for-action, motives, intentions, and the
like. I am merely trying to suggest a complexity not satisfactorily
accommodated by Nygren's own alternatives. In some ways, perhaps,
"for the sake of A" as an originative and justificatory reason is closer
to Nygren's account of a causal ethic. But his own account does not
allow for the element of active and deliberate referral which is required on the part of the agent.

Thus far I have sketched some typical replies to Nygren, concerning the linguistic convenience of using "love for God" as well as
"faith," and the theological propriety of talk of active response. An
obvious question remains: if agape as an other-regarding principle
has God as well as the neighbor for its distinctive object, how is this
substantively applicable to the making of moral judgments? There is
nothing approaching a consensus, but I think one may distinguish
two classes. First, love for God may have effects on the content of
neighbor-love itself; second, love for God may involve discrete attitudes and actions whose very intelligibility (to the believer at
least) depends on their not being reducible to neighbor-love.

That neighbor-love involves substantive overlap with love for
God has been shown. Yet love for God may also throw up certain
limits around the character and intensity of neighbor-love. Kierkegaard
in particular calls attention to such limits. He refers to God in a number of passages as the "middle term" in genuine neighbor-love.

When God is the middle term in judging love, . . . the judgment is this: divinely understood, is it really love to show de-

80. Cf. Eric D'Arcy, *Human Acts* (Oxford: Clarendon Press, 1963), pp.
130–74

votion such as is demanded by the object of love? Next, is it love, divinely understood, on the part of the object of love to demand such devotion? Every man is God's servant; therefore he dare not belong to anyone in love unless in the same love he belongs to God, and he dare not possess anyone in love unless he and the other belong to God in this same love; a man dare not belong to another human being as if the other were everything to him; a man dare not permit another to belong to him in such a way that he is everything to the other.[81]

On the level of basic *attachments* to others, the agent must avoid any transfer from equal regard to unqualified obedience or adoration. And this may often be a relevant consideration in situations of moral choice. In personal relations, my affection for my spouse or friend may grow too ardent or too embittered; hence the God-relationship sometimes cools and sometimes soothes. In social relations, my loyalty to a political leader may pass from respect to adulation; yet no human being is to be taken with the sort of ultimate seriousness which in effect idolatrizes. Attachments may thus issue in distinctive attitudes and actions. While many have objected to this theme in Kierkegaard and others[82] as implying excessive detachment from other men, and that God and man might somehow be rivals, it is important as one example of how love for God may have an effect on the content of neighbor-love.

Finally, corporate worship, prayer, and ascetic discipline are sometimes cited as instances of human activities which (1) properly refer to love for God and cannot be translated without loss into neighbor-love, and (2) are part of normative ethics. Roman Catholic moral theology typically regards all of the above as a part of its legitimate subject matter. Protestants, on the other hand, propose more restrictions, so that prayer, for example, "is not the content of ethics, but, like faith, the presupposition of ethics." [83] Here too one witnesses

---

81. Kierkegaard, *Works of Love*, p. 113.
82. See, e.g., Dewi Z. Phillips, "The Christian Concept of Love" *Christian Ethics and Contemporary Philosophy*, pp. 325–28. Cf. also Lewis, *Four Loves*, pp. 133–60.
83. Brunner, *Divine Imperative*, p. 311.

the interweaving of disputes some of which are verbal and some substantive. In the case of the former, perhaps an expansionist Catholic view of ethics does not wish to rule out from the start significant attitudes and actions which in fact are often taken as part of the Christian life; it wants to catch as many of these as possible. In the case of the latter, Protestants sometimes object to any notion of two sets of duties. One reason repeatedly given is that whenever the two sorts of activities are set alongside each other, a denigration of "ordinary earthly life" inevitably follows.[84] I shall return to this question in discussing Barth.

84. Ibid., pp. 310–11. Häring criticizes Brunner from the Catholic side, in *Law of Christ*, 2:89.

Agape and Self-Love

What he felt as a menace in himself, and what he saw at
work in the scene about him, was very like what Hawthorne
felt and saw: a complex moral reality of which one pole
was a pure and strong affirmation of the grandeur of the
individual, and the other pole a wild egoism, anarchic, ir-
responsible, and destructive, that masqueraded in the kingly
weeds of self-reliance.

Newton Arvin, *Herman Melville*

To say anything very useful about a phrase as generally ambiguous
as "self-love" may well be impossible. For it serves as a classic
example of a difficulty already noted: a single word or phrase may
shuttle back and forth between distinct experiences and different
(and sometimes rival) concepts. And value judgments may simply
reflect variant meanings not always incompatible. Thus if I deprecate
self-love or pride I may be censuring a conceit which overrates one's
own achievements or a vanity which fails to take a fair account of
other peoples' interests. Alternatively, if I commend it I may have in
mind something like personal resolution, adherence to one's own
insights won often through effort and pain, and in face, perhaps, of
social ostracism. By implication, not to commend this strength would
be to encourage intellectual and emotional "bad faith," thus perhaps
letting oneself or others get by with ideas one believes confused or
passions misplaced.[1]

---

1. Note for example the variant but compatible meanings in two separate
passages from Jane Austen's *Persuasion*. "Vanity was the beginning and end of
Sir Walter Elliot's character; vanity of person and situation. . . . He considered
the blessing of beauty as inferior only to the blessing of a baronetcy; and the
Sir Walter Elliot, who united these gifts, was the constant object of his warmest
respect and devotion."

"Anne had never seen her father and sister before in contact with nobility, and

Within this complex state of multiple uses, sometimes conflicting, sometimes not, the literature exhibits a wide diversity of its own. All I shall hope to do is identify certain characterstic issues of greatest ethical importance. These issues may be most conveniently grouped around four value judgments of "self-love": as wholly nefarious; as normal, reasonable, and prudent; as justified derivatively from other-regard; and as a definite obligation, independent of other-regard, though for some coincident with it.

Self-Love as Wholly Nefarious

A fairly prevalent impression exists that theologians have only dour and condemnatory things to say about self-love. While, as we shall see, this is untrue *simpliciter,* the impression obviously has some basis. I have already described how Niebuhr perpetuates the historic link between self-love, pride, and sin. What, more specifically, is it which is condemned? And how far does this condemnation extend across the range of actual options? Does it effectively eliminate any distinction between a culpable selfishness and a laudable or at least morally indifferent self-regard?

The single word which best connotes those attitudes and actions characteristic of nefarious self-love is, I think, *acquisitiveness.* Speaking roughly, in relation to everyone else the agent's predominant aim is individual and private satisfaction. What in particular satisfies may vary, and no single concept such as "happiness" need do all the work of elucidation. The ultimate goal of the agent's aspirations is in any case some prospective state of his own. This goal dominantly pervades every relation to others. In social relations, cooperative action is only an obvious device for securing from others whatever is instrumental to the agent's private ends. In personal relations, enrichment to the self determines the degree to which the other is found interesting and desirable. Whoever thus enriches is if possible possessed, in one way or another, without overriding regard for the other's independent needs and desires.

---

she must acknowledge herself disappointed. She had hoped better things from their high ideals of their own situation in life, and was reduced to form a wish which she had never foreseen — a wish that they had more pride."

Moreover, the sublimity of the objects to which the agent aspires may have little effect on the character of his relation to any of them. Sensuality, for example, is held to be merely one possibility along an enormous spectrum. Romantic and religious relations, while more subtle and devious, are likewise not exempt. In a well-known account of romantic love, Denis de Rougemont ascribes to eros such a basic acquisitiveness: the beloved is only a pretext for the agent's taking flight, an interchangeable occasion for the stirring of private passion.[2] Similarly, Nygren claims to identify an entire *"Eros*-religion" and *"Eros*-ethics" governed by such self-seeking.[3]

Though I have hardly touched on the complexities of acquisitive self-love, its main characteristics (popularly encompassed under "selfishness") are sufficiently familiar and it would be superfluous to labor them. That they refer to a distinct and familiar experience I think it would be idle to deny. Theoretically the most important issue is how far such acquisitiveness — invariably condemned by the writers concerned — is supposed to extend. In de Rougemont's case, he clearly purports to be doing more than describing the views of localized historical groups. He wants to explain a permanently recurrent state of affairs. Eros is not so much the peculiar passion of a given epoch

2. Denis de Rougemont, *Love in the Western World,* trans. Montgomery Belgion (Garden City, N.Y.: Doubleday and Company, Inc., 1957); in Great Britain the title is *Passion and Society* (London: Faber and Faber Ltd., 1956). His account contains a distinctive twist, to be sure, in that it traces a desire so allegedly insatiable that no earthly object can really be the occasion for fulfillment. The desire in its purest form involves a profound conflict within the self "between the intolerable laws of finite terrestrial existence and the desire after a transgression of our limits, fatal but divinizing" (p. 230). In specifying these attributes, de Rougemont focuses upon the romance of *Tristan and Iseult* as the classic dictum in the realm of myth, for it is an "archetype of our most complex feelings of unrest" (p. 4). He also undertakes, with less lucidity, to show how eros subsists down to the present day by tracing its manifestations through such ostensibly disparate phenomena as German Romanticism and modern warfare (pp. 175–283). (In his more recent volume he considers other contemporary "metamorphoses of Tristan" such as *Doctor Zhivago* and *Lolita.* See *Love Declared,* trans. Richard Howard [Boston: Beacon Press, 1963], esp. pp. 41–76). Nonetheless, the passion which is boundless is acquisitive through and through.

3. Nygren, *Agape and Eros,* e.g., pp. 208–10.

as an inveterate orientation toward human relations and the "world" itself. Even so we may still distinguish two claims: (1) acquisitive self-love is *a* discriminable set of attitudes and actions which has reappeared with depressing persistence throughout human history, albeit in extremely varied exemplifications; (2) acquisitive self-love is the *sole* spring of human behavior, the only set of attitudes and actions there is, identical for every man. In (1), acquisitiveness effectively governs *all* of the actions of *some* men (in every historical period); in (2) it effectively governs *all* of the actions of *all* men (in every historical period).[4] One doubts that de Rougemont goes beyond (1), though his account is unsystematic and one is hard put to be sure. What he says in his cryptic remarks about agape seems at any rate incompatible with (2). For he takes agape to involve a definite decision to live in an other-regarding way, which appears to be a matter of human agency and divine grace that is not irresistible. Such a decision furnishes important backing for marriage, for example, an institution de Rougemont thinks dependent more on resolution than on taste.[5] In any event, to live agapeistically seems to be an actual rather than an illusory or quixotic option, a genuine alternative to acquisitiveness.

It is possible however to find theologians who maintain something very like the second claim. Consider for instance the following statements by Nygren who — his formal protestations to neutrality notwithstanding[6] — speaks for himself as well as, or perhaps rather than, Paul and Luther. Here the condemnation of self-love is unqualifiedly sweeping and applies exhaustively to all "natural" pos-

---

4. Two other claims can be distinguished, though they are not so germane at the moment: (1) acquisitiveness affects all of the attitudes and actions of some men as a constantly corrupting influence but not always a governing one; or (2) it so affects all men. Here acquisitiveness may be one of the constant springs of human behavior, but not the only one. I shall return to such claims as they apply to both eros and agape when considering Barth.

5. De Rougemont, *Love in the Western World*, pp. 290–324.

6. Perhaps I should say explicitly that I take Nygren's treatment of Luther as normative for his own view. The claims Nygren makes of strict historical objectivity for his work are less than convincing. Note, for example, his statement that Luther's "criticism of the Catholic idea of love is . . . irrefutable" (*Agape and Eros*, p. 722).

sibilities. Any distinction between a culpable selfishness and even a morally indifferent self-regard does seem eliminated.

When . . . Paul sets self-love and neighbourly love in opposition to one another, he is not condemning merely a "lower self-love," or the natural propensity to self-assertion, but all self-love whatsoever, even in its most highly spiritual forms.[7]

Luther has departed so far from the traditional idea, which discovers a *commandment* of self-love in the commandment of love to one's neighbour, that he finds this latter to contain a direct *prohibition* of every kind of self-love. Love to one's neighbour, he holds, has the task of completely dispossessing and annihilating self-love.[8]

Does there indeed exist any other love than that which builds on the foundation of self-love? Is it conceivable or possible in human life as human life is at present constituted?

If the last two questions are put to Luther, his immediate answer is essentially negative. The fact is that the resources of natural human life are exhausted in and with egocentric love. There is nothing in the life and activity of the natural man which does not bear the marks of . . . seeking its own. It is therefore wholly under the dominion of sin, and on that basis there is no possibility of manifesting love in the Christian sense of the word, a love that seeketh not its own, but loves God with all its heart and its neighbour as itself.[9]

In this last quotation, Nygren may be propounding a version of what moral philosophers commonly call psychological egoism.[10] Psy-

7. Ibid., p. 131.
8. Ibid., p. 713; cf. pp. 217, 222.
9. Ibid., pp. 722–23.
10. The literature on psychological egoism is very extensive. See, e.g., C. D. Broad, *Five Types of Ethical Theory* (Paterson, N.J.: Littlefield, Adams and Company, 1959), especially pp. 184–92, 240–56, 273–81; Joseph Butler, *Fifteen Sermons* (London: G. Bell and Sons Ltd., 1964), esp. Sermon XI; Frankena,

chological egoism is not a normative ethical theory of the right and good so much as a theory about human motivation. It has many versions, all of which identify what is *desired* — inevitably, and despite all appearances to the contrary — rather than what is *desirable*. The underlying thesis is that acquisitive self-love constitutes de facto the sole spring of behavior, identical for every man. Men pursue their own individual and private satisfaction and they cannot help pursuing it. If their behavior at times seems ostensibly altruistic, this is only disguised acquisitiveness. Their conscious aims, if other-regarding, are never their real and determinative ones. At the deepest level, all aims are genetically derived from and may be reductively analyzed into one and only one.

It might be objected that such a theory of human motivation is irrelevant for ethics, since the theory is descriptive rather than prescriptive. One must take care not to try fallaciously to deduce ethical conclusions from non-ethical premises. The rejoinder to this objection has typically been that the theory is important for ethics in view of another common dictum, namely, "ought implies can." If it is not illogical it is at least unreasonable to urge men to follow a way of life which in fact they are incapable of following. If normative ethical principles of whatever sort, acquisitive or other-regarding, are to have much point, there must be some possibility of choosing among them. Nygren might not find such a dictum very troubling, since as we saw earlier he approaches a doctrine of irresistible grace. Would it then be too simplistic or unfair to conclude that he leaves only the following alternatives? (1) The life and activity of the natural man is unavoidably acquisitive. "*Eros*-ethics" might therefore consist in guidance for the optimal promotion of self-interest. One thinks

---

Ethics, pp. 19–21; Richard T. Garner and Bernard Rosen, *Moral Philosophy* (New York: The Macmillan Company, 1967), pp. 36–54; John Hospers, *Human Conduct* (London: Rupert Hart-Davis, 1963), pp. 141–55; Alasdair MacIntyre, "Egoism and Altruism," *The Encyclopedia of Philosophy*, ed. Paul Edwards, 8 vols. (New York: The Macmillan Company & The Free Press, 1967), 2:462–66; Bertrand Russell, "The Elements of Ethics," *Readings in Ethical Theory*, ed. W. Sellars and J. Hospers (New York: Appleton-Century Crofts, Inc., 1952), pp. 23–27; Moritz Schlick, *Problems of Ethics*, trans. David Rynin (New York: Dover Publications, Inc., 1962), pp. 56–78.

for instance of a Hobbesian warrant for societal restraints to avoid total civil war.[11] (2) The life of agape is one of utter self-giving where God is actually the subject. "*Agape*-ethics" might then be purely reportive of what such a life involves.

In order to determine just how oversimplified these alternatives are, one would have to know more than Nygren explicitly tells us. Later I shall mention some confusions concerning psychological egoism, but for the moment simply note two possible complications to the above, neither of which I think Nygren would find very palatable. These will involve a digression into some difficult theological questions, and I shall be brief.

First, if one wishes to appeal to Reformation theology, as Nygren uncritically does in the case of Luther, one need not equate the motives in the agent's relations to God and to other men. The question of "spiritual righteousness" is one thing, and before God one might be, apart from grace, a thoroughgoing egoist. The ques-

11. Under "*eros*-ethics" one might then envisage a version of ethical egoism. While ethical egoism has several possible formulations, all of them hold roughly that each man ought predominantly to pursue his own advantage, self-interest, welfare, etc. Psychological egoism is sometimes the argument about human nature cited as the basis for the normative theory, though it has also been argued that psychological egoism actually makes ethical egoism redundant ("One might as well urge people who jump out of windows to go downward rather than upward" [Hospers, *Human Conduct*, p. 141]). Another question, about which there has been a good deal of recent interest, is whether ethical egoism satisfies the minimal conditions for any moral system. However that question is decided, ethical egoism as a normative principle is clearly inconsistent with agape as a normative principle. In addition to some of the items in the preceding footnote, see Kurt Baier, *The Moral Point of View* (Ithaca, N.Y.: Cornell University Press, 1958), pp. 187–213; Richard B. Brandt, *Ethical Theory* (Englewood Cliffs, N.J.: Prentice-Hall, Inc., 1959), pp. 353–79; C. D. Broad, "Certain Features in Moore's Ethical Doctrines," *The Philosophy of G. E. Moore*, ed. P. A. Schlipp (Evanston: Northwestern University, 1942), pp. 43–57; J. A. Brunton, "Egoism and Morality," *Philosophical Quarterly* 6 (1956): 289–303 (reprinted in Joseph Margolis, ed., *Contemporary Ethical Theory* [New York: Random House, 1966], pp. 280–300); Jesse Kalin, "On Ethical Egoism," *Studies in Moral Philosophy — American Philosophical Quarterly*, Monograph 1, ed. N. Rescher (Oxford: Basil Blackwell, 1968): 26–41; Brian Medlin, "Ultimate Principles and Ethical Egoism," *The Australasian Journal of Philosophy* 35 (1957): 111–18.

tion of "civic righteousness" is another, and here one might have *some* capacity for fellow-feeling, transcendence of one's own interests, and so on. Such a capacity might be severely limited, perhaps confined mainly to social arrangements, but not wholly absent or explained away.[12] Furthermore, one might allow that it can fluctuate within the same person and vary between persons and groups.

Second, one might distinguish the resources of *natural* human life, as denoting life apart from God, from the resources of *actual* human life, where God is always present. The former would accordingly appear as a logical possibility only, though nonetheless of prime importance theologically.

> [T]here may be a concept of 'natural man' that refers to no actual individual at all but only to a purely hypothetical being; that is to say, to man as he *would* be were it not for the grace of God, but (the theologian might wish to add) as in fact he never is, since this is God's world which He has not abandoned.[13]

If this distinction is a proper one, then in a sense the wheel comes full circle. For one may once more refer to agape as an actual alternative to acquisitiveness through divine grace, as something available to men in their present confusions and trials, and as applicable

12. It may be that certain strains in Luther himself resist assimilation into Nygren's program. The difficulties in trying to reconcile Luther's various statements are of course immense. But one finds in some of his writings a view close to what I shall consider in a moment: the agent's own interests serve as the paradigm of all others, and may be taken as the standard for treating others in the sense of the golden rule. In making this point, it would seem that Luther assumes the agent has some capacity to effect the transfer. Note for instance the following from the 1535 *Lectures on Galatians*: "No one can find a better, surer, or more available pattern than himself; nor can there be a nobler or more profound attitude of mind than love; nor is there a more excellent object than one's neighbor. . . . Thus if you want to know how the neighbor is to be loved and want to have an outstanding pattern of this, consider carefully how you love yourself" (*Luther's Works,* trans. Jaroslav Pelikan [Saint Louis: Concordia Publishing House, 1964], 27:57).

13. Maclagan, *Theological Frontier of Ethics,* p. 30.

in suitably different ways toward God and other men. Moreover, if one does not accept Nygren's account of the Christian as a tube or funnel, some place may be meaningfully ascribed to human decision in response to providential action. Yet this latter ascription does imply that one rejects psychological egoism as an exhaustive account.

A related issue is whether and how agape as an actual alternative is linked to *faith*. For instance, does agape require some definite belief in God in order to be known and/or actualized? These issues go beyond my immediate concerns. I allude to them now only to observe that they may crucially affect the claims about agape as an actual alternative. In Barth's view, as we shall see, faith and agape are not properties of human nature but definite actions occurring to certain men.[14] Yet they are nonetheless correlative *with one another*. This may mean that agape as an actual alternative connects necessarily with faith.

Self-Love as Normal, Reasonable, Prudent

The second value judgment is that self-love is normal, reasonable, prudent: it is not especially praiseworthy but not necessarily blameworthy. One encounters here a relatively straightforward assumption. People do not need just in general to be urged toward concern about their own welfare. We have plenty of attachment to that, and of an immediate and unreflective kind. Thus our pursuit of it does not involve moral merit or virtue. Considered in itself it is not an obligation. At most one may call it normal, reasonable, prudent. On the other hand, one need not disparage it altogether. The elements of unease and distrust, evident in Nygren, no longer predominate; prudential self-regard need not inevitably or totally pass over into acquisitiveness. It is more likely to incline toward narrowmindedness than toward incorrigible selfishness. Hence its evils are not always set forth in comparably stark and dramatic terms.

Such an assumption, I think, stands behind one very common

14. For Barth, acquisitive self-love or eros is likewise not a property but a definite action.

interpretation of the "as yourself" clause in the second great commandment, namely, "you shall love your neighbor as you *now* love
yourself." Note, for example, the following exegesis by Rudolf
Bultmann.

> It is . . . stupid to say . . . that a justifiable self-love, a nec-
> essary standard of self-respect, must precede love of neighbor,
> since the command runs "love your neighbor *as yourself.*" Self-
> love is thus presupposed. Yes, it is indeed presupposed, but not
> as something which man needs to learn, which must be ex-
> pressly required of him. It is the attitude of the natural man
> which must be overcome.[15]

Bultmann's last sentence, to be sure, must be construed with caution.
While the pursuit of one's own interests is not a command or
obligation, it is never wrong in itself. It need not be overcome or
overridden on every occasion (e.g., not in cases of mutual cooperation), but perhaps only where a clash with the legitimate interests of
others is involved. In any event there is common agreement that we
are all far more disposed, without special prompting, toward our
own welfare than toward our neighbor's, and that the sting in the
commandment is directed against this disposition.

One may distinguish two further senses in which self-love is held
to be a natural state of affairs and not blameworthy, the first of
which holds that one's own interests serve as the paradigm of all
others; they are the most adequate index of what other-regard
means. This is the case in at least two closely-related senses. First,
self-love has been taken to be a paradigm for equal regard of others
per se because it is basically independent of idiosyncratic attractiveness and merit in oneself. To quote Paul Ramsey:

> How exactly do you love yourself? Answer this question and
> you will know how a Christian should love his neighbor. You
> naturally love yourself for your own sake. You wish your own

15. Rudolph Bultmann, *Jesus and the Word*, trans. Louise Pettibone Smith and
Erminie Huntress Lantero (New York: Charles Scribner's Sons, 1958), p. 116.

good, and you do so even when you may have a certain distaste for the kind of person you are. Liking yourself or thinking yourself very nice, or not, has fundamentally nothing to do with the matter. After a failure of some sort, the will-to-live soon returns and you always lay hold expectantly on *another* possibility of attaining some good for yourself. You love yourself more than you love any good qualities or worth you may possess. Unsubdued by bad qualities, not elicited by good ones, self-love does not wait on worth. In fact it is the other way around: self-love makes you desire worth for yourself. Regardless of fluctuations in feeling, you love yourself on one day about as much as on any other. And regardless of differences in temperament or capacity for deep emotion, one person probably wishes his own good about as much as another person wishes for his.[16]

Second, self-love has been taken to be the standard for treatment of others in the sense of the golden rule: "Do unto others as you would have them do unto you." In the recent literature there is a surprising paucity of explicit discussion of this ancient formula.[17] All I shall do now is note that self-love in accordance with the golden rule may be the source of more specific judgments of what counts as other-regard. The degree of specificity is a matter of dispute; there are absurdities in saying that if I detest sympathy I ought not to be sympathetic, if I want to be punished I ought to punish, and so on. What perhaps is assumed is that most people do not detest sympathy or want to be punished, or at least do not want to have their interests simply ignored, and that self-love may thus be cogently universalized. The agent, at a minimum, must be willing to apply the same general standard of treatment to others that he wishes to see applied

16. Ramsey, *Basic Christian Ethics*, pp. 99–100. For an earlier formulation of the same assessment, see Luther, *Lectures on Romans, The Library of Christian Classics*, trans. & ed. Wilhelm Pauck (Philadelphia: The Westminster Press, 1961), 4:366–69.

17. See Tillich, *Love, Power, and Justice*, pp. 79–80. Cf. however R. M. Hare, *Freedom and Reason* (New York: Oxford University Press, 1965); Marcus G. Singer, "The Golden Rule," *Philosophy* 38 (Oct., 1963): 293–314.

to himself. This means that the interests, aspirations, etc. of others must be taken into account, however different some of them may be from the agent's own. In this way, "selfish prudential reasoning" is turned into "moral reasoning." [18]

The final sense in which self-love is held not to be blameworthy involves the recognition of blessing or fruition to the self which may attend other-regard. Often reference is made to Jesus' teaching about finding one's life by losing it.[19] The question of sequence is important, of course; fruition cannot be the objective of one's regard, or that regard becomes a version of acquisitiveness. Blessing to the self must thus be unintended or epiphenomenal. In scholastic terminology, it is not a cause, but a proper accident. Yet such blessing is more than empathetic delight in the happiness of others, though it will include that.

One fairly representative account is Reinhold Niebuhr's. He is fond of citing the following sort of paradox: "consistent self-seeking is bound to be self-defeating; on the other hand, self-giving is bound to contribute ultimately to self-realization." [20] The paradox appears to include two elements. First, consistent self-seeking is self-defeating because the self is never rich in isolation: "Whatever spiritual wealth the self has within itself is the by-product of its relations, affections, and responsibilities, of its concern for life beyond itself." [21] Second,

18. Hare, *Freedom and Reason*, p. 94.

19. The place of reward in Jesus' teachings generally (including a defense of its prominence) is interestingly considered in K. E. Kirk, *The Vision of God* (London: Longmans, Green and Co., 1956), pp. 140–46. For a further discussion along the same lines, see Helen Oppenheimer, "Christian Flourishing," *Religious Studies* 5 (December, 1969): 163–71. She sees a danger "that the ancient and healthy Jewish and Christian concept of goodness as having something to do with flourishing, fruition, blessing, will be lost in high-mindedness" (p. 167).

20. Reinhold Niebuhr, *Man's Nature and His Communities* (New York: Charles Scribner's Sons, 1965), pp. 106–07. For other references to the paradox of self-realization through self-giving see Niebuhr, *Faith and History*, pp. 176–79; *The Self and the Dramas of History* (New York: Charles Scribner's Sons, 1955), pp. 31–32.

21. Niebuhr, *Faith and History*, p. 177.

self-giving produces self-enhancement and fulfillment — but it is unclear whether self-fulfillment follows naturally or providentially, to what degree it follows, and in what precisely the fulfillment consists. The answers will probably vary according to the individual's estimate of what consequences to the agent are likely to follow other-regarding actions in this life.[22] Hence Niebuhr sometimes refers to reciprocity in kind, noting how uninitiated love does frequently win a response definable as a this-worldly consequence. But this response is never guaranteed, for, as we saw earlier, he stresses self-sacrifice and the permanent possibility of historical failure. Self-fulfillment then does not necessarily include "physical security or historic success." Finally, the blessing is primarily a religious one: "spiritual wealth" connotes freedom from anxiety about the self's final destiny and the present significance of its striving. Kierkegaard removes virtually all references to this-worldly consequences, though no more than Niebuhr to this-worldly *actions*, i.e., on the need to serve particular neighbors in definite ways. Reward itself is received only from God and is measured by the agent's other-regarding motives and intentions. But within eschatological limits the concept of "reduplication" or "like-for-like" rigorously applies.

God is love, and when a human being because of love forgets himself and thinks of the other person, God thinks of the lover. The self-lover is busy; he shouts and complains and insists on his rights in order to make sure he is not forgotten. . . . But the lover, who forgets himself, is remembered by love. There is One who thinks of him, and in this way it comes about that the lover gets what he gives.[23]

22. I should just mention what I hope is obvious: the issue here concerns only unintended de facto consequences *to the agent*. Whether the morality of an action affecting others is to be judged wholly or in part by *its* consequences is another issue altogether and falls roughly under deciding what to count as other-regard. Niebuhr is free to say (and does) that "this-worldly" consequences in the latter sense are centrally relevant in moral judgments.

23. Kierkegaard, *Works of Love*, p. 262; see also pp. 354–56.

Self-Love as Justified Derivatively

Those who treat self-love as not especially praiseworthy in itself
sometimes go on to allow for deliberate concern about the agent's
own welfare, so long as this can be derived from other-regard.

Some definition of legitimate concern for the self must be given,
even if only as a secondary and derivative part of Christian
Ethics. For certainly as a part of vocational service grounded in
Christian love for neighbor, an individual has great responsibility
for the development and use of all his natural capacities, or else
he takes responsibility for rashly throwing them away.[24]

There is still no direct obligation to be thus concerned, independent
of benefitting others. Concern is obligatory only when it is instru-
mentally conducive, in effect, to such benefit. But when it so con-
duces, it may be justified by a process analogous to that followed
with self-denial or self-sacrifice.[25]

Given the assumption that men are typically disposed to accord
themselves, arbitrarily, a privileged position, the validity of derivative concern is acknowledged but not stressed. Our capacity for self-
deception in comparing the importance of our own welfare with
that of others is vast enough, apart from tempting theoretical opportunities to rationalize this tendency. Nevertheless, hard as it
often is to distinguish in practice between privileged and derivative
concern, it is possible to allow in theory for cases in which the self-
benefitting action is morally right because the decisive reasons remain other-regarding ones. Here I shall elaborate, in part, on the
reasons identified in chapter 1 for refusing in the name of agape to
issue a blank check.

The first consideration is that of the neighbor's own good. The
agent ought to stand up for his own welfare when others, by neglecting it, are encouraged toward their own corruption and are under-

24. Ramsey, *Basic Christian Ethics*, p. 159.
25. Thomas, *Christian Ethics and Moral Philosophy*, p. 514; cf. Brunner,
Divine Imperative, pp. 170–78, 306–07.

mining general other-regarding conditions for human community. W. G. Maclagan observes that

> [T]here can be a disciplinary value for others in our not permitting them to treat our happiness with indifference. Not only have we no obligation to make ourselves, as it were, "everybody's doormat"; we have something of an obligation not to do so. Nor is the reason for this adequately given in the form that others, considered severally as individuals, will be better men and women if they learn to respect interests not their own, though that is true enough. Inseparable from this is the further fact that the realisation of a good community, which is the moral concern of us all, is impossible on any other terms.[26]

Another sort of case, already alluded to, which seems to justify the agent's asserting his interests at the expense of another's, is one where the interests of third parties are at stake and a sacrifice of his interests would constitute an unjust betrayal of theirs. To cite an obvious instance, if I resist an aggressor the moral judgment of my action will take account of his express intention to murder my family. Here obligation and self-interest may simply coincide. A problem arises for the defender of derivative self-concern in such a case only if the moral analysis is confined mistakenly to "bilateral" rather than "multilateral" considerations.[27]

The agent may also be obligated to look after his own welfare: negatively, in order not to burden others, and positively, in order most effectively to further their good. This applies to such obvious external matters as keeping his own affairs in order so that others will not have to do so. But it may also apply in ways more personal and compelling. For example, his own basic happiness or unhappiness may be an object of concern to him because of its effects upon others.

26. Maclagan, "Self and Others," pp. 118–19. His discussion (pp. 116–22) of the other-regarding reasons for self-benefitting actions sometimes being morally right seems to me especially acute. Most of the reasons he considers, including the three I mention here, can be found in the theological literature, though in general less clearly formulated.

27. These words are used by Hare, *Freedom and Reason*, e.g., p. 117.

If he dwells on his disappointments or makes little effort to restrain his bleaker moods, his family and friends will suffer as well. He may come to realize, on a level far deeper than telling himself to "cheer up," that his own state of contentment and satisfaction is morally relevant as it enhances the prospects of serving ends beyond such satisfaction.

Self-Love as a Definite Obligation

Reasons that justify self-concern of a derivative kind leave writers like D'Arcy and Johann dissatisfied. I think they differ at the following points from the views considered in the preceding two sections. The assumption that people need not, in general, be urged toward concern about their own welfare appears too sanguine and simple. D'Arcy in particular believes that active or self-regarding love *("eros")* and passive or self-sacrificing love *("agape")* are both corruptible. I shall not discuss his own detailed account of these two loves, which he also takes up in terms respectively of *animus* and *anima,* mind and heart, essence and existence, though it seems to me bewilderingly eclectic. The point for our purposes now is that self-regard and other-regard, when carried to excess, give rise to roughly equivalent dangers. Self-sacrifice can become too prodigal almost as readily as self-regard can become too acquisitive; the relative strength and weakness of each are sufficiently alike to require independent attention and proportional exhortation.

> Selfishness is only a vice if it means an undue regard for self; unselfishness is only a virtue if it is countered by self-respect. The two loves, therefore, so far from being opposites appear to require the presence of each other.[28]

28. D'Arcy, *Mind and Heart of Love,* p. 348. Much of the disagreement between D'Arcy and the views considered earlier lies, then, in differing estimates of how disposed people are in general toward unselfishness. Cf., e.g., Brunner, *Divine Imperative,* p. 328: "I must remember that [since] by nature I oppose my will to that of the other, the first and also the surest sign of genuine love is my acceptance of the other person — that attitude which does not correct others, or 'pull people up,' or demand, or resist. For masochists are few and far between in the human race."

Moreover, self-love as self-respect may refer to laudable attitudes and actions not all of which can be either encompassed under prudence or linked necessarily with benefit to others. There are additional precepts with which prudence ought to be compared but not confused. To take a concrete instance, "that someone ought to stick to his own vocation when his heart is in it enough to make it worth risking security or health or life itself is not a precept of *prudence,* but of *courage.*" [29] Of course such talk is subject to distortions which do involve others and must be guarded against. One would not want to back the romanticist assumption that a genius in realizing his gifts has the right to wreck the lives of those around him. But when distortions such as this are set aside, some action-guiding considerations remain. They relate generally to being one's own master, to exercising self-control and resisting temptations, to tenaciously following one's own lights when the occasion arises or in defense of one's liberty. Failure to adhere to these precepts is lamentable and perhaps blameworthy. ("He deserves what happened to him, since he just goes along with whatever crowd he happens to be in.") When self-love is assessed, therefore, some allowance must be made not only for the evil of acquisitiveness, but also for the positive value of considerations allied to self-respect. [30]

Those who adduce such considerations find it hard to see how all of them are parasitic upon other-regard. Something like courage can be displayed in one's own interests as well as that of others; it cannot

29. W. D. Falk, "Morality, Self, and Others," *Morality and the Language of Conduct,* eds. Hector-Neri Castañeda and George Nakhnikian (Detroit: Wayne State University Press, 1965), p. 34. Cf. Gabriele Taylor and Sybil Wolfram, "The Self-Regarding and Other Regarding Virtues," *Philosophical Quarterly* 18 (July, 1968): 238–48.

30. Moreover, a trait like self-respect need not be taken as incompatible with the traditional Christian stress on humility. "What then is humility? Humility does not consist in thinking one is a failure when one is not. Indeed, a man who does this may be guilty of pride, if it indicates that he feels he ought to be judged on higher standards than other people for no good reason. Humility is rather the recognition that there is infinite room for improvement and that the minimum standard which is connected with self-respect is no great achievement" (Elizabeth Telfer, "Self-Respect," *Philosophical Quarterly* 18 [April, 1968], p. 121).

be derived altogether from likely advantage to them, however often it may be compatible with such advantage. Some are prepared to grant that the bulk of imposing moral considerations are indeed other-regarding ones. They may even concede that at least in everyday usage the notion of a moral obligation is reserved pretty largely for a commitment to others. Nonetheless, they hold that self-regarding commitments are sometimes closely akin to other-regarding ones in being directives for action, and that self-regarding commitments may on occasion override commitments to others. This last point is of course a critical one. In theory at any rate, the decisive action-guiding reasons cannot always, exhaustively and without remainder, be other-regarding ones. There may be cases where interests conflict, and where the loss to the agent is unacceptably greater than the loss to the other, even when the latter is not morally negligible.

> It might . . . be that . . . someone ought to stand up for his own good even to the detriment of another. It could be sound advice to say to a woman in strife with herself and tied to a demanding parent, "You ought to consider yourself, and so break away now, hard as it may be on the parent." [31]

For D'Arcy and Johann, however, to say that the bulk of imposing moral considerations are other-regarding may already be conceding too much to the view that we have plenty of unreflective attachment to our own welfare apart from other-regard. In any event, the issue of the relation between self-regard and other-regard is then wrongly conceived. This is not because of the major difficulties in any so-called bias theory: what criteria should we employ to determine how far the

31. Falk, "Morality, Self, and Others," p. 49. See also E. F. Carritt, *Ethical and Political Thinking* (Oxford: Clarendon Press, 1947), pp. 113–16. In a case like that of the woman in strife, someone wishing to justify self-benefitting actions as derivative from other-regard could allow that in many instances she ought to break away. He would only insist that her reasons ought to relate to reasonably foreseeable benefits to others. She might break away for example in order to become a medical doctor. Here there could be an other-regarding justification to begin and to stick to one's vocation, which might override *explicit* commitments to others, especially to a single other, such as the demanding parent.

scales ought to be tipped in favor of the neighbor? [32] Rather, the possibility of basic conflicts of interest appears simply to be ruled out, perhaps by definitional fiat. For self-love and neighbor-love are taken as *coincident,* not in some cases so that there is merely no need to concern ourselves to disentangle the former, as morally indifferent, but in all cases. This is implied in D'Arcy's account of the roughly equivalent dangers to agape and eros and the way the two loves require the presence of each other. Johann is even more explicit. Self-love is a manifest obligation, yet its proper and enlightened pursuit is never an alternative to neighbor-love, but is rather correlative. Any attempt to oppose them denies in fact the constituted nature of the relationship: I cannot choose to love the other simply in addition to loving myself or even as much as I love myself. Rather I am not fully myself until I am present and open to the other; I only love myself when I am able to love him, just as I love him only when I overcome acquisitiveness. Enlightened self-love is impossible apart from love for God and neighbor. "Only when drawn into communion with other selves is my own person confirmed in being and my own love equal to the perfection to which it secretly aspires." [33] *Ex hypothesi,* enlightened self-love will then dictate approximately the same course of action as neighbor-love.

A final observation should be noted in passing about the position of coincidence. Its proponents do not seem interested in what an unsympathetic critic might call an eschatological escape clause. That is, the coincidence of which they speak does not appear to require, necessarily, a reference to a world to come. Here and now, discrepancies between giving and getting are held to be more apparent than real. In refusing to love others, one's own welfare is damaged in

32. These difficulties may be marshalled in support of altruism. See, e.g., Maclagan, "Self and Others," pp. 114–15.

33. Johann, *Meaning of Love,* p. 44; cf. pp. 33, 42. "Our actions will be true to ourselves and to the requirements of all our relationships only if they are deliberately ordered in the direction of a universal love. The commandment to love universally is not something imposed on us from outside; it is simply a formulation of the very exigencies of our beings as persons" (Johann, "Love and Justice," *Ethics and Society,* ed. Richard T. De George [Garden City, N.Y.: Doubleday, 1966], p. 40).

this life. Naturally coincidence is not immediately evident in every case, but a generalization based on a temporal "long run" is defensible. And of course a man may in fact love badly. But this will be reflected not only in his indifference toward God and cruelty toward others, but also in the division and alienation within himself.[34]

34. Johann, "Love and Justice," p. 37.

3

Agape and Justice

> Amongst an association of saints, if such a community could really exist, the disputes about justice could hardly occur; for they would all work selflessly together for one end, the glory of God as defined by their common religion, and reference to this end would settle every question of right. The justice of practices does not come up until there are several different parties . . . who do press their claims on one another, and who do regard themselves as representatives of interests which deserve to be considered.
>
> John Rawls

Let us now consider the second principle with which agape is most often compared. Here too one finds a complex state of multiple usage, sometimes conflicting, sometimes not. Of course everyone agrees that justice has something to do with at least an inchoate sense of *suum cuique:* the rendering to each man of his due. Moreover, in most of the treatments before us the stress is on justice as a predicate of societies and of their actions and institutions. Thus I shall be primarily though not exclusively concerned with social justice rather than, say, commutative justice (involving rights between two individuals).

But this clearly does not limit us very much. And despite the agreement about *suum cuique,* a conceptual vagueness surrounds "justice" in the literature. The difficulties include how to determine what is "due," and also how agape may affect the definition of what is due and/or may add to it. It seems wisest again to begin inductively, for the proposed relations between agape and justice range from opposition to equation. In the first three sections of this chapter, I shall set out some of the major senses in which they have been related. In the last, I shall underscore the way in which many of these differences reflect varying conceptions of the principles involved.

Agape and Justice Opposed

Once more the figure who offers the clearest account of opposition is Nygren. This is nicely illustrated in his discussion of the parable of the laborers in the vineyard (Matt. 20:1–16), which he takes to be a particularly illuminating example of the incompatibility between agape and justice.

The kingdom of heaven is like this. There was once a landowner who went out early one morning to hire labourers for his vineyard; and after agreeing to pay them the usual day's wage he sent them off to work. Going out three hours later he saw some more men standing idle in the market-place. "Go and join the others in the vineyard," he said, "and I will pay you a fair wage"; so off they went. At noon he went out again, and at three in the afternoon, and made the same arrangement as before. An hour before sunset he went out and found another group standing there; so he said to them, "Why are you standing about like this all day with nothing to do?" "Because no one has hired us", they replied; so he told them, "Go and join the others in the vineyard." When evening fell, the owner of the vineyard said to his steward, "Call the labourers and give them their pay, beginning with those who came last and ending with the first." Those who had started work an hour before sunset came forward, and were paid the full day's wage. When it was the turn of the men who had come first, they expected something extra, but were paid the same amount as the others. As they took it, they grumbled at their employer: "These latecomers have done only one hour's work, yet you have put them on a level with us, who have sweated the whole day long in the blazing sun!" The owner turned to one of them and said, "My friend, I am not being unfair to you. You agreed on the usual wage for the day, did you not? Take your pay and go home. I choose to pay the last man the same as you. Surely I am free to do what I like with my own money. Why be jealous because I am kind?" [New English Bible]

Nygren treats the parable as pointing both to the character of God's love (which is in turn the prototype of human agape) and the principle of justice. God's love is "unmotivated"; i.e., fellowship with men is established for no reason extrinsic to the love itself. "The point is directed against the thought of worthiness and merit, against every attempt to regulate fellowship with God by the principle of justice." [1] The clash between the position of the owner and that of the laborers who came first is genuine and uncompromising. Only agape makes the position of the owner intelligible. For neither work nor indolence evokes agape. But from the standpoint of justice the laborers are clearly right to argue as they do. The more and less deserving ought not to be treated in the same way; some proportion between work and wages is surely fair. Nygren explicitly rejects one possible compromise to the effect that the owner dealt justly with those who came first by adhering to a contract, and he exercised kindness toward the rest by aiding those poorer than himself. Nygren argues that those who came first are right to protest if the principle of justice is to be introduced at all. Thus, "it is futile to try to eliminate from this parable that which is offensive in it from a juridical point of view. The offence only ceases when the principle of justice itself is eliminated as inapplicable to the religious relationship." [2]

We should notice at once that the principle of justice is here equated with what is elsewhere often taken as one particular conception of justice, namely, "to each according to his desert or works." Justice is then a grading concept in terms of which various achievements and acquired characteristics are assessed.[3] High marks are given because or insofar as someone has done something meritorious. Advantages are allocated in accordance with particular conduct and not because the several parties are all human beings. The value which agape attaches to each man prior to his doing anything in particular is obviously never reducible to any such grading criterion. Agape

1. Nygren, *Agape and Eros*, p. 86.
2. Ibid., pp. 88–89.
3. Gregory Vlastos, "Justice and Equality," *Social Justice*, ed. Richard B. Brandt (Englewood Cliffs, N.J.: Prentice-Hall, Inc., 1962), pp. 43f.

prohibits us from grading persons as such. They ought never to be valued only for their merits, however often they are in fact so valued.

Nygren has therefore identified an important contrast between agape and "to each according to his works." The difficulty is that in the literature other conceptions of the principle of justice have also been proposed—or more frequently, vaguely assumed—and some of these conceptions have far more overlap with agape. I shall try to enumerate them more systematically toward the end of the chapter.

Agape and Justice Distinguished

Whatever one may decide about the substance of Nygren's position, it has the virtue in this instance of being clear and delimited. The same cannot be said for many of those positions which reject thoroughgoing opposition between agape and justice, but also maintain a degree of distinction between them. Nevertheless, I think such positions, however unclear in specific respects, capture more of the basic relation usually held to obtain between agape and justice than does Nygren or someone like Fletcher who collapses any distinction. This is because such positions are founded on the assumption that, even when the various conceptions comprising justice are viewed as incommensurable, they have something in common: in every situation in which disputes about justice occur, claims are being pressed and the several parties "do regard themselves as representatives of interests which deserve to be considered." [4] Nygren of course assumes this as well, but he appears to tie it without reservation to a particular conception of justice involving desert. Others, by accident or design, do not. The interests which are to be considered are not necessarily connected with desert. They can involve basic *needs* shared by everyone, quite apart from what men

4. John Rawls, "Justice as Fairness," *Philosophical Review* 67 (1958): 164–94; reprinted in *Philosophy, Politics and Society,* 2d ser., ed. Peter Laslett and W. G. Runciman (Oxford: Basil Blackwell, 1967), pp. 132–57. See also Brian Barry, "On Social Justice," *The Oxford Review* 5 (Trinity, 1967): pp. 29–52.

have individually made of their respective talents, environmental opportunities, and so on. The point then is that justice applies in a general way to a certain kind of moral situation, namely one in which mutually interested parties confront each other and where we may safely assume that each will insist on what he takes to be his rights. But nothing very definite is usually forthcoming about whether such rights are given by virtue of "common humanity," acquired by effort, bestowed by decree, or whatever.

Beyond this common assumption, the positions vary enormously. I shall document in brief fashion the characterization above and identify several variations.

We considered previously how Reinhold Niebuhr contrasts agape and justice without opposing them altogether. Emil Brunner, for one, has objected that Niebuhr never states very specifically what he means by justice;[5] but in a sense, this lack of definition substantiates the point about a common assumption. Justice for Niebuhr is above all an ethical principle which both warrants participation in the claims and counterclaims of historical society, and typically admits the claims of self-interest.

> The effort to substitute the law of love for the spirit of justice . . . is derived from the failure to measure the power and persistence of self-interest. It is because self-interest is not easily overcome in even the life of the "redeemed" that most of the harmonies of life are not the perfect harmonies of fully co-ordinated wills but the tolerable harmonies of balanced interests and mutually recognized claims.[6]

> In so far as justice admits the claims of the self, it is something less than love.[7]

In denying any thoroughgoing opposition between these concepts, however, Niebuhr also reasons as follows: "[T]he final law in which

---

5. Emil Brunner, "Some Remarks on Reinhold Niebuhr's Work as a Christian Thinker," *Reinhold Niebuhr*, pp. 30–31.

6. Niebuhr, *Love and Justice*, pp. 25–26.

7. Ibid., p. 28.

all other law is fulfilled is the law of love. But this law does not abrogate the laws of justice, except as love rises above justice to exceed its demands." [8] Such a statement may give trouble. To say that agape exceeds but never abrogates what justice requires may mean that the two principles are always substantively compatible. Then presumably agape involves, first, an acceptance of the requirements of justice, and second, an addition of further compatible requirements of its own. Elsewhere, however, Niebuhr hardly takes the two sets of requirements to be always compatible. As we saw in chapter 1, justice is a workaday moral principle, agape only partly so. In short, agape sometimes involves doing more than justice requires, but never less; at other times, the two principles imply conflicting kinds of actions between which one must choose, and without the advantage of an absolute priority either way.

I think at least three different ways of relating agape and justice have been put forward by those who deny either total opposition or equation. But the waters here are exceptionally muddy, and distinctions cannot be made with any great confidence. (1) In those situations where interests are being pressed, agape as self-sacrifice acts only as a restraint, but an indispensable one if justice is not to degenerate into inordinate self-seeking. (2) Sometimes agape and justice are contrasted in self-other relations and identified in other-other relations. Agape warrants sacrifice (if need be) where the self's own interests are at stake, as perhaps justice does not. At the same time agape warrants the active, impartial promotion of interests where the welfare of many *others* is at stake, as does justice.[9] (3) While agape and justice are distinguished conceptually, they nonetheless overlap in some cases, and whenever they do agape may require more but never less than justice does, in *both* self-other and other-other relations. Though passages in Niebuhr may be cited in support of

8. Ibid., p. 25; see also, e.g., E. Clinton Gardner, "Love and Justice," *Theology Today* (July, 1957: 212–22; reprinted in *Social Ethics,* ed. Gibson Winter (London: SCM Press, 1968), pp. 66–77.

9. "Justice may be defined as what Christian love does when confronted by two or more neighbors" (Ramsey, *Basic Christian Ethics,* p. 243).

(2) and (3), most of the time he appears to adopt (1), for reasons given earlier.

Brunner takes a position which seems to be largely a version of (2). On the one hand, at least in collective other-other relations, love *requires* justice. "In the world of systems" one "cannot give effect of his love except by being just." [10] This is because such a world by virtue of its constitutive requirements involves the kind of situation to which justice applies, where men are representatives of institutional interests which deserve to be considered. Brunner is careful not to depreciate justice thereby. It is in no way inferior to love, for "as long as we live in this world, where there are systems, justice is as indispensable as love." [11] Brunner sometimes goes so far as to approach (3): love requires more but never less than justice does. Love has justice as its "pre-condition," love can never neglect justice, and loving actions are never performed at the expense of justice but "only beyond and through" it.[12]

On the other hand, however, the two principles do not overlap. The "real gift of love only begins where justice has already been done, for it is that which is beyond justice." [13] This is a bifurcation to which many have objected.[14] Reasons for the absence of overlap include the following. First, love applies pre-eminently in personal ethics and cannot be made intelligible in relations between collectives. "If in the world of institutions, a man did not turn love into justice, he would destroy such a world." [15] Here Brunner assumes the normative content of agape to be roughly an equal regard which finds its quintessence in I Thou relations. Agape is distinguished in self-other relations not so much because of the greater sacrifice it

10. Emil Brunner, *Justice and the Social Order,* trans. Mary Hottinger (New York: Harper and Brothers, 1945), p. 128.
11. Ibid.
12. Ibid., p. 129
13. Ibid., p. 130.
14. See, e.g., Ramsey, *Basic Christian Ethics,* pp. 346–47, and *Nine Modern Moralists* (Englewood Cliffs, N.J.: Prentice-Hall, Inc., 1962), p. 207; Thomas, *Christian Ethics and Moral Philosophy,* pp. 250–53.
15. Brunner, *Justice and the Social Order,* pp. 128–29.

may involve but because of its greater personalism. Only when two people meet each other in openness and affection does agape come fully into its own. This is at once the sublimest kind of relation and one which has no direct relevance for the world of institutions. Second, agape differs from justice in that it does not measure itself out very carefully. The nicely calculated more and less is out of place; there is instead a certain carelessness about the self's own welfare and generally more spontaneity and freedom. Third, occasionally Brunner appropriates after all a theme from Nygren: concern for what is due is taken as synonymous with what is deserved. Justice then involves a fair appraisal of worth. Alternatively, agape involves an independent bestowal of worth.[16] But this is still ambiguous. Worth may or may not be assessed entirely on the basis of particular conduct. For Brunner and Nygren at this juncture, worth seems clearly tied to individually acquired desert. Yet worth has also been taken to refer to each man as irreducibly valuable apart from particular conduct. Can one plausibly speak of what is due a man qua human existent? Does the principle of justice apply when one does so speak? This sort of question is rarely addressed in explicit terms in the literature, a state of affairs which seems to me to vitiate a good deal of the discussion which does go on. Again, the relation between agape and justice may depend on particular conceptions held about the latter as well as the former.

Gérard Gilleman adopts a position closest to (3): while agape and justice are distinguished conceptually, they nonetheless overlap in some cases, and whenever they do, agape may require more but never less than justice does, in both self-other and other-other relations. Gilleman too finds that questions of justice arise when rights are being actively pressed by self-interested parties. Such pressure occurs instinctively and spontaneously at both individual and collective levels, and usually in a fashion which is at best morally indifferent. The principle of justice occupies something like an intermediary position between instinctive self-interest and agape or charity. Self-interest at every level is to be justly constrained, i.e., by fair or non-arbitrary arrangements to which all parties may subscribe. In

16. Ibid., p. 126.

this way justice is both distinguished from and yet fully compatible
with charity. Justice is "a more limited and strict obligation" not because it is more perfect than charity but "because it assures the
minimum of charitable relations necessary to safeguard further progress in love." [17] Justice is more "external" and applicable largely to
goods, possessions, services rendered, and the like. Charity is a far
richer and more complex principle; for example, it refers to communication and help where people are aware of the inner lives of
one another. A personalist strain thus appears in Gilleman as well.

Yet there is overlap in some cases. By the application of the
principle of justice a minimum of *charitable* relations is assured.
Likewise, charity is not confined to I-Thou relations, but has direct
relevance for the world of institutions. This may be illustrated by the
change Gilleman believes charity effects on the character of the nicely
calculated more and less. Such calculation may often be governed
by what Gilleman calls the "vindictive instinct": each side presses
its own claims without attendant regard for any other party except
as an object from which concessions must be extracted. Each side
views the other as an opponent who is responsible for grievances
and who will try to take advantage of any weakness. Crudely, justice
applies then as a kind of adjudicating principle whose goal is a
rough equilibrium of contending social forces with concentrations of
power dispersed as widely as possible. Gilleman thinks charity alters
the vindictive instinct and in effect elevates the goal of justice itself.[18] The relations between collectives ought to be judged and may
be judged (in terms of actual possibilities) not simply by a negative
respect for other parties' rights, but by their positive promotion. While
all of this remains rather vague, his own specific example suggests
something of what he has in mind.

An industrialist, remarking the insufficiency of his workers'
wages and the social risks they run in his factory, spontaneously

17. Gérard Gilleman, S.J., *The Primacy of Charity in Moral Theology*, trans.
William F. Ryan, S.J., and André Vachon, S.J. (Westminster, Md.: Newman
Press, 1961), p. 334. The French edition is *Le Primat de la Charité en Théologie
Morale* (Bruxelles: Desclée de Brouwer, 1954).
18. See also Thomas, *Christian Ethics and Moral Philosophy*, pp. 246–61.

raises their wages and insures them against these risks, because
his conscience tells him that in justice he must respect the rights
of these men who are bound to him by personal ties and, therefore, have a special title to his love in charity. Such a Christian
attitude—in the ideal hypothesis that it were to become general
—would permit and even compel the workers to adopt a similar
disposition. A second attitude is that of workers and employers
alike vindicating their right by every means in their power,
especially by the economic constraint of lockouts and strikes.
Such is the attitude of instinctive justice, which . . . opposes
two groups who are thinking primarily of themselves. The
former attitude tends to union, the latter to division and strife.
. . . We do not say that this second attitude is always illegitimate, but it is only justified as a makeshift, when the former
attitude is absent.[19]

Niebuhr would probably regard this as a semi-quixotic attempt to
apply the ideal of harmony and brotherhood too directly to the realities of collective life. One could never be certain, to take Gilleman's
example, that the first action of the industrialist would elicit (to say
nothing of compel) a similar response from the workers. Yet Gilleman might also reply to Niebuhr as follows. Could one not agree
that the industrialist's first action was just rather than agapeistic? To
question whether the first action would elicit a similar response could
be construed as questioning whether it is prudential to be more just
than one *has* to be, rather than whether justice is still the principle
in accordance with which one acts.[20] A Niebuhrian treatment of justice appears sometimes to assume that everything one party gives
another without being forced to or without the assurance of reciprocation falls under a principle other than justice. But this perhaps goes

19. Ibid., p. 339.
20. Two claims seem not very clearly distinguished in the writings of Niebuhr
and many others: (1) agape as self-sacrifice *motivates* one to give up inordinate
self-seeking and thus be more just; (2) agape accepts the state of inordinate self-
seeking as the characteristic situation of justice and enjoins one to be *more* than
just.

beyond the common assumption that in a situation to which justice typically applies the several parties regard themselves as representatives of interests which deserve to be considered. Justice itself may require some fair promotion of various interests even when the parties involved are not forced to it. Gilleman, then, distinguishes far more than Niebuhr instinctive justice from the virtue of justice as elevated by charity. And he displays a basic optimism about the prospects of realizing the latter as a general social ideal. In any event, Gilleman gives us a rough version of (3). Justice and agape overlap in part because the areas of cooperativeness and consensus in group relations are stressed more than the elements of conflict.

Agape and Justice Identified

The final sense in which agape and justice have been related is far different (ostensibly at least) from anything so far considered. Joseph Fletcher writes, "Love and justice are the same, for justice is love distributed, nothing else." [21] I shall try to describe Fletcher's proposition and then discuss in slightly more detail its professed connection to utilitarianism.

Fletcher expressly rejects the relation between agape and justice proposed by Nygren, Niebuhr, Brunner, and a Catholic position such as Gilleman's.[22] But it is not easy to trace the definite alternative in the hail of assertions he offers on this subject. Much of the time the pivot of Fletcher's discussion is a refusal ever to confine love to one-to-one relations. (He stipulates that such relations, if they can be successfully isolated in any sense, fall under philia or eros.) The second great commandment ought to read "You shall love your neighbors as yourself." [23] In situations of moral choice, the agent always confronts in effect more than one neighbor, for there are always multilateral considerations to be weighed in any of his actions. If we say that justice is "being fair as between neighbors," then it is

21. Fletcher, *Situation Ethics*, p. 87.
22. Ibid., p. 93.
23. Ibid., p. 91.

really no different from love. Since "each of the claimants must be heard in relation to the others," with no "selective blindness" permitted, justice is simply "the many-sidedness of love" or "love coping with situations where distribution is called for." [24] And distribution is always called for. It is not enough to allow that agape *includes* justice as part of its normative content so that no independent principle of distribution is required above and beyond agape.[25] Rather, they are to be coalesced altogether.

But Fletcher also equates agape with utilitarianism. "Let's say plainly that agape is utility; love is wellbeing; the Christian who does not individualize or sentimentalize love *is* a utilitarian." [26] This immediately poses the complicated question of whether his two equations can be mutually compatible, whether one can identify agape and justice as well as agape and utilitarianism. While I would digress too far if this question were considered very fully, it bears so directly on the proposed relation between love and justice that some brief comment is required.

How then are utility and justice customarily related? Can Fletcher have it both ways? One influential sort of relation has been to define utility or beneficence as "the principle that we ought to do the act or follow the rule which will or will probably bring about *the greatest possible balance of good over evil* in the universe." [27] The principle of beneficence here presupposes and follows from the more basic principle of benevolence: "we ought to do good and to prevent or avoid doing harm." [28] On this scheme the principle of justice is independent of beneficence and has to do not with the *quantity* of good over evil, but the *manner* in which it is distributed.[29] An action may maximize the amount of good in the world and still not distribute the good very equally over the population as a whole.

24. Ibid., pp. 88–90, 95.
25. Ibid., p. 94. Cf. Frederick S. Carney, "Deciding in the Situation: What is Required?", *Norm and Context in Christian Ethics*, pp. 7–9.
26. Fletcher, "What's in a Rule?: A Situationist's View," *Norm and Context in Christian Ethics*, p. 332.
27. Frankena, *Ethics*, p. 37.
28. Ibid.
29. See also Frankena, "The Concept of Social Justice," *Social Justice*, p. 4.

Justice requires us to distribute the good more equally, even if this demands on occasion the adoption of a less beneficent rule. In any case, on this understanding the principles of utility and justice are distinct, and the latter is capable of overriding the former. What is just cannot be ascertained simply by an appeal to utility, much less by being identified with it.

If this is what Fletcher means by utility (and the principle of beneficence above is often taken to be pure utilitarianism), then it clearly is contradictory to equate agape with both this principle and justice. But I think one may regard it as fairly certain that Fletcher does not mean to equate agape or utilitarianism with beneficence in this sense. He may mean that the principle of utility enjoins us to promote the greatest good of the greatest number. But then, as William K. Frankena points out, we still have a double principle: "it tells us (1) to produce the greatest possible balance of good over evil and (2) to distribute this as widely as possible." [30] Thus we abandon pure utilitarianism for the principles of both beneficence and justice. Yet Frankena takes this move still to involve an acceptance of the possibility that the two principles may conflict and that no formula is available for deciding when one or the other takes precedence. Considerations derived from each principle must be coordinated as far as possible, but they cannot be equated merely by fiat. Fletcher neglects then to discuss how his own program can deal with a standard difficulty which has plagued utilitarians (and which ought to concern agapists more than it does), namely: "maximization versus equalization," or the so-called " 'meshing problem' of balancing the total amount of good at issue in a given putative distribution against the fairness of the distribution in cases where these two desiderata cut against one another." [31] To say that distribution is always called for does nothing toward meeting the difficulty.

As utility and justice are customarily related, therefore, it does not appear that Fletcher can have it both ways. But there is another meaning sometimes ascribed to justice which might not require us

30. Frankena, *Ethics,* p. 34.
31. Nicholas Rescher, *Distributive Justice* (Indianapolis: The Bobbs-Merrill Co., Inc., 1966), p. 40.

to give it such an independent and delimited status. Here what is
due a man is whatever is required by valid moral principles.[32] Justice
is acting in conformity with such principles. Just-making considerations are on this view not simply one species of right-making
considerations but rather are synonymous with the latter. To judge
that an action is right is to judge that it is just, and to judge that
an action is wrong is to judge it as unjust. Hence if one's valid moral
principle is agape, justice may be identified with it after all.

> The point is that "just" and "unjust" seem to play a double role.
> On the one hand, they refer to certain sorts of right-making
> considerations as against others; on the other hand, they have
> much the same force as do the more general terms "right" and
> "wrong," so much so that one can hardly conjoin "just" and
> "wrong," or "right" and "unjust." [33]

By and large however, the more restricted meaning is ordinarily
ascribed to justice.

None of this is considered very carefully by Fletcher so that his
own proposition remains obscure. And perhaps I have said enough
to indicate the vagueness generally surrounding the meaning of
justice which characterizes much of the literature. Thus it should
prove helpful if some of the major conceptions of the principle are
sketched in more detail, even though still only briefly. I may then
be in a better position to assess the possible kinds of relations to
agape.

Different Conceptions of Justice

I shall, then, consider some of the possible conceptions of justice
often not distinguished very carefully in the literature.[34]

32. Frankena, "Concept of Social Justice," esp. pp. 3–6.

33. Ibid., p. 6.

34. I shall draw here on discussions mostly by C. Perelman, *The Idea of
Justice and the Problem of Argument,* trans. John Petrie (London: Routledge and
Kegan Paul, 1963) esp. pp. 1–60; A. M. Honoré, "Social Justice," *Essays in*

1. *Similar treatment for similar cases.* There is, as I have said, an interpretation of justice which virtually equates it with judgments of right per se. In such cases it is often taken as a formal requirement of reason, and sometimes identified with golden rule arguments and the logical requirement of universalizability.[35] Hence the principle of justice stipulates that what is right for one person cannot be wrong for another similarly circumstanced. No one ought to apply a different standard to himself than to others if this in effect means that he accords himself a privileged position. In later chapters I shall consider this interpretation in several contexts.

2. *To each according to his merit or works.* The laborers in the vineyard who worked longest complained because wages were not allocated on the basis of the amount of labor. Generally advantages or disadvantages are to be proportioned to the particular conduct of men and not simply to their character as human beings, roughly in accordance with Nygren's principle of justice. Several further distinctions might be made, e.g., between "to each according to his efforts" and "to each according to his achievements." The first refers mainly to intention and taking pains. Fair procedures are those which allocate advantages and disadvantages on the basis of expenditure of effort. Yet the criterion of effort has been criticized as too difficult to apply in a wide number of cases. A partial alternative is to allocate advantages in proportion to actual achievement, to the results of actions. A student is graded on the answers he gives on the examination, irrespective of effort exerted. In the case of both effort and achievement, however, particular conduct is the basis of allocation: "the principle of justice according to desert explains only how the fair demands of men as men on their fellowmen may be modified by their conduct, not what these demands are apart from their conduct."[36] Merit or desert is clearly part of the notion of justice for most people. To this extent Nygren is right.

Legal Philosophy, ed. Robert S. Summers (Oxford: Basil Blackwell, 1968), pp. 61–94; Frankena, "Concept of Social Justice"; Vlastos, "Justice and Equality"; Rescher, *Distributive Justice.*

35. See, e.g., Frankena, "Concept of Social Justice," pp. 8–9; M. G. Singer, "The Golden Rule," pp. 302–03.

36. Honoré, "Social Justice," p. 73.

Whether one ought to construe agape and meritarian justice as mutually exclusive in every case to which both may apply is not so clear, and would require more discussion than I can now give it. In part it depends on whether one characteristic of the neighbor always valued by agape is taken to be freedom, and if so, whether and how freedom connects with desert. By and large "to each according to his merit" is thought to link with freedom. Allocation of benefits in proportion to industry is sometimes considered a just procedure in the sense that it acknowledges the differential exercise of an equal liberty by the recipients. Yet as a realistic criterion for social practices such a notion is generally considered far too simplistic. And even if meritarian justice is not always incompatible with agape, the latter would appear to be far closer to a conception of justice that allows for the demands men make on other men apart from particular conduct.

3. *To each the same thing.* This conception has been called "the only purely egalitarian one" in that all the others involve some degree of proportionality.[37] And there is clearly overlap here with the notion of agape as equal regard. Indeed, one might ask whether this formula and agape are not identifiable in the way Fletcher desires. For the formula implies that no characteristics of "each," other than those which apply to everyone alike, must be taken into account. Differentiations between neighbors based on particular conduct are irrelevant. We saw how the corollary of independent and unalterable regard is the attribution to everyone alike of irreducible worth and dignity. It could then be said that agape requires the same thing in the case of every neighbor: equal consideration of and identification with his interests. In this sense at least agape does mean to each the same thing.

Yet there are objections to equating agape with justice in this sense. For the formula does not explicitly stipulate that the class of beings to which it applies includes every man. While this may be assumed by some of its proponents, it cannot be derived from the formula itself. "Each" might be limited to a much smaller category, e.g., each mother, each member of the aristocracy, and so on. The

37. Perelman, *Idea of Justice,* p. 17.

essential characteristics of the class to which it applies are not specified. Moreover, the formula implies not only that all members of a class must be viewed as identical but also that all must be accorded identical treatment. Yet in the literature equal regard may be confined to equal consideration, without the corollary of identical treatment. I have already noted how even Kierkegaard maintains that the neighbor must be cared about "appropriately." This seems to allow for differing capacities and needs. And traditionally agape has been thought to involve a rectifying bias toward the disadvantaged, handicapped, and defenseless.

4. *To each according to his needs.* This conception perhaps more than any other can be said to overlap with agape, in at least the following senses. The notion of needs, however complex they may be, is not based on particular conduct alone. It includes those things essential to the life and welfare of men considered simply as men.[38] This conception is also close to agape in that what is often sought above all is to lessen suffering, and usually without reference to desert. Furthermore, unlike "to each the same thing," it allows for differential treatment. Needs differ and treatments must vary accordingly; thus at least a certain kind of inequality is recognized.

A standard criticism of this formula is that it warrants only one kind of inequality and fails to provide for other sorts of relevant differences based on other sorts of claims. Claims of potential recipients differ not only in relation to need, but also in relation to special promises and contracts, special ties of kinship, etc. In a striking way, however, precisely the same kind of objection has been lodged against agape. As I shall try to show in the last chapter, one of the characteristic problems with interpreting agape as equal regard is to explicate its connection with the particular obligations of some special moral relations. But in any event to speak of the neighbor qua

38. Note for example this proposition of social justice: *"all men considered merely as men and apart from their conduct or choice have a claim to an equal share in all those things, here called advantages, which are generally desired and are in fact conducive to their well-being"* (Honoré "Social Justice," pp. 62–63). He then goes on to allow for but to play down the set of factors ("principles of discrimination") which justify any departure from the principle embodied in the proposition.

human existent does not necessarily commit one to the concept of needs as the sole characteristic to be taken into account. The agapist is formally at liberty to distinguish between needs and preferences, for example, and contend that both count in regarding the neighbor's well-being. In the case of both he reasons solely from equalitarian premises. It is here, as I shall also try to show in the last chapter, that the overlap is greatest between agape and a notion of justice which is equalitarian.

Other conceptions, some closely related to the ones above, might be elucidated, e.g., "to each according to his choice"; "to each according to the covenants he has made"; "to each according to his legal entitlement"; "to each according to his actual productive contribution to the society"; "to each according to the best prospects for enhancing the common good". But I hope the different conceptual possibilities have been adequately illustrated to make my general point. In short, the positions identified earlier often assume very different notions of justice. The issue about the relation between "love and justice" would be a good deal clearer if such different possibilities were acknowledged. For example, not only could various conceptions be distinguished, but possible conflicts between them — merit and need is the most obvious case in point — could be recognized. And if one were to opt for some sophisticated combination, this too could be clarified and the question of priorities considered. One issue agape is likely to affect is that of priorities. For agapeistic pressures appear to extend by and large in the following directions: needs typically will be emphasized before merit, other sorts of differences between persons (beyond differential treatment based on different needs) will be played down, and privilege will always have to be justified.

4

Agape and Subsidiary Rules[1]

> It should be clear that to love one's neighbour as thus com-
> manded does not *mean* to succour him in distress, any more
> than to love God *means* to keep his commandments. It is a
> separate question, in what kind of behaviour must the
> love of God or neighbour be exhibited and its genuineness
> verified?
>
> John Burnaby

Some of those who concentrate on the general meaning of agape
irrespective of circumstances have comparatively little to say about
whether there are definite kinds of action in which agape ought to
find expression. While clearly agape involves the performance of
concrete actions, are there specifiable classes of action which the
agent ought always to do or refrain from doing? How precise can
one be, in advance of the actual situation, in identifying rules which
permit or prohibit certain kinds of conduct? Are any such rules unbreakable, whatever the consequences?

These questions arise even when one holds — as the vast majority
do in the literature before us — that agape is never to be materially
equated with a given moral code. For while almost everyone agrees
that the expression of love includes many things beyond formulated
rules, it nonetheless may involve them as well. Such rules may be
part of the application of agape. What then is their nature and authority?

The issues here are difficult and could readily warrant a volume to
themselves. All I shall try to do is to characterize one recent discussion of some importance, that focusing on situation ethics. For

1. Portions of this chapter first appeared in D. Brezine, S.J., and J. V. Mc-
Glynn, S.J., eds., *The Future of Ethics and Moral Theology* (Chicago: Argus,
1968), and are incorporated here by permission of the publisher.

purposes of a single chapter, that literature has the advantage of being relatively self-contained and so manageable. However, I would argue that many of the problems which fall traditionally under the heading of "love and law" are addressed.

Versions of Act and Rule Agapism

For the sake of clarity, I must first attend to the terms used in the discussion of situation ethics. Some of the most recent and influential writings are dependent on William K. Frankena's formulation of the options.[2] Appropriating in part a parallel debate among moral philosophers on forms of utilitarianism, Frankena distinguishes a number of possible sorts of authority which more specific principles and rules may possess in relation to agape. (1) Such rules may be bypassed altogether. All of them may be regarded as unhelpful or clear barriers to personal freedom and "authenticity." (2) They may be taken seriously as useful summaries of past cumulative wisdom, to be set aside whenever love appears to dictate alternative action in a particular situation. (3) They may be morally decisive in any situation to which they apply. (4) There may be combinations of the above.

The most extreme position Frankena calls *pure act-agapism.*

This admits no rules or principles other than the "law of love" itself, and it also does not allow that there are any "perceptual intuitions" about what is right or wrong in particular situations independently of the dictates of love. It insists that one is to discover or decide what one's right or duty in a particular situa-

2. William K. Frankena, "Love and Principle in Christian Ethics," *Faith and Philosophy,* ed. Alvin Plantinga (Grand Rapids: William B. Eerdmans Publishing Co., 1964), pp. 203–25. Cf. Frankena, *Ethics*; John Rawls, "Two Concepts of Rules," *Philosophical Quarterly* 64 (January, 1955): 3–32. Examples of the appropriation of Frankena's formulation are Joseph Fletcher, "Situation Ethics Under Fire," *Storm Over Ethics* (Philadelphia: United Church Press, 1967), pp. 149–73, and "What's in a Rule? A Situationist's View," *Norm and Context in Christian Ethics,* pp. 325–49; Paul Ramsey, *Deeds and Rules in Christian Ethics* (New York: Charles Scribner's Sons, 1967).

tion is solely by confronting one's loving will with the facts about that situation, whether one is an individual or a group. Facts about other situations and ethical conclusions arrived at in other situations are, for this extreme view, simply irrelevant, if not misleading. It adopts with complete literalness, as the whole story, St. Augustine's dictum, "Love, and do as you please." Here belong at least the more drastic of the views sometimes referred to as anti-nomian, nominalist, existentialist, situationalist, simplistic, or contextualist.[3]

This description of situation ethics is widely held to be an accurate one. Specifically, it is assumed that situation ethics is committed, in principle, to a doctrine of radical discontinuity between discrete situations. For example, when in 1952 Pope Pius XII condemned a movement he alternately called the "new morality," "situationsethik," "ethical existentialism," "ethical actualism," or "ethical individualism," he described it as follows.

The distinctive mark of this morality is that it is not based in effect on universal moral laws, such as, for example, the Ten Commandments, but on the real and concrete conditions or circumstances in which men must act, and according to which the conscience of the individual must judge and choose. Such a state of things is unique, and is applicable only once for every human action. That is why the decision of conscience, as the advocates of this ethic assert, cannot be commanded by ideas, principles and universal laws.[4]

It may be, as this statement seems to imply, that we finally have a strict either/or before us, that one must argue the case for "universal moral laws" which obtain for all men at all times in all places,

3. "Love and Principle in Christian Ethics," p. 211.
4. *Acta Apostolicae Sedis* 44 (1952): 413. A brief bibliography of the German language discussion of situation ethics from roughly this period may be found in Karl Rahner, S.J., *Theological Investigations,* trans. Karl-H. Kruger (Baltimore: Helicon Press, 1964), 2:217–18. See also J. Fuchs, S.J., "Morale théologique et morale de situation," *Nouvelle Revue Théologique* 76 (1954): 1073–85.

or capitulate to a belief that every situation is unique, to be assessed by an agent whose final authority is his own distinctive lights. But many consider this view of situation ethics as far too simplistic, or at least ambiguous, for reasons that will be evident as we proceed. I would only add here that the question of a strict either/or is complicated by at least three considerations.

1. The notion of a fully discrete situation is problematical and its analysis by proponents of situation ethics generally obscure. Various elements often suffer neglect. For example, the agent's standpoint, including his interests and ideals, may sometimes determine which of several possible accounts of a given point in space and time he offers as the decisive characterization. Furthermore, the distinctions between situations are often fluid and somewhat arbitrarily drawn, since all of the agent's own perceptions and acts are nuanced, at least to some degree, by past conditions and future expectations as well as by the personal and social relationships in which he finds himself. In short, "in the absence of a thorough exploration of what is to count as a constituent of a moral situation, little is said in speaking of 'situational ethics.' " [5]

2. From the other side, those who do argue for universal moral laws are not always clear about just how much they wish to claim. It is one thing to say that there *are* such laws "in reality" (perhaps ontologically). It is another to claim one or more of the following regarding any of them. (a) They are adequately *known* (at least to some) to be universally binding, even given all-pervasive "conditions of estrangement" and/or the fluctuations of history. (b) Claim (a) may signify in addition that what is known has been actually formulated in exhaustive (or at least sufficient) detail so that such laws are universally binding *as explicitly stated*. Some thinkers who stress historical development or evolution in the apprehension of the mean-

5. George Woods, "Situational Ethics," *Christian Ethics and Contemporary Philosophy*, p. 334. Fletcher has acknowledged the fairness of at least part of this criticism: "Situationism is better served by a more integrative definition of the situation than I gave it. . . . The book should have done more to indicate that there is usually a 'network of situations' to be considered rather than just *the* situation" ("Situation Ethics Under Fire," p. 163). Cf. however Ramsey, *Deeds and Rules*, pp. 192–220.

ing of all universal moral laws do not appear to make this additional claim. (c) The laws in question include some which apply not simply to certain fundamental principles, values, attitudes, relations, and the like, all of which may transcend fixed spatio-temporal delimitation, but also to classes of conduct which are so delimited, and which may be indisputably identified by a "neutral" observer. Though at least parts of, e.g., the Decalogue refer to very tangible kinds of behavior, it is important to note that some of those who affirm universal laws have in mind various principles, relations, etc. which possess a high degree of generality rather than specific, neutrally describable classes of conduct and the rules placing and governing them.

3. The two most prominent exponents of situation ethics in the English-speaking world, Joseph Fletcher and John A. T. Robinson, self-consciously repudiate *pure act-agapism*. Formally one may say that they adhere rather to the second option, which Frankena calls *summary rule* or *modified act-agapism*.

> This admits rules but regards them as summaries of past experience, useful, perhaps almost indispensable, but only as rules of thumb. It cannot allow that a rule may ever be followed in a situation when it is seen to conflict with what love dictates in that situation. For, if rules are to be followed only in so far as they are helpful as aids to love, they cannot constrain or constrict love in any way. But they may and perhaps should be used.[6]

Fletcher has explicitly endorsed Frankena's formulation of summary rule or modified act-agapism as correctly characterizing situation ethics.[7] This is the point at which the situationist attempts to establish a mediating position between what he takes to be the excesses of extemporism and legalism. Though Fletcher has been criticized in the past for being curiously preoccupied with exceptions to rules,

---

6. Frankena, "Love and Principle in Christian Ethics," p. 212.

7. Fletcher, "What's in a Rule?", pp. 331–32. Cf. Fletcher, "Situation Ethics Under Fire," pp. 155–57.

in the form of selectively describing atypical cases, he has more recently stressed his opposition to the extemporists or spontaneists. Their error, as he sees it, lies precisely in their belief "that moral experience is radically discontinuous and therefore cannot provide any meaningful carry-over from one situation to another." [8]

> It is flogging a docetic horse to treat the problem as one of "context *versus* principles." That issue only arises as between moralists who are impromptu, unprincipled, and spontaneous in their ethical method — for example, the ancient antinomians and modern existentialists — *and all the rest of us.*[9]

Robinson places, if anything, a more pronounced emphasis on the need for rules.

> *What* "love's casuistry" requires makes . . . the most searching demands both upon the depth and integrity of one's concern for the other . . . and upon the calculation of what is truly the most loving thing in this situation for every person involved. Such an ethic cannot but rely, in deep humility, upon guiding rules, upon the cumulative experience of one's own and other people's obedience. It is this bank of experience which gives us our working rules of "right" and "wrong" and without them we could not but flounder.[10]

Yet for both men, love remains the governing agent in any alliance with rules, retaining in every instance the freedom to dissolve it. The rules, using Fletcher's language, are to be understood as illuminative maxims rather than directive precepts.[11] Extemporists may

8. Fletcher, "What's in a Rule?", p. 328.
9. Fletcher, "Situation Ethics Under Fire," p. 155. Cf. James M. Gustafson, "Context versus Principles: A Misplaced Debate in Christian Ethics," *Harvard Theological Review* 58 (April, 1965): 171–202.
10. John A. T. Robinson, *Honest to God* (Philadelphia: The Westminster Press, 1963), pp. 119–20. See also Robinson, *Christian Morals Today* (London: SCM Press Ltd., 1964).
11. Fletcher, *Situation Ethics*, p. 31.

err in rejecting altogether the principle of analogy, i.e., "that what applies in one case should apply in all similar cases." But analogy must not be pressed too far: "Situationists ask, very seriously, if there ever are enough cases enough alike to validate a law or to support anything more than a cautious generalization." [12] Maxims, then, have validity solely as "statistically preponderant generalizations."

It seems fair to conclude the following about Fletcher's view of summary rules or maxims.[13] First, all such maxims are established inductively. "The most that can be hoped for any normative rule, such as the one against lying, is that it will be 'summary' or based on a wide, long and mature experience." [14] Second, maxims are to be suspended, ignored, or violated if and whenever more good can be effected than by adhering to them.[15] Third, while it is possible to find references to remote as well as immediate consequences and to a "network of situations," the center of gravity is the particular situation and its specific consequences. Maxims are always relative to definite, concrete situations; they illuminate what normally produces good consequences in an individual case. This is perhaps most clearly illustrated in Fletcher's rejection of the universalizability requirement (in a particular situation of moral choice one logically commits himself or someone else to making the same judgment in any similar situation), the generalization argument (what if *everyone* were to perform a given action in a given situation?), and the wedge argument (what will happen if I perform a certain action? Will others be influenced to do likewise with harmful overall results? Will this mean that the camel's nose will be inside the tent?).[16] All

12. Ibid., p. 32
13. Fletcher does not distinguish between the two terms, though it is possible to do so. "The term 'maxim' is better than 'summary rule' because a maxim is a *general* truth, a generalization. It is *based* on past cases which can be summarized, but it is not itself merely a summary of those cases. A moral maxim tells us what kind of action usually produces the best consequences" (Donald Evans, "Love, Situations and Rules," *Norm and Context in Christian Ethics,* p. 382).
14. Fletcher, "What's in a Rule?", p. 331.
15. Joseph Fletcher, *Moral Responsibility* (Philadelphia: Westminster Press, 1967) pp. 31–32.
16. Fletcher, *Situation Ethics,* pp. 130–31.

of these Fletcher dismisses as obstructionist efforts of a legalistic
mentality to establish rules which are or might be obligatory even
when they are not conducive to the greatest general good in the
particular case. The moral agent must decide in each situation
whether the maxims in question will serve love then and there, and
if not, must discard them. It appears, therefore, that Fletcher would
agree that

> the crucial question is always whether telling the truth in *this*
> case is for the greatest general good or not. It can never be right
> to act on the rule of telling the truth if we have good independent
> grounds for thinking that it would be for the greatest general
> good not to tell the truth in a particular case.[17]

This statement is a description of what some philosophers currently
call act-utilitarianism. Despite the sketchiness of Fletcher's treatment
of many issues, Donald Evans, Basil Mitchell, and Paul Ramsey
have extrapolated from his view of maxims that Fletcher propounds
(or should, if he worked it out fully) a version of modified act-
utilitarianism.[18]

I cannot consider here the extensive philosophical discussion of
act- and rule-utilitarianism.[19] The only comment I would make is that,
assuming at least for the present that this is a justified extrapolation
and Fletcher is a consistent act-utilitarian, he is obliged to try to meet
the traditional objections.[20] To illustrate such objections, let us consider a very commonplace example. Suppose I take my family to a
restaurant. My three year old son is a very poor eater and is generally

17. Frankena, *Ethics*, p. 30.
18. Evans, "Love, Situations and Rules," pp. 367–414; Basil Mitchell, "Ideals,
Roles, and Rules," *Norm and Context in Christian Ethics*, pp. 351–65; Ramsey,
Deeds and Rules, pp. 145–225. Though Fletcher rejects it, the wedge argument
can be used by the act-utilitarian.
19. See, e.g., David Lyons, *Forms and Limits of Utilitarianism* (Oxford:
Clarendon Press, 1965). Cf. however Gertrude Ezorsky, "A Defense of Rule
Utilitarianism," *Journal of Philosophy* 65 (September 19, 1968): 533–44.
20. The objections mentioned here are summarized in Frankena, *Ethics*, p.
32.

anaemic. He is served meat, green beans, and french-fried potatoes and proceeds to eat only the latter. After repeatedly urging him (to no avail) to eat his other food as well before he fills up, I contemplate two alternatives. (1) I can take away the rest of his french fries and hide them in a napkin while he is looking the other way. When he asks for more, I can reply "There are no more french fries," knowing that he will not remember with certainty and will be disposed to believe me. (2) I can take away the rest of his french fries while he is watching and when he asks for them I can reply "There are no more french fries for you because you have not eaten your other food." In either case I can safely expect that he will then eat his other food. Let us assume for the sake of argument that (1) and (2) are identical in terms of the amount of good resulting from the act. The only difference is that (1) involves telling a lie. In such a case, the objection runs, the consistent act-utilitarian has to judge that (1) and (2) are equally right. But the most elementary appeal to "common moral consciousness" leads to the conclusion that (1) is wrong and (2) is right.

Suppose, however, that we alter the case slightly. The alternatives are the same but I cannot assume that in situation (2) he will happily or even necessarily eat his other food. He may respond with three-year-old irrationality and perhaps throw a tantrum: so there is a risk in telling him the truth. Here let us assume that (1) may result in a slightly greater amount of good. The act-utilitarian must then judge that it is right. Yet, again appealing to common moral consciousness, (2) is, or at any rate might be, right. The question, then, is whether "there are or at least may be cases in which rules like keeping promises and not lying must be followed even when doing so is not for the greatest general good in the particular situation in question." [21] This an act-utilitarian and hence presumably Fletcher, cannot allow.

My purpose in noting these traditional objections is not to claim that they are necessarily decisive against act-utilitarianism, but merely to indicate the direction of some of the recent criticism of situation ethics. The general contention is that in confining the legitimate use

21. Ibid.

of rules solely to illuminative maxims, Fletcher has overlooked some essential moral considerations which transcend the specific consequences of actions in a particular situation. It simply will not do for him to excoriate as "legalistic" all views which hold that rules may have other legitimate uses. Further distinctions are required. Examples of such possible distinctions may be found in Frankena's final two options. The first is what he calls pure rule-agapism.

> It maintains that we are always to tell what we are to do in particular situations by referring to a set of rules, and that what rules are to prevail and be followed is to be determined by seeing what rules (not what acts) best or most fully embody love. . . . We may and sometimes must obey a rule in a particular situation even though the action it calls for is seen not to be what love itself would directly require.[22]

This option embodies especially the second of the two objections above and is parallel to rule-utilitarianism. But it is not the only alternative to situation ethics or modified act-utilitarianism. There is also the possibility of combinations of rule-agapism and act-agapism.

> Here would fall, for instance, the view that, while we may and should appeal to rules when we can in deciding what should be done in a particular case, as the rule-agapist holds, we may and should appeal to the "law of love" directly in cases for which there are no rules or in which the rules conflict, just as the act-agapist does. Such combinations may, in fact, be more plausible than either pure act-agapism or pure rule-agapism by themselves.[23]

This formulation serves to point up the actual complexity of possible alternatives to situation ethics. One common way to understand the contention that we should appeal to rules when we can in deciding what ought to be done is as follows. Some rules, when they are

22. Frankena, "Love and Principle in Christian Ethics," p. 214.
23. Ibid.

applicable to a case in question, are always, if not determinative, at least relevant to one's final decision. We cannot ignore or discard them as having no moral weight. We move into a situation with this relevance assumed; we do not debate then and there whether they are relevant or helpful or illuminative or not, as the situationist appears to do. In this sense we may say that there is an established presumption in their favor, and that a decision that they are not decisive has a special burden of proof.

I shall utilize at this point a well-known distinction by W. D. Ross: certain rules or duties possess a *prima facie* if not always actual authoritativeness.[24] They are to be followed "all other things being equal," i.e., unless other unusual moral considerations are taken to be determinative. One's reasons for asserting such a presumption in their favor may vary. In the case of truth-telling, one might argue, speaking very roughly, that a general subscription to this rule is essential to the notion of the self's own integrity in its relations to others, and that without it one has difficulty in conceiving of integrated and consistent personal identity. There is no need to conclude, of course, that we must conform to the rule on every possible occasion, but only that non-conformity requires special attention and warrants. One might believe, in addition, that all profound personal relationships, such as genuine friendship or parenthood, demand a general policy of truthfulness which, while again not always a literal or indefeasible requirement, is a characteristic of the relationship on which we may typically count. For the sake of the relationship at any rate, rather consistent adherence to the practice may sometimes be more important than certain short-term or immediate advantages which may accrue from permitting another consideration to override it. One might say, finally, that truth-telling does have indispensable social utility, that one's society must rely generally on this social practice.

On the other side, in saying that rules may conflict and that one must sometimes appeal directly to love I am (or may be) acknowledging that such rules, at least as explicitly formulated, are not uni-

versal or unexceptionable. I do *not* mean by this acknowledgment
that they are omitted from consideration, but only that while always
relevant, they are not automatically decisive (or may not be, theoretically, at some future point in time). Hence, in denying that rules
are "unexceptionable" one simply refuses to allow that rules are
invariably free from other, and possibly overriding, moral objections.
Their binding character is prima facie rather than actual. On this
side, one may therefore distinguish two issues: is the only acceptable
rule a maxim in Fletcher's use of that term? and, are there *actually*
any unexceptionable rules? These issues are by no means equivalent.
To say that there are only summary rules or illuminative maxims is
to say less than many would — still without contending that there
are unexceptionable rules governing conduct (in the sense I have
explained). I shall now try to sort out these issues in more detail as
we consider some of the major criticisms of situation ethics.

Representative Criticisms of Situation Ethics

It will be necessary to confine myself to a brief explication of the
views of two thinkers, Paul Ramsey and Donald Evans, whose criticisms seem to me to be representative, detailed, and generally acute.

Ramsey groups his criticisms of situation ethics as Fletcher expounds it under three headings. The first is that in execution if not
in strict intention, Fletcher seems to endorse pure act-agapism. He
is located "in the upper left hand corner of the kingdom of situa-
tionalism, from which when pressed he can readily take sanctuary
across the border into an ethics of the unique moment without taking responsibility for the defense of the inhabitants of that territory." [25] Why is this the case? Ramsey believes at least part of the
answer is to be found in the logic of summary rules or illuminative
maxims. The summary rule position, in and of itself, he takes to
be always unstable. One of its major defenders, Fletcher, is constantly
inclined de facto to stress the unique and unrepeatable features in
each situation whereas another defender, Robinson, emphasizes the
need for "working rules" to such an extent that they appear virtually

25. Ramsey, *Deeds and Rules,* p. 149.

unbreakable. Such instability is due on the one side, Ramsey holds, to the logical priority which the particular case invariably retains in relation to any summary rule. Certainly the situationist is prepared to admit that many such rules may be practically indispensable in helping us to expedite the routine matters of daily existence. But they are not formally indispensable in any way. They may always be ignored or discarded, they are not (even) assumed to be relevant prior to the situation, nor is special justification required before they may be overriden. Whether the situationist "follows or violates a summary rule or principle, he still goes about deciding in that act of self-elected sovereignty, by a *direct* application of agape to that particular case, what is the right thing to do." [26]

Ramsey does not mean to deny that a great part of moral life is appropriately governed by a direct appeal to love and the illumination furnished by summary rules. What he rejects is the claim that the *only* legitimate use of rules is as maxims or summaries of past experience. This claim neglects any number of factors, including the rules of social practice, an adequate philosophy of law, a comprehensive doctrine of justice and human rights, and a minimally probing view of "the covenants of life with life." [27]

The instability of summary rule agapism likewise is reflected in the tendency toward general rules of some of its exponents. Though Ramsey has Robinson in mind here, he points out that, in an earlier book on the ethics of medical practice, Fletcher himself defended as a general rule "the patient's right to know the truth." [28] The right was "not a conclusion that awaits, or would vary according to the particularities of, an individual medical or personal diagnosis." [29] Ramsey argues that the defense of this general rule is inconsistent with Fletcher's subsequent views, but it nicely illustrates the instability. "*One* quite general rule . . . would be quite sufficient to subvert the exclusive claims of situation ethics." [30]

26. Ibid., p. 161.
27. Ibid., p. 163.
28. Joseph Fletcher, *Morals and Medicine* (Boston: Beacon Press, 1960), pp. 34–64.
29. Ramsey, *Deeds and Rules*, p. 167.
30. Ibid., p. 165.

A second heading under which Ramsey undertakes to criticize situation ethics concerns its allegedly exclusive stress on the consequences of actions. Ramsey thinks that the price paid for this stress is disastrously high because it permits an arbitrary characterization of what is really going on.

> It looked like a good beginning as well as a good story — that one about the young woman who said Yes, she'd sleep with a man who offered her $100,000 and again replied affirmatively for $10,000 but when the offer dropped to $500 grew indignant and exclaimed, "What do you think I am?" — to be met with the answer, "We have already established *that,* now we're haggling over the price." But if not exactly the price, still "what she accomplishes for herself or others" does have according to Fletcher . . . the power to change the characterization of what she'll be doing. Given $100,000 and a couple of additional suppositions, the events that night could be described not as high-priced prostitution but as "a lovely young woman building parks for the children of the poor to play in." [31]

In principle, such a stress allows also for the possibility that every human relationship may be used as an instrument for some more ultimate set of consequences. Ramsey acknowledges that some of the traditional doctrine of intrinsically right and wrong means is vulnerable to legitimate attack and that no action can be altogether independent of ends. Nonetheless, "it may be the case, for example, that there are some kinds of essentially non-menial human actions that have a moral order of their own which does not need and does not find positive warrant in ends, but which would be voided if bad consequences regularly flowed from such behavior." [32] If this possibility is not granted, Ramsey maintains, then all relations and covenants among men are subservient in principle to the criterion of consequentialism. He finds this line of reasoning potentially dangerous.

31. Ibid., p. 186.
32. Ibid., p. 186.

A final heading is closely related to the second. Ramsey contends that a primary reason for what he regards as the arbitrariness of Fletcher's assessment of individual cases is that Fletcher fails to make clear how he proposes to describe the actions he wants to evaluate. On this point in particular Ramsey thinks that Protestant ethicists have an appreciable amount to learn from Roman Catholic moral theology, past and present, and from discussions within contemporary moral philosophy. As an example of the latter, Ramsey is indebted to Eric D'Arcy's work on the description of human actions.[33] Ramsey is convinced that certain classes of conduct are so significant morally that the terms describing them ("moral species-terms") cannot be "elided" into terms describing their consequences. Fletcher re-describes many actions without admitting it, while he continues to count on the older, non-elided descriptions for his posture of radicalism and sensationalism.

It is necessary to restrict attention by and large to criticisms of situation ethics, with less emphasis on the constructive proposals of the critics. Thus I shall only note that Ramsey distinguishes roughly two sources of general rules in Christian ethics. The first is "the meaning of essential humanity," derived from both religious and rational insights. In every immediate situation one confronts a person or persons who have an essence or nature. No effort to bring in some purely "extrinsic" state of historical affairs in the future, however desirable, can be cited as a legitimate warrant for contradicting this nature. Certainly, if one holds that there is an essential humanity and that some rules can and must be understood only in relation to it, then there is a clear basis for their general or universal authority. His acceptance of this basis helps to explain why Ramsey regards the situationist's claim that he cares about persons instead of rules as bogus and pernicious. There may be rules which ought to be generally held for the sake of persons in every situation. Situationists usually have trouble with any notion of an "essential" human nature (preferring perhaps an "actual" or even a "possible" one?).

The second source of general rules is for Ramsey the set of condi-

33. Eric D'Arcy, *Human Acts*.

tions for the best possible social existence. Here he has appropriated John Rawls' discussion of "rules of practice" such as promise-keeping or truth-telling.

> If there are any Christian moral or social practices, there cannot be exceptions that depart from them by direct general appeals to *agape* overriding the rules in particular cases in which the agent does not take the weighty responsibility of criticizing the practice as a whole and attempting to replace it with another. *Agape* justifies no exception to the practice.[34]

Deliberation ought to center on the meaning of "rules of practice," including the precise conditions of their application, the qualifications, excuses, and exemptions which further specify their content.

Donald Evans is much more explicitly sympathetic than Ramsey to Fletcher's attack on legalism. He also believes "that much Catholic and fundamentalist legalism is morally repugnant." [35] But he finds Fletcher's own positive alternative seriously deficient. Evans understands situation ethics as it is expounded by Fletcher to involve two principal claims: the acceptance of only those rules which may be construed as illuminative maxims and the rejection of all unexceptionable moral rules. Evans agrees with the latter and indeed seeks to improve on Fletcher's case, but is painstakingly critical of the former.

As I have said, Evans interprets Fletcher's view of maxims as a form of act-utilitarianism. His criticisms parallel Ramsey's to an important degree, though his views are notably different on such questions as the authority of "rules of practice." In addition to maxims, Evans distinguishes two other main classes of rules which he regards as necessary for any minimally comprehensive normative ethics, and which the situations neglects or scorns.

The first class he calls *promissory* rules.

---

34. Ramsey, *Deeds and Rules*, p. 137.
35. Evans, "Love, Situations and Rules," p. 367.

A man who makes a promise to do X commits himself in advance *not* to decide whether to do X *solely* on the basis of his judgment concerning the probable consequences of doing X in the particular situation of decision. He already has one moral reason for doing it: "because I promised." When he has to decide, this reason may be overridden by reasons arising from a consideration of consequences. . . . But the reason does have a distinctive weight of its own, which depends on the obligation created by a promise.[36]

Promising is a definite linguistic act with performative force. When freely made, and assuming one acknowledges the general obligation to keep promises, promising constitutes a moral reason transcending one's assessment of the specific consequences in the particular situation. It also assumes the *institution* of promise-making and -keeping as well as the value of each specific act. Such an institution is justified because a society requires a certain level of assurance about the future behavior of its members if it is to be a society at all. This is the case in two distinguishable ways. First, "society" implies, in part, "a group in which mutual expectations depend partly on promise-keeping rather than entirely on mere regularities of behavior." [37] The institution involves not only conventions about promising, but also — and far more importantly — the belief that there is an "intrinsic value" to the kind of personal relations which are founded on mutual commitments.

The "usefulness" of the institution of promise-keeping depends on an assumption that mutual human relations based on the moral obligation created by promise-making have an intrinsic value; a society based morally on mutual trust and mutual commitment is better than a "pack" based non-morally on mutual expectations concerning regularities of behavior.[38]

36. Ibid., p. 385.
37. Ibid., p. 387.
38. Ibid.

Second, there is a purely utilitarian consideration: the satisfaction of basic needs such as food and shelter requires mutual dependence and reliability and thus promise-keeping.

The second principal class Evans terms *rule-utilitarian rules.*

> A rule-utilitarian rule is one which is justified by considering the consequences of its being followed by most people or by everyone, as compared with the consequences of its being broken by most people or by everyone. . . . A rule-utilitarian rule is established by considering the *compound* effects of many people, or all people, observing the rule in comparison with the *compound* effects of their violating it. One considers the overall utility of the rule, not the utility of each separate act.[39]

Evans' account of such rules is important, but it goes beyond my immediate concerns here. I want only to emphasize that, on the one hand, he is able to regard the appeal to rule-utilitarian rules as *often* a legitimate way of deciding moral questions. From this standpoint, Fletcher is mistaken in refusing to give rule-utilitarian rules their due, in not really allowing societal rules a place at all. *The only genuine issue is how extensive that place should be.* Any serious allowance (as opposed to an occasional favorable reference) must observe at a minimum that these rules introduce considerations which transcend one's own judgment about the particular consequences of his action at a given moment.

On the other hand, Evans is sympathetic with Fletcher's concern that a stress on rules, especially rule-utilitarian rules, may result in a tacit legalism. They may constitute a barrier to moral maturity and result in "perpetual moral infancy for the masses." Evans does not want to slight either the decisional responsibility of the individual or the dangers of "code-morality." In attempting to avoid legalism as well as a restriction of rules to maxims, he argues roughly as follows. First, he distinguishes in a very broad fashion between personal and societal rules. In opposition to Fletcher he grants that the generalization argument is often a legitimate part of morality. But he does

39. Ibid., p. 393.

not regard it as essential to every moral judgment. Every moral judgment must be in principle universalizable, but need not require the agent to ask: what would happen if *everyone* acted thus? For there are personal or non-societal (though still universalizable) as well as societal rules. Some rules are personal because they are not explicitly formulated. "The more a moral judgment resembles an artistic judgment in its subtle sensitivity and creativity, the more likely it is that the moral rule which is implied cannot be formulated or is formulated so that it applies only to the one case." [40] Others are formulated, yet for various good reasons the moral agent may not wish to legislate for their blanket adoption.

These reasons include: (1) one's inability in some cases to estimate even roughly the consequences if everyone adhered to the personal moral rule; (2) the fair certainty that if everyone adhered to the rule the overall consequences would be bad, combined with the reasonable assurance that one's own action conforming to the personal rule in a particular situation produces good consequences; (3) an unwillingness to allow the rigidity involved in societal adoption, since one wishes to keep the personal rule in question open to revision in relation to changed social conditions; (4) the concern that societal adoption result in hypocrisy, since the personal rule may, for example, be so demanding that few people will actually conform to it. [41]

Second, Evans attempts to avoid legalism by denying that there are unexceptionable moral rules. By moral rules in this connection he does not mean analytic rules (those which are right by definition), statements of fundamental obligations such as agape or benevolence, and indefinite rules (e.g., "never be indifferent to suffering") which are often so vague as to be of no clear assistance in a specific situation. The rules he has in mind are all rather definite and appear typically to involve moral species-terms such as the prohibitions against lying, stealing, and killing. Furthermore, by "exceptions" to a moral rule he is not arguing that there are *singular* exceptions, purely random or unique cases. This permits him to accept the

40. Ibid., p. 398.
41. Ibid., pp. 397–402.

universalizability requirement. "The universalizability requirement does not show that universal exceptions are impossible; it only shows that any exceptions must be universal ones." But he makes clear that the requirement is a formal one and does not necessitate that all rules be explicitly formulated in every detail or universal*ized*. They need not constitute part of an elaborate casuistry. "It is usually better to regard both societal and personal moral rules as non-universalized directives to consider important morally-relevant factors in a situation." [42] The decisive question for Evans regarding one's acceptance of unexceptionable moral rules is, then, whether any additional universal exceptions are allowed. Evans construes his response to this question as a *moral* decision, not a logical conclusion: "One ought not to set aside in advance the possible moral relevance of unmentioned possible consequences." [43]

In the case of Evans, as with Ramsey, I have not been able to consider very specifically his own proposals. But while concentrating on the criticisms, I hope I have said enough about each of the critics to illustrate the complexity of possible alternatives to situation ethics.

Two Senses of Situation Ethics

In fairness to Fletcher and the situationism he expounds, however, I must comment on another possible reading of his position. There are passages in his recent writings which may call into question the interpretation by Evans, Mitchell, and Ramsey, however understandable their extrapolation from his earlier cryptic and deliberately popularized work. At least it is legitimate to inquire whether he may wish to give some rules more weight than the illuminative maxim view appears formally to allow. This would take him roughly toward the position which, as I described it earlier, allows that some rules have a prima facie authority. On the other hand, it may be that Fletcher has simply altered his view without acknowledging it, or has made inconsistent claims, or meant to hold the prima facie view all along. This is a matter I shall not try conclusively to decide.

42. Ibid., p. 407.
43. Ibid., p. 410.

What I want to do is note the difference between the illuminative maxim and prima facie views.

This difference becomes readily apparent if one considers one of Fletcher's now famous cases. At the end of World War II a German woman was taken to a prison camp in the Ukraine. When her husband, who had been captured in the Bulge, returned to Germany he successfully located his three children, but searched in vain for his wife. She heard about her reunited family and the search. The rules of the camp allowed a prisoner to be released only because of illness, in which case treatment was provided in a Soviet hospital, or pregnancy, in which case the prisoner would be returned to Germany because she was then regarded as a liability.

> She turned things over in her mind and finally asked a friendly Volga German camp guard to impregnate her, which he did. Her condition being medically verified, she was sent back to Berlin and to her family. They welcomed her with open arms, even when she told them how she had managed it. When the child was born, they loved him more than all the rest, on the view that little Dietrich had done more for them than anybody.[44]

Clearly Fletcher has cited this case to show how "unloving" absolute adherence to a moral rule can turn out to be, in this case the rule prohibiting adultery. But it is important to note that at least three distinguishable kinds of authority may be attached to this rule.

First, it may be taken strictly as an illuminative maxim in the sense I have discussed. Presumably the woman then decides whether in her situation the rule serves love and if it does not, she *disregards* it. She should do so without remorse, without a sense of conflicting moral considerations all of which are relevant but some of which are disjunctive. She applies love directly to her situation and in so doing decides that the rule prohibiting adultery is unhelpful. It does not have to be overridden; her sexual relations with the guard do not require some special moral burden of proof. This is true even if

44. Fletcher, *Situation Ethics*, p. 165.

(assuming she is a situationist) she attaches to the rule prohibiting adultery the greatest possible experiential importance open to her, if she believes "the wisdom of the race" overwhelmingly supports the prohibition. (I am not interested here in determining whether the rule against adultery *can* be finally justified, even as an illuminative maxim, given the widespread de facto variation in sexual practices, past and present, etc. For my purposes now, such justification may be assumed.) She decides that reunion with her family will bring about the greatest general good and so she does what she has to do. For any and every maxim may, in principle, be discarded.

Second, the rule is regarded as always relevant (though not necessarily decisive) in any situation to which it is applicable. This is approximately the prima facie view. Certain rules (I shall include this one) have such authority that they are never disregarded but only overridden. I suggested earlier some of the formulations by which such relevance can be underscored. The rule has a presumption in its favor and the reasons overriding it have a special burden of proof. It has a prima facie if not an actual authoritativeness. There is an assumption in advance that generally the rule should be followed; one brings this assumption to a given situation. Here the woman makes her decision with compunction. She is forced to decide between rules which conflict or, perhaps more accurately in this case, between a rule of conduct which she regards as generally right and a more significant marital relationship to which she is committed (and in reference to which the rule prohibiting adultery has its intelligibility and weight). In this instance it seems fairly clear that the rule prohibiting adultery should be overridden, particularly since this violation will ensure the very relationship which makes the rule intelligible. But the prima facie view would maintain that at least some rules should be adhered to in virtually every case, with exceptions justified only in the most remote and theoretical sense of Evans' "unmentioned possible consequences." (An example of such a rule might be the prohibition of torture.)

Some recent statements by Fletcher suggest he may be willing to allow this second kind of authority for certain rules. For example, in stressing his opposition to the extemporists, he indicates that he no longer sees a significant difference between situation ethics and the views of John Bennett.[45] Bennett's position is not always explicit or detailed, but in the particular essay to which Fletcher alludes, he states: "My chief concern is to insist that we in deciding do not set aside an important principle. It may be subordinated to another, but the way in which we act will be determined in part by the subordinated principle." [46] This is very much like saying that certain rules may never be disregarded but only overridden and that decisions between rules which conflict are only made with the most serious compunction. If Fletcher really intends his position to be substantially the same as Bennett's, then one of the two principal claims of situation ethics as construed by Evans — that the legitimate use of rules is confined to illuminative maxims — seems either meaningless or muddled. In this case, only the claim that there are no unexceptionable rules would unequivocally remain as the sine qua non of situation ethics.

One might put the question this way. For someone to be designated as a situationist, is his rejection of unexceptionable moral rules a *sufficient* as well as a necessary condition? Can rules be allowed which introduce considerations transcending the consequences of the particular situation? Has Fletcher himself moved to the "right" to such an extent that situationism as he represents it is indistinguishable from the position of Evans? I think not. Yet the question is certainly debatable, as we have seen. My major concern now is not with an exegesis of Fletcher's very cryptic formulations but with the characterization of situation ethics as it is presently being discussed. In some respects the discussion is not very far advanced. The illuminative maxim and the prima facie views need to be distinguished more frequently if one is to be clear about the sufficient conditions for situation ethics.

The rule prohibiting adultery may be accorded a third kind of authority, which the situationist would view as sheer legalism. Here the rule is given indefeasible rather than presumptive priority. No

45. "It seems to me that there is no substantial issue as between Bennett's published view and situationism's" (Fletcher, "Situation Ethics Under Fire," p. 157).
46. John C. Bennett, "Principles and the Context," *Storm Over Ethics,* p. 19.

appeal to intentions or consequences, however laudable in themselves, can override what by prior determination has been judged to
be intrinsically immoral. In the case I have been considering, this
would mean that it would not be licit for the woman to commit adultery in order to achieve some highly praiseworthy future state of
affairs. The most loving thing to do would be to remain a faithful
wife where she is, hoping for an eventual reunion with her family
by means which are not in themselves illicit. But there may be more
potential flexibility to the position than this. In the work of prudence
in applying the rule to particular cases, the very meaning of the
rule is made more precise. An act might be *exempted* from being
classified as adultery when fidelity is attested to and the act is for the
sake of the familial relation. In a final and crucial sense, the rule
remains unexceptionable because a thoroughgoing appraisal may show
that it does not apply to this particular case, even as a consideration of
this case may render the meaning of the rule more exact. This third
kind of authority is beyond our purview. I mention it only to suggest that even the view which allots indefeasible priority to certain
rules governing conduct need not be as rigid and "prefabricated" as
is often supposed.[47]

Concluding Assessment

As the discussion of situation ethics has proceeded so far, one cannot help thinking that much of the disagreement about the authority
of rules reflects (too often unacknowledged) disagreements which
begin further back. That is, determinative reasons why people differ
have often to do with varying material accounts of agape itself and/or
varying further premises about human nature and human good.
Several examples follow.

---

47. These options, including a detailed inquiry into the third kind of authority, are discussed in Paul Ramsey. "The Case of the Curious Exception," *Norm
and Context in Christian Ethics,* pp. 67–135. For Evans' own account of the
relation of his position to Ramsey's, see "Paul Ramsey on Exceptionless Moral
Rules," *The American Journal of Jurisprudence* 16 (1971): 184–214.

For Fletcher, as observed in chapter 3, agape is materially identified with utilitarianism. Whatever obscurities remain about his identification, he usually means that whether an action is loving or not depends solely upon the goodness or badness of its consequences. And, as noted earlier in the present chapter, Ramsey wishes to retain a deontological element in the sense of "the covenants of life with life." Fidelity to such covenants has a distinctive moral weight independent of any consideration of consequences. Either consequence-features only, fidelity-features only, or a hybrid of the two, are then sometimes built into the content of agape. Whether either kind of feature issues in general subsidiary rules is a logically independent question and disputable on each side. But the material characterization of agape may affect the outcome decisively. If one holds for example that agape itself involves covenant relations, then the obligations internal to such relations may be formulable in general rules which bind apart from a consideration of welfare production for the greatest number.

Moreover, differing material meanings of agape are often based on differing premises about human nature and human good. If man has a morally relevant essence or nature which exists beyond the flux of human history, past, present, or future, then certain rules reflecting this nature may well be invariant. To cite one historical instance, it is doubtful whether Augustine would entirely approve of the use Frankena makes of his famous "Love, and do as you please." While a motive of love was a necessary condition for a good action, Augustine never held that it was a sufficient condition. "Love, and do as you please" did not mean that any action whatever might be good, since certain actions were prohibited by nature. He would probably have said that someone genuinely motivated by love would not *want* to do what was so prohibited.

Situationists in general assume significantly less about any essential human nature. The "raw material" has, perhaps, no tropism except toward the pleasant. Certainly it includes no characteristics sufficiently immutable, so far as moral judgments are concerned, to warrant the claim that some classes of action are prohibited because they do not accord with such characteristics. One ought to stress instead that moral judgments follow solely from basic principles of action-guidance to which the agent has freely committed himself. Agape is one such principle.

It is possible to identify among situationists certain closely related assumptions about human nature and human good as these have to do with moral decisions. The most obvious concerns a stress on the freedom of the agent to assume responsibility as a burden to be justified as Dostoyevsky did in *The Grand Inquisitor*. This appears to be one of Fletcher's principal positive reasons for situationism; he proposes to relinquish what is seen as childish dependence on rules which simplify, externalize, and attend exclusively to uniformities. Another assumption is that attention to uniformities neglects the distinctiveness of the agent's own moral wrestling, the particularities of every present situation, and the individual character of one's own vision of the meaning of human action. Fletcher would presumably concur with the following statement by Iris Murdoch.

> I want . . . to consider whether there are not positive and radical moral conceptions which are unconnected with the view that morality is essentially universal rules. I have in mind moral attitudes which emphasize the inexhaustible detail of the world, the endlessness of the task of understanding, the importance of not assuming that one has got individuals and situations "taped," the connection of knowledge with love and of spiritual insight with apprehension of the unique.[48]

Still another assumption sometimes in evidence is that a motive of love is a sufficient condition for a good action. Or at least the sphere of moral accountability may be confined totally to attitude and intention. The agent ought to be as certain of his facts as possible, but an error in empirical judgment is altogether different from moral culpability. The latter pertains solely to a general unloving attitude

48. Iris Murdoch, "Vision and Choice in Morality," *Christian Ethics and Contemporary Philosophy*, p. 208.

or a specific intention not to bring about the greatest amount of good in a particular set of circumstances.[49]

A final sense in which claims about an essential human nature may be set aside is more social in character. Openness is required because of historical institutional change and evolution as well as personal uniqueness. A certain autonomy and in some instances even "norm-forming" authority is bestowed upon social institutions (and hence upon data about them, especially as studied by the social sciences) and historical changes in these institutions. One can distinguish three sides to the morally relevant authority a changing social context is sometimes said to have. The context frequently governs the *appropriateness* of a response and thus requires sound and relevant judgments, not simply individual moral uprightness. It may also *elicit* certain responses, and limit or prevent other ideally preferred ones. It may contribute to the *creation* of normative rules or at least issues which require innovative normative assessments. What situationists are disposed to stress are not the moral limitations which "realism" demands but the creative possibilities of new social configurations. These possibilities, often linked to the profound changes wrought by science and technology, are taken as markedly discon-

49. At one point Fletcher endorses the *Gesinnungs-ethik* legacy (*Situation Ethics*, p. 79). Yet the characterization offered above, while applicable to some proponents of situation ethics, may not adequately represent Fletcher. In a recent article he distinguishes right from good as follows. The rightness of an action depends on its actual consequences; the goodness of an action depends upon its intended consequences. Moral assessment thus involves both an "objective" side — rightness determined by the de facto results of the act in question — and a "subjective" one — the goodness of the agent's intention to bring about optimally beneficial effects (Joseph Fletcher, "Virtue is a Predicate," *The Monist* 54 [January, 1970]: 81–82. See also Brand Blanshard, "Morality and Politics," *Ethics and Society*, pp. 10–13). One can also distinguish more than Fletcher appears to do between actual and reasonably foreseen consequences, and hold the agent accountable for the latter. Moral assessment would then include the agent's general loving attitude, his intention to bring about the greatest amount of good in a particular set of circumstances, and his judgment about reasonably foreseen consequences among alternative ways to execute his intention. For instance, he might intend well and nonetheless be careless in estimating how the balance of advantage was likely to go.

tinuous with past conditions. At least historic claims about an immutable human nature may thereby be called tacitly into question. Assumptions such as the above which support situation ethics as a self-conscious movement also serve to illustrate its selectivity. For other reasons have been advanced in support of a stress on concrete circumstances and the relativity of rules. Two of these reasons are specifically theological and neither appears very congenial to situation ethics as currently discussed. The first is put forward by Barth, among others, and will be considered in chapter 7. For Barth, the divine sovereignty is infringed upon unless there is a final sense in which it is *God* who commands in each present moment. As I shall try to show, one may distinguish theological contextualism from empirical situationism. A second theological reason concerns the effects of a doctrine of sin as a constant datum with which one is forced to reckon. The doctrine may support an insistence on the relativity of rules in the following ways. Suppose one agrees with Niebuhr that agape will never be progressively realized to the point where all contradiction between it and competing wills and interests is removed, and that the latter reflect corruption arising incurably from human nature. Specific rules (including societal laws) do not escape this corruptibility. For specificity itself, however unavoidable, always means compromise. The "world" involves pervasive conflict and cultural conditioning never fully reconcilable with love. To deny such conflict and conditioning risks utopianism; but to admit this account of the "world" is to acquiesce to tentativeness. "Relevance" is at once required and a moral concession. Particular situations often demand a highly sensitive, *appropriate* response which may render formally preferable principles and rules unhelpful or even distortive. It may be impossible and really wrong to demand that such principles be applied in any other way than as residual critical resources. Furthermore, many specific formulated rules should be regarded with some degree of tentativeness because they are susceptible to an "ideological taint"; they express not simply the pure demands of love and justice, but also the inordinate self-interest of parochial historical groups. All socially sanctioned behavior patterns and all institutions are tainted with an ambiguous mixture of moral and amoral motives and unacknowledged pressures toward self-perpetuation. If such patterns and rules are made absolute and unbreakable, they may be imposed on new conditions to which they are alien and thereby foster lawlessness among those most affected by the changed circumstances.[50] Finally, because of the pervasiveness of conflict and cultural conditioning, one is confronted with "borderline situations" of various sorts, with the necessity of compromise, with choices (over which he may have little control) between the "lesser of evils." In such a world the hope of "conflictless" rules is superficial and an illusion. On some of these points Niebuhr is joined by many Reformation-oriented ethicists. Helmut Thielicke, for example, writes:

> The borderline situation . . . has its origin in a communal guilt which already stands behind our situation and which we for our part ever increase and intensify. We are thus both the object and the subject of this communal guilt: it lays us under the constraint of necessity, yet at the same time we are summoned to act in freedom, responsibly. . . . Our own action needs forgiveness, but so too does the situation within which it occurs.[51]

The point about the moral consequences of a doctrine of sin is perhaps the least attractive to a situationist like Fletcher. He resists any notion of a transcendent love ideal which leads one to regard every action as partially deficient and normally a choice between evils; he wants to remove any free-floating uneasy conscience. *"The situationist holds that whatever is the most loving thing in the situation is the right and good thing. It is not excusably evil, but is positively good."* [52] While Niebuhr is by no means unrelentingly dour or pessimistic (as we have seen), he would probably in turn suspect Fletcher's statement as expressing quite unwarranted moral self-confidence. To try to reduce love to what is actually the maximum amount of good achievable in a particular situation might seem to

50. Niebuhr, *Faith and History,* pp. 183–84.
51. Helmut Thielicke, *Theological Ethics,* ed. William H. Lazareth, 2 vols. (Philadelphia: Fortress Press, 1966), 1:602.
52. Fletcher, *Situation Ethics,* p. 65.

him too prosaic and insensitive to both the heights of self-giving to which man may aspire (or at least which he may inwardly sanction) and the permanent prospect of inordinate self-seeking. It is wrong to demand unambiguous solutions in any situation, and it is also wrong to be sanguine about what is achieved. In addition, Niebuhr would insist not only that all specific rules must be invested with some degree of tentativeness but also that they are at least part of the time lamentably necessary to prevent injustice and exploitation. They may serve to correct the taint of self-seeking as well as be conditioned by it. One must beware of the curative powers of unbridled love. This cannot be pressed too far, but Niebuhr might find some of the situationist's confidence in "mature" men responsibly making free decisions to be naive if not ludicrous.

I shall say more in chapter 6 about the effects of wider beliefs and assumptions on agape itself. My present point has simply been that disputes falling generally under "love and law," and specifically under the debate about situation ethics, often reflect such prior disagreements. These disagreements need far more attention than they have thus far received.

5

Agape as a Virtue of the Agent

A normative ethics which is even minimally complete does more than affix an ethical predicate to a term signifying an act or a quality. It also specifies what we may generically call the "psychological conditions" in the agent, in virtue of which the agent's act or quality has, or deserves, that ethical predicate. . . . In judging an act to be good, such an ethics refers not only to the act itself but also to the "condition" or "mental disposition" of the agent.

Alan Gewirth

At the beginning of the last chapter it was observed that for almost everyone agape is never to be equated with a given moral code. Agape encompasses far more than formulated rules placing and governing definite classes of action, even if one agrees that in certain instances it is positively expressed by them. Consider the following statement identifying a broad distinction often made in moral reflection which is relevant to the inquiry now to be undertaken.

By the morality of the act I mean the morality of specific willed actions. By the morality of the agent I mean a morality whose central conception is a man's moral character. The former is especially prominent in the analysis of right and wrong — did so and so do what was right on such and such an occasion? The latter is usually more general in its methods and is frequently an ethics of virtue rather than an ethics of right. Where it specifies, it usually specifies the quality of the motive or "spring of action" in the agent, not as something completely isolable (since the agent possesses at least a certain unity) but as something relatively distinct and in that way examinable. There are somewhat similar distinctions between an ethics of works and an ethics of faith and the spirit, between an ethics of righteousness and an ethics of moral goodness, between a legalistic ethics and an ethics of inward sweetness and light.[1]

I propose to shift attention roughly from judgments of conduct to judgments of character, from rightness to goodness, doing to being, rule to virtue. For agape has often been taken to apply to both sorts of judgment.

> And though I have no doubt that the Christian concept of *agape* refers partly to external behaviour — the agapeistic behaviour for which there are external criteria — yet being filled with *agape* includes more than behaving agapeistically externally: it also includes an agapeistic frame of mind.[2]

I shall examine then in the present chapter some possible meanings of an "agapeistic frame of mind," the "mental disposition" included in agent-commitment.

To remain within manageable limits, illustrations — showing how agape is taken to apply to the variety of features relevant to the assessment of character — will be confined to the following crudely distinguished topics. First, a combination of feeling with striving or conation is frequently attempted. Some position is sought between love as overwhelming compulsion and as austere obedience. Second, even if one allows a large role to feelings (including perhaps unconscious purposes) in the agent and recognizes that different kinds of love have been linked to them, for most thinkers agape is of course also connected directly to conscious attitudes and intentions. I shall consider one treatment where deliberate attitudes and intentions are combined as part of what agape enjoins. Third, one repeatedly finds the claim that love ought to be the agent's ultimate, dominating motive, sometimes reminiscent of the legacy that love is the form of the other virtues. Agape may serve more or less as an

---

1. John Laird, "Act-Ethics and Agent-Ethics," *Mind* 55 (April, 1946): 113. See also Frankena, *Ethics,* pp. 8–9.

2. R. B. Braithwaite, "An Empiricist's View of the Nature of Religious Belief," *Christian Ethics and Contemporary Philosophy,* p. 65.

abstract noun identifying an attribute which organizes and integrates the several attitudes and intentions oriented toward practice: the agent acts in certain ways because he possesses the attribute. In these first three sections I shall identify some of the typical reasons for independent concentration on character as well as conduct. But the final status of an ethics of virtue in relation to an ethics of right conduct remains unclear in much of the literature generally. So, fourth, I shall suggest some of the issues at stake in the relation between being and doing. Finally, I shall append a discussion of some distinctively theological issues concerning grace and personal agency in accounting for the presence of the virtue.

Feeling and Will

An elaborate treatment of this topic is provided by Dietrich von Hildebrand. He draws on materials from both traditional Roman Catholic sources and phenomenology (with a stress especially on value theory). Von Hildebrand begins by distinguishing between intentional and unintentional activities and assigns love to the former. But, following Husserl, he means by intention not "something done on purpose" but "any conscious meaningful relationship to an object." [3] This rules out "mere states" which "exist in us as simple facts," natural teleological trends such as hunger and thirst, and passions which, as given, must be indulged or controlled.[4] (Love, however, has some affinities to passion, as we shall see.)

He next distinguishes within intentional experiences between cognitive acts on the one side and responses on the other. Cognitive acts are more passive; one is conscious of something, one observes, listens and receives. Responses have a much more spontaneous character. The "content" is heavily on the side of the apprehending subject. The sphere of responses includes belief, conviction, doubt, hope, fear, joy, sorrow, enthusiasm, indignation, esteem and contempt, trust and mistrust, love and hatred. Thus love, for example, is not "con-

3. Dietrich von Hildebrand, *Christian Ethics* (New York: David McKay Company, 1953), p. 191.
4. Ibid., pp. 192–95, 204.

sciousness *of* something but is itself a conscious entity, a consciously accomplished reality." [5]

Within the sphere of responses there are three further distinctions between theoretical, volitional, and affective kinds. The first includes conviction, doubt, and expectation, the second refers to "willing in the strict sense of the word," and the third to the "plentitude" involved in such responses as love and hatred, enthusiasm and indignation.[6] Von Hildebrand admits that will has often been used more inclusively to encompass both volitional and affective responses, but he argues in Augustinian fashion for circumscription so that will and love are not quite identified.[7] The narrow sense of will "dominates the whole sphere which is accessible to our free intervention." [8] Admittedly volitional and affective responses share "the theme of importance"; "they equally presuppose the importance of an object and an awareness of this importance, and they are motivated by it." [9] But the two kinds of responses nevertheless differ significantly. Affective responses possess a certain human richness which the will lacks. They are "voices of our heart" in which the entire personality is engaged. The will has a more "one-dimensional, linear character." [10] Finally, only the will is free in an unqualified sense. The affective responses cannot be engendered by pure effort and are therefore not under the agent's immediate control.

5. Ibid., p. 196.
6. Ibid., p. 197.
7. Ibid., pp. 199–200, 205. Cf. John Burnaby's Introduction to his translation of *Augustine: Later Works, The Library of Christian Classics,* eds. John Baillie, John T. McNeill, and Henry P. Van Dusen (Philadelphia: The Westminster Press, 1955), p. 36: "It is important to observe that both *amor* and *caritas* include feeling as well as striving or conation: indeed it is the affective element in love that supplies its dynamic. In virtue of this affective element, love does not cease to exist when it has attained its object. So Augustine can define love as 'nothing else but the will, seeking after *or holding in possession* an object of enjoyment' . . . a definition which makes clear the difference in connotation between 'will' and 'love.' The two words denote one and the same activity, but *voluntas* fixes attention upon the conative element in this activity, while *amor* always connotes feeling."
8. Von Hildebrand, *Christian Ethics,* p. 200.
9. Ibid., p. 202.
10. Ibid.

How then can love be commanded? The richness which involves responses like delight and joy cannot be created by resolve. Von Hildebrand's principal answer is that human freedom at its profoundest level has "the capacity of sanctioning and of disavowing our own spontaneous attitudes." [11] Though they cannot be simply engendered or dissolved, a man can identify implicitly with them and thereby bring them to definite fruition as well as permit them increasingly to influence the total personality. "Affective responses . . . depend above all upon that which we call the character of a man, his heart, his sensitivity to good, . . . his general inner direction." [12] In this way he is "indirectly" responsible for their influence if not for their presence. Love for God and neighbor can be legitimate obligations "as soon as we take into account the existence of cooperative freedom and indirect influence, and the responsibility connected with them." [13]

It is hardly feasible to identify in detail, much less try to assess, von Hildebrand's various premises concerning human nature. For one thing, that task would require extensive attention to the range of phenomenological concepts he employs. Yet it seems plain that generally (and here I think typically) he wishes to attend to character traits which combine modes of feeling and thought as well as action. Assessments of a person's character may properly include all of these modes. Let me add three possible extrapolations. The first two follow rather clearly from von Hildebrand's account, the third less obviously so, but it is a point often made elsewhere in any case.

1. Certainly one may grant that usually no clear boundary bisects the agent's "general inner direction" from external movements. The former, insofar as it is genuine, and when there are no obstructions, naturally manifests itself in observable behavior the evaluation of which may lead in some instances to formulated rules. And naturally a general inner direction or virtue is not something which may or may not be exercised. That is, a person could not say that he had the virtue of love but never exercised it. Even those who wish to

11. Ibid., p. 231. For a summary statement of the role of freedom in the affective sphere, see pp. 334–36.
12. Ibid., p. 338.
13. Ibid., p. 341.

accord "unqualified worth" to the virtuous motive alone do not
seem strictly obliged to maintain that a man motivated by love can
be indifferent to whether or not he acts at all or to the effects of
his action; or that a loving motive is a sufficient and not only a
necessary condition for a good action; or (though this may be more
seriously controversial) that they wish to hypostasize the will. All
that is often insisted on is that a normative ethical principle such as
agape applies to a variety of distinguishable features which constitute the whole person, all of which are sometimes subject to moral
assessment.

> One is free from the prejudice that the concept of action itself is
> by itself sufficient to mark the domain of the essential human
> virtues. One has before one, for reflection and comment, whether
> in one's own person, or in the person of another, always a
> whole person, including the way he thinks and expresses his
> thoughts and feelings, the things that he notices and neglects,
> the attitudes that he adopts, the feelings that he restrains and
> the feelings to which he allows free play, the words that he
> chooses to use or that he uses unreflectingly, the gestures and
> physical reactions that he controls or suppresses, the plans that
> he makes and the sudden impulses that occur to him.[14]

2. Virtues and vices pertain then not just to acting well or ill, but
also, for instance, to important attachments one forms and to pleasures one takes. The agent may make an effort to keep them out of
his announced purposes and overt behavior. He may struggle against
the malicious pleasure he takes, for example, in the misfortune of a

14. Stuart Hampshire, *Thought and Action* (London: Chatto and Windus,
1960), p. 91. See also Murdoch, "Vision and Choice in Morality," p. 202: "When
we apprehend and assess other people we do not consider only their solutions
to specifiable practical problems, we consider something more elusive which
may be called their total vision of life, as shown in their mode of speech or
silence, their choice of words, their assessments of others, their conceptions of
their own lives, what they think attractive or praise-worthy, what they think
funny: in short, the configurations of their thought which show continually in
their reactions and conversation." Note as well Iris Murdoch, *The Sovereignty of
Good* (London: Routledge and Kegan Paul, 1970).

rival. More may be at stake for him than neglecting to do publicly what he ought. The presence of the pleasure, and the struggle against it, he may regard as morally significant even if he succeeds in avoiding public diagnosis.

Such internal disharmonies account in part for an insistence that virtues and vices are integrally related to — but not identified with — what may be witnessed by others. There are moral reasons for insisting on their integral relation, yet the experience of intra-psychic struggle may prompt one to draw back from identifying them. Moreover, we then approach the widely-held assumption (one finds it in von Hildebrand) that it makes sense to refer to intra-personal as well as inter-personal action. What the agent may want to be is not always reducible to the cumulative impact of expectations and responses from others, to any public consensus regarding what in general anyone ought to be; or to what is detectable in fact by others in the same way it is detectable by himself (even if necessarily detectable in some way by others). The agent is also self-moving. He acts upon himself as well as being acted upon by other persons.

3. There may be fear of a sophistic, conventional measure of human excellence. Every instance of acting lovingly toward others need not have an identical explanation. A certain ambiguity is frequently taken to surround conformity to rules as such.[15] The ambiguity derives from two sorts of complex relations. In assessing oneself or another, it may be hard to discern the link between a perceived and an unconscious mental state. The agent's reasons for acting in a certain way often seem opaque, or at least not always readily identifiable. Secondly, it may prove difficult to close the gap in any single fashion between a mental state, either perceived or unconscious or both, and behavior. A breach may exist unavoidably between carry-

---

15. Note the following strong assertion: "There is no set of statements about behaviour which *entail* or *are entailed by* any statement about mental or spiritual characteristics. However carefully, fully and exactly we specify our tests before we shall never be able decisively to discriminate between . . . being honest and seeming honest. For the heart is deceitful above all things, and whatever criteria we adopt, it always *may* succeed in conforming outwardly to our requirements while inwardly repudiating the standards we have set" (J. R. Lucas, "The Soul," *Faith and Logic,* p. 141).

ing out the prescribed action, for whatever reason, and carrying it out specifically for the sake of love. For conformity may also be fortuitous or inspired by acquisitive intent. To aim for a sensitive assessment, one may wish to attend to inner thoughts and feelings not all of which can be captured in behavioral formulas.

Attitude and Intention

Attitude and intention are frequently held to form the core of the agent's conscious "psychological conditions," and combined as part of what agape enjoins. Consider a treatment by Evans, in a book which considers J. L. Austin's work on performative language and applies it to the biblical understanding of creation. Evans argues that many attitudes are characterized by something for which he coins the word "onlook." He notes the following examples:

> 'I look on death as the mockery of human hopes (or as the gateway to a higher form of life).'
> 'I look on suffering as a wise discipline, imposed by God (or as an opportunity for self-discipline, or as something trivial compared with my growing inner wisdom, or as an annoying interference with my work).'
> 'I look on my work as a way of making money, no more (or as my one reason for living, or as my calling from God).'
> 'I look on sex as a sordid animal urge (or as an expression of a profoundly spiritual relation).' [16]

Onlook is thus the substantive for looking on something as something else, though it need not be restricted to a specific linguistic formula where the words "look" and "on" are actually used. It is more seriously self-involving than "view," "opinion," "outlook," or "perspective," and less intellectual than "conception."

Two features of onlooks are stressed particularly. The first Evans calls *commissive.* There is "a declaration or redeclaration of policy;

16. Donald Evans, *The Logic of Self-Involvement* (London: SCM Press, 1963), p. 125.

or, at least, there is an expression of intention, a minimal under-taking."[17] The speaker commits himself to regard someone or some-thing and to behave in a certain way. "Insofar as an utterance is commissive, it is not true-or-false; it is fulfilled-or-unfulfilled."[18] The second feature is the *verdictive*. Here opinion and judgment are paramount. The speaker places someone "within a structure, organ-ization or scheme. This often involves the ascription of a status, func-tion or role to *x* in my own mind."[19] There are many differences of course, between onlooks. Some are literal while others are more "ana-logical" and "parabolic." Justifications vary accordingly: some are empirically verifiable; others may involve an appeal to revelation, and so on.

An example of a religious-ethical onlook given by Evans is "I look on each man as a brother for whom Christ died."[20] The principal element of interest for our purposes is his contention that such an onlook legitimately fuses verdictive and commissive features. He op-poses any attempt to reduce such hybrid affirmations. Deciding *that* each man is a brother, I am also deciding *to* think and behave in the appropriate ways. My decision-*to*, on the other hand, is not totally divorced from my decision-*that* each man is to be looked on as a brother (my judgment being based perhaps on Christ as the para-digm, etc.).[21] Such a religious-ethical onlook then is both attitudinal and intentional in nature, i.e., it includes both a judgment and an undertaking, both a viewpoint and a declaration of policy — in short, both a decision-*that* and a decision-*to*. Moreover, the stress is on an orientation toward someone rather than on a quality which inheres in the agent.

Such dispositions as humility, pride and trustfulness are attitudes in so far as I am humble *towards* some definite person or group,

17. Ibid., p. 126. For two other important works by philosophers on intention, see Hampshire, *Thought and Action*; G. E. M. Anscombe, *Intention* (Oxford: Basil Blackwell, 1963).
18. Evans, *Logic of Self-Involvement*, p. 32.
19. Ibid., p. 127; cf. pp. 36–37.
20. Ibid., p. 129.
21. See ibid., pp. 136–37.

proud *of* something definite or *towards* someone definite, and trustful *in relation* to someone definite.[22]

A combination of attitude and intention clearly forms a major part of the meaning of agape as a virtue of the agent. Concerning the verdictive feature, it should also be observed that there may be different sorts of loving and unloving attitudes which issue or fail to issue in action. The agent may fail to act concretely due more perhaps to lack of attention than to active malice. Various attitudes then may stand behind inaction, such as indifference, insensitivity, malice. To say that thoughts, feelings, attachments, and so on, are subject to assessments founded on agape fosters attention to such attitudinal complexities. Certain beliefs may likewise be relevant. Wrong attachments may imply a false view of what is to be valued. I mentioned earlier Kierkegaard's contention that one may care too much or in the wrong way.

In the case of the commissive feature, the crucial question centers on fulfillment rather than truth or falsity. The concern may therefore be to give an account of a certain moral-psychological state, about being the sort of person who helps others rather than concentrating on what, specifically, will help them. One asks then about the extent to which love organizes and dominates various thoughts, feelings, and actions; and about the depth, intensity, or genuineness of whatever love the agent exemplifies. For love ought to show in the set of a person's life. In order to judge that an agent is loving we need more than one notable performance, and more than a limited class of actions which he habitually performs or refrains from performing. There ought to be a variety of exemplifications which reflect a long-range policy. The policy persists through time and integrates a cluster of specific objectives. Love ought to be genuinely inward, so that the more one comes to know the agent, the less one senses a discrepancy between manifest operations and deeper aims. These latter points bring us to the claim that love ought to be the agent's ultimate, dominating motive.

22. Ibid., p. 122.

Love the Form of the Virtues

Charity in the Roman Catholic tradition is one of the supernatural virtues and its traditional pre-eminence forbids us from regarding it as merely a virtue alongside others. It is usually represented as the causative source of the other virtues; it gives to them their basic direction. So love ought effectively to govern all of the attitudes and actions of the agent. Such governance differs from what occasions his passing moods and momentary impulses.

Von Hildebrand refers also to love in this wider sense. He distinguishes three spheres in which moral goodness is to be found: actions, concrete response (which we considered earlier), and virtues and vices, i.e., "the lasting qualities of a person's character." [23] A virtue is for him more than a given ability or a temperamental disposition or even a good intention because it must be capable of dominating the whole pattern of someone's life. The entire demeanor of a man will express the virtue of love; actions in "qualitative affinity" with it will be forthcoming; affective responses congruent with it will arise spontaneously. Indeed, every action and attitude finally attests to a homogeneous point of origin, a "loving, reverent, value-responding center." [24] The word "center" is meant to express a "fundamental approach to the universe and to God, a qualitatively unified 'ego' which is always more or less actualized when the person accomplishes a morally good act." [25] The elements of "self-donation" and "participation" make love "the most total, central and intimate of all value responses." [26] Love subsists, he contends, even when it is not con-

---

23. While von Hildebrand holds that the virtue of love is not constitutive but must be realized, he believes it is nonetheless linked to man's raison d'être just as pride and concupiscence are perversions. Yet presumably the latter might still effectively dominate the attitudes and actions of some men. Others, particularly certain Protestants, insist more emphatically on the dominance of vices in some men and that wickedness seems often incorrigible.
24. Ibid., pp. 412–13.
25. Ibid., p. 352.
26. Ibid., p. 413.

sciously experienced, and so may be called a "superactual response." [27] It need not invariably be that for the immediate sake of which a given action is performed, in order still to remain the finally integrative reason or standard of the good.

Yet no consensus exists in the literature about the precise sense to be given to the claim that love is not merely a virtue alongside others, but the causative source of them. Catholics themselves have differed on the nature and extent of charity's dominance.

> Some theologians so stress the importance of charity that they seem loath to give any value to other virtues, such as courage or justice or purity, unless they explicitly fall under that of charity. . . . They cannot, however, mean that we must *always explicitly refer* what we do to the love of God, and once we admit that a virtue has an intrinsic excellence of its own and that only some kind of overruling *principle* of life or motive is needed, the edge of the difficulty is removed. All our actions are to some extent affected by our central love; when a man is selfish at heart even his virtues are *slightly tinged* with this *attitude,* and it is a common experience to find that a man who has changed his convictions, undergone a testing and shaking experience and survived it, without permanent harm, talks, speaks and acts as a "different person." The *whole man* is in *each* of our acts, and that is why love does have some say as to the dress in which we clothe our virtues and our vices.[28]

This statement hardly resolves all of the difficulties. To some extent it reflects them. Issues arise which warrant further identification and comment.

References to "causative source," the "whole man," and "our central love" include but often exceed committal regarded as sincerity, genuineness, or as we say, "meaning it." The decision-to-love (waiving the question as to whether "decision" is the right word) appears to dominate in a stronger sense as well. It refers to what constitutes

27. Ibid., pp. 235–36, 241–43.
28. M. C. D'Arcy, *Mind and Heart of Love,* p. 92. Italics mine.

one's personal identity. That is, it implies totality in the sense of integrating all of one's powers; and determination of one's consciousness in the sense of providing continuity of meaningful action from the past, in the present, and into the future.

D'Arcy's endorsement of love as an overruling principle or motive claims less for the dominance in question than is frequently done. Two major claims may be distinguished.[29] The first allows that love is basic in relation to other attitudes and principles in that wherever a conflict occurs between what love and other attitudes or principles require, love should have priority and overrule. D'Arcy might deny that such conflicts are possible if love and other moral attitudes and principles are rightly construed. Such a denial would reflect of course a certain view of the moral life, and a widely contested one. Even if someone accepted such a view, he might argue that love with authority only to overrule still permits other virtues to exist as isolated and independent entities. So a stronger claim is often found. Love is paramount in that it is the basis of other virtues and principles; it provides the fundamental justifying reason for their existence, or the purpose or intent underlying them. One may even assert that other virtues and principles are to be *explained* only in terms of love.

A recent version of the stronger claim has been called *pure agapism*. Its proponents

> all hold that the "law of love" is the sole basis of morality — that on it hang "the whole law and the prophets," i.e., that the rest of the moral law can and must be derived from love together with relevant non-ethical beliefs and knowledge, empirical, metaphysical, or theological.[30]

Yet pure agapism may itself have a restricted and a very wide meaning. The more restricted meaning may in turn take two forms: agapism is "*the* proper form for Christian or Judeo-Christian ethics to take, or at least that it is *a* proper form for it to take."[31] As *a*

29. Cf. Downie and Telfer, *Respect for Persons*, p. 33.
30. Frankena, "Love and Principle in Christian Ethics," p. 211.
31. Ibid., p. 310.

proper form, other valid normative schemes are allowed, both religious and non-religious. The last word is thus deliberately modest:
here is one way to account for the varied dimensions of the religious
and moral life. As *the* proper form within Christian ethics, all other
virtues and principles must somehow be explained in terms of agape.
So Fletcher, for example, asserts that there is "only one 'thing' . . .
intrinsically good; namely, love: nothing else at all." [32] James Gustafson objects to love as *the* proper form, or what he calls "love-
monism." [33] There are other virtues and principles which must be
considered independently if the complexities of the religious and
moral life are to be adequately addressed. A far wider meaning has
also been allowed for pure agapism. Love is not only the paramount
attitude and principle in Judeo-Christian ethics but it is finally the
most adequate basis for *any* morality. Tillich contends for instance
that the "silent voice" of man's own nature has love as its final
normative standard, and to deny this is to engage in self-destructive-
ness. For "every valid ethical commandment is an expression of man's
essential relation to himself, to others and to the universe. This alone
makes it obligatory and its denial self-destructive." [34]

   This last statement in particular opens up issues to be considered
in the next chapter. For the present it is enough to observe that the
discussion about pure agapism seems on the whole unduly abstract.
What is chiefly unacknowledged is how decisive different sorts of
normative content can be for the formal outcome either way. Only
certain kinds of content may permit one to hold consistently that
other attitudes and principles can be explained in terms of agape.
This point should be clear from the various relations between love
and justice, and the various kinds of content which these reflect, indicated in chapter 3, and to be taken up again in chapter 8. Similarly,
if one conceives of agape as solely an other-regarding attitude and
principle, then pure agapism is possible only if one agrees that self-
benefitting actions never have independent moral justification. Cour-

   32. Fletcher, *Situation Ethics*, p. 57.
   33. James M. Gustafson, "How Does Love Reign?" *The Christian Century*
83 (May 18, 1966): 655.
   34. Tillich, *Love, Power, and Justice*, p. 77.

age, for example, displayed on one's own behalf, would have always
to be justified derivatively from other-regarding considerations. Another large question of substance is whether pure agapism refers
both to love for God and neighbor-love, and if so, how these are
related. I shall consider it further in the chapter on Barth. We
have already noted efforts to transpose love for God altogether into
neighbor-love so far as normative ethics is concerned. Others however wish to integrate various attitudes and principles, including
regard for the neighbor, under a notion of final active referral of all
things to God. To love God is to cultivate one's capacity to recognize
providential action and to conform to it, to attend to the vision of
reality which religious beliefs serve in part to identify, and to connect the vision to what one experiences in his spatio-temporal world.

Being and Doing

It is not difficult to imagine a modern interlocutor who would confess to a growing restlessness with much of the foregoing. "Doubtless," he might say, "some of the reasons which have been given for
independent attention to the subject of virtue are well-taken. But I
am still uncertain about the final status of an ethics of virtue in relation to an ethics of right conduct. How are we to understand the
formal relation between the two kinds of assessment so recurrent in
moral reflection? Specifically, are we committed in principle to two
different sets of objects each capable of separable evaluation and irreducibly different in their status? If so, I find this incoherent. For
what precisely *is* the irreducible element in virtue which can be
diagnosed and evaluated in oneself or in others apart from its correlative actions? Is one left with a finally incorrigible inner-outer
problem, with an inscrutable 'motive' to be forever contrasted with
'mere' external acts?"

There is no single answer in the literature. Part of the diversity reflects the different legacies at work. Among the influences which
stand behind the independent concentration on virtue or character
one thinks for example of the traditional theological references to the
soul and to the inner spiritual man, the existentialist claim that the

life of "inwardness" remains always incommensurable with "out-
wardness," and the phenomenological account of the activity of in-
tentionality — the "movement" of the self toward some object of
consciousness.

I cannot hope to treat such topics very fully in a single chapter.
But in order to identify further some issues concerning the status of an
ethics of virtue, I will consider the following statement, which represents a characteristically modern approach to the subject.

> To be or to do, that is the question. Should we construe mo-
> rality as primarily a following of certain principles or as primarily
> a cultivation of certain dispositions and traits? Must we choose?
> It is hard to see how a morality of principles can get off the
> ground except through the development of dispositions to act in
> accordance with its principles, else all motivation to act on them
> must be an *ad hoc* kind, either prudential or impulsively al-
> truistic. Moreover, morality can hardly be content with a mere
> conformity to rules, however willing and self-conscious it may
> be, unless it has no interest in the spirit of the law but only in
> its letter. On the other hand, one cannot conceive of traits of
> character except as dispositions and tendencies to act in certain
> ways in certain circumstances. Hating involves being disposed to
> kill or harm, being just involves tending to do just acts (acts
> which conform to the principle of justice) when the occasion
> calls. Again, it is hard to see how we could know what traits to
> encourage or inculcate if we did not subscribe to principles, for
> example, to the principle of utility, or to those of benevolence
> and justice.
>
> I propose therefore that we regard the morality of principles
> and the morality of traits of character, or doing and being, not
> as rival kinds of morality between which we must choose, but as
> two complementary aspects of the same morality. Then, for every
> principle there will be a morally good trait, often going by the
> same name, consisting of a disposition or tendency to act accord-
> ing to it; and for every morally good trait there will be a
> principle defining the kind of action in which it is to express

itself. To parody a famous dictum of Kant's; principles without traits are impotent, traits without principles are blind.[35]

This passage is not without its own ambiguities and implicit assumptions. Clearly a pure agapist would want the "same morality" in the sense of a morality finally unified by the same normative criterion, the same basic ethical principle. Yet even on the supposition that character traits and specific actions are both to be governed by agape, it is not altogether clear how these two objects of evaluation relate to one another; thus it is hard to determine in what such governance consists. If "one cannot conceive of traits of character except as dispositions and tendencies to act in certain ways in certain circumstances," then character traits appear to *reduce* in the end to dispositions to act in certain ways and agape defines only the sorts of *acts* enjoined. The principle may not apply directly then to traits which combine modes of thinking and feeling as well as acting. Hating would be solely comprised in the disposition actually to kill or harm; the attitudinal complexity noted earlier, for instance, which may stand behind either action or inaction, seems to go unrecognized. However, there are also references which seem less reductionist. One needs, it is maintained, both kinds of judgment. Principles without traits are impotent; one should exhibit concern for the spirit, not only the letter of the law. To go beyond mere *ad hoc* motivation, we need to ask ourselves explicitly how we cultivate dispositions to act in certain ways. And attention to the spirit might conceivably allow for attitudinal complexities and the like.

Perhaps it is unfair to analyze this single passage beyond a certain point. But one common modern view which I think it reflects may be called the complementarity-thesis. There is a relation of symmetry or complementarity between judgments of character and of conduct. One stays within the limits of complementarity when one agrees to an exchange in principle between references to character and to ac-

---

35. Frankena, *Ethics*, pp. 52–53. For a comparison of this modern view with the Socratic one, see M. F. Burnyeat, "Virtues in Action," *The Philosophy of Socrates*, ed. Gregory Vlastos (Garden City, N.Y.: Doubleday and Company, Inc., 1971), pp. 209–34.

tions. The same ground is covered from different directions. Yet while formally the two judgments cover the same ground, there are decisive practical reasons always to retain the two ways of talking. Such reasons in themselves suffice to justify independent attention to the subject of virtue.

Let me again extrapolate, in this instance to specify first, the status of an ethics of virtue accorded by such a complementarity-thesis, and second, how the thesis might accommodate many of the considerations suggested in earlier sections. It makes practical sense to attend separately to virtue or character, a proponent of the thesis might argue. Such separate attention should not imply an irreducible difference in formal status. It means rather that to identify character traits is often convenient. Actually to catalogue a complete list of loving action-patterns would be impossible. There is too much inexhaustible contextual detail. The spontaneity, context-dependence, and complexity involved cannot always be captured in behavioral formulas. Character traits extract from such detail.[36] They serve to select and generalize on the basis of actions which are necessarily manifold and multiform. They permit one to organize distinctive long-term patterns and identify their moral importance. They call attention to these patterns, which an act-by-act description does not in itself illuminate.

Assessments of a particular person's character and of given actions also differ in their respective points of concentration. In practical terms the two sorts of judgment are concerned often with different jobs, even if always overlapping ones. Sometimes one wishes to concentrate on a given action and its effects on all of the parties. ("I don't care how much he has loved his daughter in the face of many trials and deep suffering; for any one to do what he did to her yesterday is just wrong. I am judging that, not the sort of father he has been in general.") At other times one wishes to attend to the person himself, to the cumulative impact on others and on himself of his past actions, and perhaps to what he is likely to do in the

36. They are also convenient in that once a generalization is formed about someone, it may remain even after one has forgotten all of the specific actions which led to it. There are hazards in such a process of course: generalizations either pro or con may become fixed so that one is unable to perceive changes in characteristic action-patterns, or perceives them falsely.

future. ("All of the years I have known him on the bench, he has tried to be scrupulously fair. He panders to no one. I think that is the sort of person we need in Congress.") Perhaps one might also allow references to the struggles a particular agent has undergone and the handicaps he has faced, in order to assess him appropriately, with due recognition of the complexities in his case. One would not then simply estimate in uniform fashion the total value to others of all the separate acts of every agent. More is required of those to whom more is given.

How moreover might the complementarity-thesis accommodate many of the considerations noted previously? In some of the earlier contrasts (e.g., between acting well and the attachments one forms and the pleasures one takes), the notion of acting seems rather narrowly conceived. It appears to have to do only with "external behavior." A wider notion is implied however when allowance is made for intra-personal as well as inter-personal action. Suppose we accept such an expansive notion of action (and a commensurately wide application of "principle"). Accommodative moves might then include the following. Thoughts and feelings would not be subject to independent moral assessment, but one might often need a reference to them as part of a full description of the action being evaluated. The initial feeling of pleasure in the misfortune of a rival, for example, would likely be characterized as a temptation where assessment must await the outcome. What is subject directly to moral evaluation is not the temptation, but the observable reaction to it; whether one succumbs to or resists it successfully. Still, an account of the temptation may be needed to furnish a context of intelligibility. Similarly, only those configurations of thought which *show* continuously in reactions and conversations could be assessed. Even so, this would encompass far more than solutions to specifiable practical problems. One could likewise concede the peril of a sophistic, conventional measure of human excellence and acknowledge that every instance of acting lovingly need not have an identical explanation. Nonetheless, in the case of any single agent, a history of such instances is the criterion for an evaluation of character, especially if we cast the action-net widely enough to include reactions, conversations, and so on. And how else do we know that there is no discrepancy between manifest operations and

deeper aims except by witnessing a history of specific instances of acting lovingly? Finally, the doctrine that love is the form of the virtues
need require no more than an insistence that love predominate (in
either of the two ways construed earlier) in every decision made. If
D'Arcy means more than this when he says that "the whole man is
in each of our acts," he does not make it clear. In short, so far as
moral assessments of character are concerned, it seems most coherent
to hold that the biography is the man, including the autobiography.

Whether the complementarity-thesis as described above encompasses
all that agape as a virtue of the agent can intelligibly mean is
another question which warrants far more attention than it has so far
received in the theological literature. Here also the answers will reflect
wider assumptions. For example, one approaches the fluctuating
boundary between ethics and the philosophy of mind, and peers at
epistemological problems centuries old. I can linger now merely to
identify several points which might profitably be pursued if one
were to discuss the question further.

A traditionalist might offer the following sort of response to the
modern interlocutor. "You have sketched a formidable case for some
version of the complementarity-thesis. But I am troubled that you
did not consider very carefully the formal status of your own account.
Do you wish only to make a perspectival point? That is, do you want
simply to stipulate the epistemological conditions which set the
boundaries for *human* inter-personal awareness and assessment? I
think I am prepared to agree that there is no way to get at any
irreducible element in virtue which can be diagnosed and evaluated *in
others* apart from its correlative actions. In order to evaluate the
character of another one depends on references to those of his actions
which may be witnessed by others. I myself want to cast the action-
net widely to include those more subtle expressions of character,
spontaneous reactions, conversations, and the like, and not only the
individual's solutions to specifiable practical problems. If we do include these expressions, then yes, by their perceptible fruits you shall
know them. But I am uncertain whether you mean to stop with the
human conditions for the acquisition of knowledge of other persons.
Does it follow that you wish to rule out as well all possible moral
significance to intrapsychic states in the agent, when they do not

involve exercise, and when in a given case they are known fully
only to the agent, or perhaps only to God? I do not think I need
deny that all such states are susceptible in principle to public description in general terms. They apply to what *any* agent may himself experience. While admittedly contingent and factual then, they
are not all immediately observable by others. Von Hildebrand's account of the activity of the self toward some value would be an
instance of morally evaluable intra-psychic activity. I want to allow
that there may be factual intra-psychic consciousness which in itself
has meaning and value for the agent and perhaps for God, even
when it is not altogether manifested empirically to others or does
not impinge directly on them. Otherwise (among other losses) I
risk reducing everything of conceivable moral value about a person
to what he does which may be seen by men."

The traditionalist's response is of course fraught with implicit assumptions of its own. One of these he shares with the modern interlocutor. They both appear to assume that something material — an
observable grimace, gesture, artifact, and so on — must be perceived,
whether by hearing, seeing, reading about, touching, etc., as a necessary condition for inter-personal awareness and potential assessment.
But some have claimed that there may be co-consciousness of a kind
which is totally independent of any observable item in the material
world. So, for instance, a person might be said to communicate loving attitudes to others even when he is in solitude by virtue of a
certain state of consciousness, perhaps through meditation and prayer.
Suppose however one agrees to this shared assumption. What does
the traditionalist want which he suspects complementarity fails to
provide?

Perhaps he wants only terminological expansion of "moral assessment." He may want to go beyond the admission that we often need
a reference to thoughts and feelings as part of a full description of an
action being evaluated. He may want to hold that all mental phenomena, at least his own, may sometimes have direct moral relevance,
at least to himself and to God. It may seem to him natural to link
the concept of morality to whatever is taken to be of overriding
human significance. Morality must apply to the whole person and
hence to traits of character which combine modes of thinking and

feeling as well as acting. The proponent of complementarity may not disagree in substance. He may merely contend that it is verbally muddling to insist on such combinations if this means that all mental phenomena may sometimes have independent moral significance. All such phenomena need not be placed under the umbrella of action. But he may nonetheless accept the existence of mental affairs and the non-moral importance of thoughts and feelings, including their indirect moral relevance. He simply regards it as terminologically clearer to draw the moral lines more sharply in his own case as well as for others.

Such an irenic verbal difference may not however satisfy certain camps under the traditionalist's banner. Some have wanted to reject extroverted behavior toward others as the realm of final moral significance. They have wished to give pre-eminent value to the individual's own interior states. This approach would involve a concentrated effort to heighten inner self-awareness, to develop a profounder interpretative vision of all experience, to struggle against evil impulses within oneself, and to attain self-mastery. The struggle for inner integrity may be thought to be damaged when one strives or even hopes to do it full justice by that which can be witnessed directly by others. Others need to experience it for themselves.

In general, the agent's interior state is a place where religion and morality have traditionally been thought to coalesce. One finds Gilleman extolling as a matter of course "the importance of the interior life, the value of the least of our thoughts, which all remain inscribed in our psyche. Even omitted acts have a moral meaning." [37] So far as the agent himself is concerned, then, thoughts and feelings must be taken into account because they too are finally evaluable by God. Consider this passage from Dostoyevsky's *The Possessed* (trans. Constance Garnett):

> "There is no forgiveness for me," Stavrogin said gloomily. . . .
> "As to that, I will give you joyous tidings," said Tihon with emotion; "Christ too will forgive you if you reach the point where you can forgive yourself. . . . Oh, no, no, do not believe

37. Gilleman, *The Primacy of Charity in Moral Theology*, p. 329.

that I am uttering blasphemy: even if you do not achieve reconciliation with yourself and self-forgiveness, even then He will
forgive you for your intention and your great suffering. . . . Even
if you don't [hold out], the Lord will take account of your
original sacrifice. Everything will be taken into account; not a
word, not a movement of the spirit, not a half-thought will be
lost" (pp. 727–28).

All of the above requires further explication and argument. I have
already remarked on the recent comparative neglect of such issues
in much of the theological literature. Before ending this chapter, let
us consider a subject on which theologians have had considerably
more to say: the psychological dependence of a life of love upon
grace.

Grace and Personal Agency

Special questions arise for those who wish both to give independent attention to human virtue and to regard grace as more than
a deistic or impersonal power. For the very notion of virtue has often
been supposed to imply something not dependent on factors outside
the agent's control. Virtue further implies sustained effort. It is not
acquired easily or automatically. And it may involve incessant
struggle against a temptation which corresponds. Yet grace is seen in
part as enabling power. It has genuine effect in relation to personal
agency. It is a gift and allows the agent to do what he cannot do by
himself. How then is it compatible with the conditions of virtue?

Such questions are ancient ones and certain characteristic answers
are well-known. Traditional Roman Catholic and Protestant disputes
about operative and cooperative grace and merit are reflected in such
answers. And, as noted in chapter 1, these are sufficiently familiar to
make a detailed summary unnecessary. Here I shall first introduce
some of the special questions which arise within religious circles,
particularly among Protestants, about commending love as a virtue. I
shall then distinguish more formally several claims in the literature
concerning psychological efficacy or the relation between grace and
personal agency in accounting for the genesis of love in the self.

To speak of virtue and character strikes many nowadays as archaic. Occasionally such talk offends. The term "virtuous man" may conjure up an image of someone who is colorlessly "straight," unwilling or unable to play, and who masks aggression and anxiety. There may be theological offensiveness as well. Protestants have frequently objected to any claim that certain agents *possess* something laudatory or that such a state can be deliberately cultivated. One then comes to rely, so they hold, on the virtuous state rather than grace. The state is fostered by techniques which seem to manipulate and presume to unlock every man's heart.

The objection having to do with possession and cultivation is nicely illustrated in the following statement.

> The Bible ethic remains throughout an *ethic of present decision.*
> . . . Obedience is too concrete to be reduced to a qualitative
> attribute. Man does not obey by learning the *art* or developing the
> *habit* of obedience. Obedience to God cannot be absorbed into a
> stable character pattern so that each subsequent decision becomes
> easier and more assured. . . . However many times repeated, it
> does not become a fixed personality trait. Every present moment
> presents a new occasion for disobedience as well as a new need
> for divine help. When one objectifies obedience as a virtue to
> be cultivated, his choices become determined by his relation *to*
> *that virtue* rather than by relation to God. And obedience to one's
> own virtue is far removed from obedience to God. When trans-
> ferred from the area of contemporaneous demand to the area of
> character development, obedience may easily be turned into its
> opposite.[38]

An agent's past resolutions and achievements are insufficient grounds for him to predict his future ones. It is better to concentrate on repetition than on growth.

Once more genuine and putative disputes are hard to distinguish. Clearly some Protestant accounts of Catholic teaching on virtue are

38. Paul Minear, *Eyes of Faith* (Philadelphia: The Westminster Press, 1946), p. 48.

neither subtle nor fair. The claim that one prefers reliance on grace over one's own virtue seems little more than a theological strawman. Häring as a Catholic can also write in the manner of religious commonplace: "The ultimate end of the good is not the virtuous quality of one's own self but obedience to God and love for Him." [39] And von Hildebrand denies any insight into the degree of change. "We are not ourselves able or entitled to determine the measure of our transformation." [40] Yet some deeper differences may be at stake. Häring does for example hold out for a gradual accretion which, if not exactly making subsequent decisions easier, does progressively enhance the agent's perception of value and obligation. [41] Consider also another statement.

> The acquisition of virtue presupposes all the sweat and toil of tremendous effort. But the pain and sweat of effort do not constitute the virtue. They cannot even produce virtue, for virtue is above all else a "free gift of grace" for whose joyful acceptance all effort and strain of will are only the necessary preparation. [42]

This is a puzzling claim to many Protestants. Häring seems to hold that only the serious moral man has the chance of grasping grace (or at least of accepting it). Sustained effort becomes a strict precondition which affects "joyful acceptance" and, some would argue, intrudes on the free gift itself.

Not all Protestant ethicists repudiate virtue-language unqualifiedly, however. It will be instructive to examine briefly one partially accommodative treatment.

Brunner argues that love cannot be a virtue if by virtue one means either of two things. First, love "is not a quality which can be

---

39. Häring, *Law of Christ,* 1:494. For another contemporary Catholic statement, see Joseph Pieper, *The Four Cardinal Virtues* (New York: Harcourt, Brace and World, Inc., 1965).

40. Dietrich von Hildebrand, *Transformation in Christ* (Garden City, N.Y.: Doubleday and Company, Inc., 1962), p. 19.

41. Häring, *Law of Christ,* 1:495.

42. Ibid., p. 496.

assigned to man as such." [43] Such a quality for ancient and medieval schemes of morality is realized, he thinks, always through personal effort rather than divine action, and ends in self-justification. The state of "living in love" in the sense of agape cannot be simply one human option alongside others; its possibility is created by grace.[44] Second, love is not as individualistic as Aristotelian and Scholastic conceptions of virtue require. Agape as a virtue is not "*my* quality, something which can be thought of as belonging to the individual, but it is always a 'co-existence,' a way of being related to others." [45]

If, however, one agrees that the term "virtue" should only be used in a relational sense, then, Brunner allows, one may legitimately employ such language. Virtue then is "non-substantial"; it is regarded as an "*awareness* of the claims of others, as a *readiness to re-act.*" [46] Brunner is prepared to qualify even further his rejection of the Catholic doctrine of virtue. As a "secondary consideration," after all I have summarized above has been made clear, a "region of the habitual" can be acknowledged, an element persisting through time which may be called character, "a relative *constancy,* an *attitude,* a certain stamp." [47] Though "persons" do not differ at the most basic level from one another, the "character" of persons may.

> There is therefore an "exercise in love," a process of *growth* in love, a *more* or a *less,* a "treasure," a power at the disposal of the moment of action, which distinguishes the mature soul from the beginner, there is a really present "excellence" and even a virtuosity of loving. In brief: there does exist what Aristotle and the Catholic moralists mean when they speak of virtue.[48]

This is indeed a major admission for a modern Protestant ethicist who endeavors to reproduce Reformation theology (and it is not

43. Brunner, *The Divine Imperative,* p. 165.
44. Ibid., p. 164.
45. Ibid., p. 166; cf. p. 168.
46. Ibid., p. 167. Italics mine.
47. Ibid., p. 168. Italics mine.
48. Ibid. Italics mine.

always easy to see how it can be consistent with such theology). Brunner finally seems to maintain that love may be conceived as a virtue provided that virtue does not become the de facto preoccupation of ethics since this would alter priorities in a way injurious to "justification by grace through faith"; that love as the controlling character-trait must always have an object; and that love must proceed "downward" through faith rather than "upward" via native or divinized aspiration (here Brunner, like Nygren, distinguishes an ethics of causality from teleology). This certainly goes very far toward a position that a contemporary Catholic such as Häring could accept. And could not Brunner, for his part, agree with Häring that the power of love "at the disposal of the moment of action" does enhance accordingly the self's perception of value and obligation? It would seem that the precise status of many disagreements is very much in doubt. I shall try to distinguish the claims further.

Four claims appear with some frequency.[49] That is, agape as a human virtue may be accorded four different kinds of status vis-à-vis grace: it may be the instrument of invading grace; it may be infused by grace; it may be acquired irrespective of grace; it may be elicited by grace. In the first instance, grace is an *invasive* reality, though without consequent accretion of power in the agent which is then at his disposal, proper to him as such. Divine love is more than the pattern and prototype for human action; it also intervenes decisively and awakens effectively. In chapter 1 we saw how Nygren makes this claim and in his case approaches a doctrine of irresistible grace. The believer is merely the tube or the channel through which grace flows. Nygren appears to mean both that the source of human agape is outside man's own power of initiation and sustenance *and* that the subject in all genuine neighbor-love is actually God. Nygren denies, of course, that he wants to annihilate the agent.[50] But critics such as D'Arcy argue that a love expressly devoid of everything human and personal is, ipso facto, divine.

49. For a discussion of the latter three, see Ramsey, *Basic Christian Ethics*, pp. 209–26, and Thomas, *Christian Ethics and Moral Philosophy*, pp. 505–21.
50. Anders Nygren, *Essence of Christianity*, trans. Philip S. Watson (Philadelphia: Muhlenberg Press, 1961), p. 57.

Such an extreme form of the Agape theory [as that of Nygren] will not work out. God is Agape, and we should naturally expect someone to be the beneficiary of that love, and as beneficiary to respond. But if this theory is taken literally there is no one to respond. There is no need of that intercommunication which is essential to love. We are told that no Eros (in Nygren's sense) should enter in man's return of love, that it should be all Agape. But . . . God is Agape. There is nothing human or personal on this interpretation. In the elimination of Eros man has been eliminated.[51]

D'Arcy wants to avoid the doctrinal extremes of the right and left. Grace can be prevenient without being obliterative; the agent can aspire and respond without supposing that he can save himself.

The next two claims involve the Thomistic bifurcation between *infused* and *acquired* virtue. Gilleman, for example, refers to both in his account of natural love transformed into charity.[52] In the case of infusion, sanctifying grace elevates the whole man, including faith in the intellect and hope and charity in the will. Charity becomes the agent's divinized active principle. It commands all of the active powers in moral activity; it extends its divinizing influence to the depths of the self. Barth will argue that the difficulties with a traditional notion of infusion are notorious. Does one have to do with a "thing-like substance" poured into the agent from without, an uncreated attribute dwelling in the heart? The claim that grace is infused usually implies at least that natural human capacities are miraculously extended. It is otherwise with acquirement, which seems close to a straightforward acceptance of the notion that to say a man ought to do something is to imply that he can do it, and by virtue of his own effort. There is self-activation of a potency by directly working on one's own character. The conditions of virtue mentioned earlier are fully satisfied. Moral seriousness may then be taken as the narrow gate leading to the religious life.

The distinction between infused and acquired virtue strikes many

51. D'Arcy, *Mind and Heart of Love*, p. 82.
52. Gilleman, *Primacy of Charity*, e.g., pp. 16, 162–65.

as on the one side too mechanical and on the other too Pelagian. Hence a fourth claim is found: elicitation. Grace elicits rather than invades in that the agent must actively respond, not just passively receive. Grace elicits rather than infuses in that nothing fundamentally non-human is introduced as an extension of given human powers. The creaturely response considered in itself is never more than creaturely. Elicitation also differs from acquirement in that virtue is evoked and sustained from without; it is not simply self-activated and self-directed. The agent is drawn to do what he cannot do by himself. The relation between grace and human love may be called interpersonal, but it is also asymmetrical.

Such claims all remain of course within the "theological circle." In that circle, however, one finds differing accounts of the work of grace and differing estimates of native human capacities. In order to safeguard divine sovereignty, some characterize the working of grace as totally unpredictable. It comes and goes. The agent confronts at most a choice-offering. Others regard grace in terms more of abiding presence and as sustained, patterned activity. It makes sense to speak of growth at least in conscious awareness of the relation, of the character in general terms of the patterned activity, and what is involved in conformity to it. Moreover, while it is important to distinguish formally between questions of content (*what* the creature should do when he lives by grace) and of psychological efficacy, the answers to both in certain instances seem bound closely together. What the agent understands grace to seek in every situation may affect, for example, the degree of deliberateness on his part which he accepts as theologically warranted. Suppose the agent believes that what is always sought includes community and communion between men, and that this in turn requires among other things the maximization of social justice. He may then concern himself deliberately with long-term policies which serve to bring about more justice, and the stable and dependent attitudes and actions on his part which contribute to that end. Whether he considers himself authorized, as it were, to deliberate may depend therefore very much in some cases on his view of grace as pattern and prototype.

I shall return to issues about psychological efficacy in discussing Barth, who appears to want his own version of elicitation, where grace frees man to do what he cannot do by himself and where the creaturely response, while genuinely a response, is never more than creaturely. In any event, issues about efficacy or obligation and ability, including claims about the psychological dependence of a life of love upon grace, constitute only one sort of inquiry within ethics. One is still left with the range of issues concerned with justifying the life of agape itself.

6

The Status and Justification
of Human Agape

> For Christian believers . . . the use of the word *"Agape"*
> . . . would imply the whole religious and, in the field of
> theory, the whole theological context in which the concept
> of Agape is incorporated.
>
> W. G. Maclagan

Put most simply, the basic question one must now consider is, *why*
be loving? Here one enters territory often called meta-ethical. The
issue of justification arises irrepressibly, it may be argued, in the
case of all standards, ideals, or visions for the guidance of life. Does
the status of any normative standard — agape, survival-of-the-fittest,
etc. — rest finally on the agent's own resolution or postulation? Is
the agent required logically at least to allow that any standard he
accepts pass the requirement of universalizability? Or can one appeal convincingly to certain facts about the agent himself, or the
society of which he is a part, or the universe which surrounds him?
If so, what are these facts and how are they known?

I must confine myself to an examination of how agape is supported, justified, or defended. In the literature before us justificatory
reasons are typically part of complex theological schemes. It is time
to consider how this comes about, and what sorts of issues arise
as a consequence. Because philosophers have written so much and
so illuminatingly on meta-ethical questions, it is especially tempting
at this point to shift the theological center of gravity. One might
proceed, for example, by summarizing various views as discussed by
philosophers (definist, intuitionist, noncognitivist or nondescriptivist,
and so on) and asking which theologians hold one or another of
them. Obviously far more could and should fruitfully be done along

these lines.[1] I shall appropriate some of this discussion in what follows. But here again, rather than shift the center of gravity, I shall try mainly to see what theologians themselves believe the status and justification of agape to be. I am concerned then with the principle of agape in a religious context and the reasons within that context for holding the principle. Whether the principle is susceptible to other, nonreligious sorts of ultimate justification is an issue not at the center of most of the literature. I shall have occasion to refer to it only cryptically at the end.

To begin with, I shall identify some religious beliefs which furnish justification for the *content* of human agape as that content was characterized in chapter 1. The primary focus will be on the content of grace for which human agape is the practical corollary. Then will follow some more general observations about how theologians characteristically approach this exceptionally tangled subject. Here I shall try to begin far enough back to locate certain basic assumptions, some of which are unexamined or unargued by the writers themselves.[2] Finally, I shall note some possible non-theological grounds.

Justifying Reasons for Equal Regard

Attempts to support and justify an agapeistic way of life reflect differences in substantive schemes in their entirety. What is most

---

1. For one illuminating general example of how one can proceed, see William K. Frankena, "Ethical Theory," *Philosophy,* ed. Roderick M. Chisholm et al. (Englewood Cliffs, N.J.: Prentice-Hall, Inc., 1964), esp. pp. 420–35. For a detailed examination of a single thinker see D. J. O'Connor, *Aquinas and Natural Law* (London: Macmillan, 1967).

2. But there will be limits. I shall not consider at any point, for instance, the problems connected with allegedly incompatible statements regarding divine beneficence and untoward suffering. For many people, any affirmation that God loves the world is invalidated by the human experience of ambiguity, terror, and extinction. Naturally believers themselves have not refrained from posing such dilemmas or agonizing over such apparent contradictions. Yet much of their reflection possesses a somewhat special character, where suffering is taken to be purposive and not a reason to repudiate a life of love. In any event, most of the questions surrounding the classical problem of evil, for example, cannot come directly under our scrutiny.

directly relevant for ethics will be in circuit with all the rest, with a particular view of revelation, assumptions about human nature, the significance of Christ for man's moral life, the authority of scripture, eschatology, and so on. I must be content to break into the circuit at the points most central to this inquiry. I shall begin with justificatory reasons which are decidedly theological: with appeals to the character of divine grace as pattern and prototype. Schemes differ, moreover, in the degree of openness allowed to autonomous moral insight allegedly independent of religious belief. Some authorize in-principled appeals to such insight. Others treat these appeals as ill-conceived and the insight itself as fatally inconclusive given the heterogeneous theories produced in its name. I shall also illustrate the way in which schemes differ concerning the relevance of any common core of native moral insight.

The most influential formulation of the content of God's grace or agape (used interchangeably in this case), especially for Protestants, has come from Nygren. In a section called "The Content of the Idea of Agape" he lists four features.

First, "agape is spontaneous and 'unmotivated.'"[3] To say this is not to imply arbitrariness or fortuitousness, but rather to rule out any extrinsic motivation arising from the particular worth of particular men. Jesus' own action is the paradigm in that he seeks out the lost and consorts with publicans and sinners. Here again Nygren attacks the notion of legality which, as we have seen in considering justice, he always ties to desert. Love directed to sinners is intended to disclose its independence and sovereignty. So he likewise repudiates any attempt to reverse the conventional canons of rightness and wrongness whereby the sinner, or at least the person aware of his sin, deserves grace. In both cases — exalting either the sinner who acknowledges his state or the man distinctively meritorious through his own efforts — some notion of "better" is smuggled in, some grading concept which distinguishes between superior and inferior human beings. That is, something some human beings do in particular, as contrasted with other men, is a prerequisite for *whether* and not only how God loves. But divine love has no motive outside

3. Nygren, *Agape and Eros*, p. 75.

itself, in idiosyncratic worth. To say such love is unmotivated is a judgment about God rather than man. God loves because of who He is but He does not love particular men for those acts which distinguish them from others.

Second, and this simply defines the first feature more explicitly, God's love is "indifferent to value." [4] Grace involves more than a "transvaluation of all values"; it is a rejection of any notion of valuation whatever. Yet this seems essentially to mean again that one cannot understand what God's grace is until one abandons all thought of the worth of the particular human object. "God's love allows no limits to be set for it by the character or conduct of man." [5]

Third, God's love is "creative," i.e., it is "value-creating." [6] Nygren calls this feature the most important reason for the uniqueness of agape.

> God does not love that which is already in itself worthy of love, but on the contrary, that which in itself has no worth *acquires* worth just by becoming the object of God's love. Agape has nothing to do with the kind of love that *depends* on the *recognition* of a valuable quality in its object; Agape does not recognise value, but creates it. Agape loves, and *imparts* value by loving. The man who is loved by God has *no value in himself;* what gives him value is precisely the fact that God loves him. *Agape is a value-creating principle.*[7]

Nygren then proceeds to criticize those like Ritschl and Harnack who refer to "the infinite worth of the human soul." He takes this phrase to mean value *inherent* in human nature, proper to man qua human existent.

Fourth, God's love is the "initiator of fellowship" with God.[8] This is a traditional point about the necessity of grace. Man, by his

4. Ibid., pp. 77–78.
5. Ibid., p. 77.
6. Ibid., pp. 78–80
7. Ibid., p. 78. My italics, except for the last line.
8. Ibid., pp. 80–81.

own resources, cannot know God. If fellowship is then a reality it can only be due to God's own action.

This list is important because it expresses with peculiar force what many theologians have taken to be the authoritative religious justification for the content of human agape. Certain points of material overlap between grace and human agape on this scheme are obvious. Not only is there explicit backing for the exhortation to love the neighbor, but where this understanding of grace is operative, the content itself is supported and affected, most clearly on the point that agape is independent of particular worth of particular men. If the believer is to conform to God's love as pattern and prototype, he too must set no limits to his love on the basis of idiosyncratic character and conduct. So presumably at the beginning of any moral judgment, nothing that some men do in particular is to be a condition for whether their well-being is to be considered.

How this understanding of grace provides warrant for speaking of the neighbor qua human existent as irreducibly valuable is not quite as obvious. In part the answer depends on what Nygren means by contending that agape is a value-creating principle and that the human object acquires worth through being loved by God, and what he thinks such value creation implies for the human agent. I propose then to devote closer attention to issues centering on a religious justification for holding that each human being is irreducibly valuable. This may instruct us on some difficult and ambiguous points in the literature which turn up again and again. It may also prove instructive concerning the more general relations between religious beliefs and ethical principles.

Here I must return to a distinction noted in passing when discussing Brunner's treatment of justice. Brunner, appealing explicitly to Nygren, contrasted justice as an appraisal of worth with agape as a bestowal of worth. To appraise implies to weigh properly those characteristics already present in an object. To bestow implies to impart worth to an object not possessing it inherently. When Nygren holds that agape is a value-creating principle, he plainly has in mind bestowal as contrasted with appraisal. He also appears to believe that the contrast reveals a central theological disagreement. But this may be too simple. For a pair of distinctions seems to lie behind the two terms in question.

The first distinction concerns appraisal. At times it is held that divine agape is not conditioned by anything men do or are in particular, as contrasted with other men. Ruled out thereby are idiosyncratic traits, most notably moral merit attained by special effort. If by appraisal one means the apportionment of love in accordance with idiosyncratic traits, and the evaluation of such traits to determine whether love should be present as well as how it should be expressed, then it clearly does fall outside of agape. At other times the rejection is more sweeping. Any worth or value men are thought to have as a constitutive property, possessed by all and logically prior to their doing anything in particular, is also denied to be the reason they are loved. Here one seems to appraise generic characteristics which all men are said to have, and perhaps to share equally. Nygren, Brunner, and others reject the latter appraisal also because they believe it makes love dependent on the recognition of a worth already existent and thus does not allow grace really to be grace.

The second distinction has to do with bestowal. At times this seems to imply what may be called an "as if" judgment: conformity to God's love signifies that one ought to regard each man as if his well-being were equal to that of every other man. In one commentary, Kierkegaard and Nygren are held to agree completely on this point: "Such love is a kind of creative fictionalism which always views the neighbor with compassion and as one's equal, regardless of what he is in fact." [9] Religious backing and warrant appear in this case not to include any reference, for instance, to a doctrine of creation. From the vantage point of the "facts," which for some include objectively valuable characteristics (waiving now the epistemological issues about such characteristics), to bestow or create value seems a matter of pure agent-commitment.

At other times bestowal appears to mean the ascription of a status. On the one side, the status is other than a creative fiction. For the neighbor's ultimate status does not depend on the agent's self-imposed

9. George E. Arbaugh and George B. Arbaugh, *Kierkegaard's Authorship* (Rock Island, Ill.: Augustana College Library, 1967), p. 260.

choice. One does not simply regard him *as if* he had this status. Nor does one assign him such a status on one's own authority. The status has been conferred by God in unmerited grace or as a sovereign creation of value; and while the status is one subordinate to Him, it is often taken as one shared by all men equally in relation to each other.[10] Here is a major reason then for concluding that one person's well-being is as valuable as another's. Consider the following passage from Kierkegaard:

> Your neighbour is every man, for on the basis of distinctions he is not your neighbour, nor on the basis of likeness to you as being different from other men. He is your neighbour on the basis of equality with you before God: but this equality absolutely every man has, and he has it absolutely.[11]

Such equality every man *has*. The equality is warranted by a belief about a state of affairs, in this case by a religious belief about equality before God.

It is hard to see how Nygren, in his effort to be consistently theocentric, can allow that bestowal is simply a creative fiction. At least God's grace surely cannot be so. But if grace cannot, it follows that the agent's bestowal cannot. And not only must "fiction" be ruled out: obedience to God's grace seems to imply at this point something other than strict conformity to it. In a sense even for Nygren, if God does *bestow* value, man ought to *appraise* his fellow man in light of God's bestowal. To put the matter in this way need not undermine the governing theological interest of Nygren, Brunner, and others that "worth is worth only in relation to God." [12]

It is also hard to see how every scheme involving appraisal of generic characteristics all men have and perhaps share equally can be held always to undermine grace. That question depends on what those objectively valuable characteristics are, and how they are known. One might still relate such characteristics to beliefs in God's

10. Cf. the interesting discussion by Evans of status and role in *The Logic of Self-Involvement*, e.g., pp. 67, 147–66, 233.

11. Kierkegaard, *Works of Love*, p. 72.

12. H. Richard Niebuhr, *Christ and Culture*, p. 18.

action. They could be tied, for instance, to a doctrine of creation which need not idolize the creature or require that grace be explained or justified by something outside itself. Any generic worth or value already existent may precisely reflect God's sovereign creative action. I alluded in chapter 1 to Maritain's reference to a "metaphysical center" deeper and more mysterious than all observable qualities. Whatever one may think about Maritain's own formulation, Maritain himself is not forced to concede that this characteristic is in any sense discontinuous with religious beliefs concerning God's grace. It may be incorporated into a doctrinal scheme which, while different from Nygren's, need not according to its own criteria imply worth apart from God or which God merely recognizes. An account of characteristics to be appraised will not necessarily treat them as simply belonging to the person in some utterly autonomous way or as traits which the person has attained by his own initiative. One may appraise not an autonomous nature or individual merit, but rather characteristics common alike to the "non-meritorious" and "meritorious," by virtue of which a person is related to God.

Even to distinguish several different senses of appraisal and bestowal, and to note how some accounts of appraisal are not independent of religious belief on their own terms, suggests the complexity of the theological schemes which the reader confronts. Let me illustrate the effects of such schemes in slightly more detail. To do so manageably, I shall distinguish further between appraisal in the sense of acknowledgment-of-a-claim and bestowal in the sense of ascription-of-a-status. I shall consider acknowledgment first and then compare it with ascription as previously discussed.

> I look on every human being as a person. . . . What I mean is this: In every person there is something which claims my concern, reverence, personal involvement and acknowledgment of value . . . my *"agape"*, to use the New Testament word. This attitude does not depend on his particular, observable qualities. A person is a being such that *"agape"* is the appropriate attitude.[13]

13. Evans, *The Logic of Self-Involvement*, p. 134.

To put the judgment about irreducible value as Evans does catches a persistent meaning of appraisal. There is something in each person which *claims* the agent's acknowledgment of value, his agape. Moreover, to stress a concept of "person" independent from particular, observable qualities is not unlike Maritain's account of a metaphysical center or entity. The self is held to be more than a conjunction of observable properties and not identifiable with behavioral tendencies.

Loving the neighbor as acknowledgment-of-a-claim is also elucidated by Farrer. He argues that

> . . . if we are going to *regard* anything we must be convinced not only that it is there, but that it really possesses in itself, and not merely in our sense of it, those characteristics in virtue of which we regard it. . . . The first step to regard our neighbour as ourself is to see that he is as real as oneself, and that his reality has the same sort of actual structure and quality as our own.[14]

When we consider the case of rescuing a drowning stranger, the action of rescuing him is not the result of an arbitrary decision to assist neighbors in danger instead of laughing at them, about which there is nothing further to be said. Rather, "it is natural to say that we *see* something about him, viz. that his humanity claims our succour."[15] Other human beings *call for* what devotion freely gives. If we urge others to regard their neighbors, the nature of our persuasive argument must be rightly conceived. "It is not a persuasion towards adopting a policy or taking up an attitude, although it involves doing both. No, primarily it is the persuasion to acknowledge a claim."[16] Such acknowledgment is not simply a matter of agent-commitment. It is not something about which we are at liberty to please ourselves. An action such as rescuing a drowning man "is

14. Farrer, "Examination of Theological Belief," p. 23. See also Farrer, *The Freedom of the Will* (London: Adam & Charles Black, 1958), pp. 308–09.

15. Farrer, "Examination of Theological Belief," p. 29.

16. Ibid., p. 27.

not due because we decide it shall be. What we decide, or come to a common mind about, is that it is due." [17] To acknowledge is thus to discover more than to choose. We do not decide to endow the neighbor with irreducible value, but rather to acknowledge that he has such value.

Farrer also undertakes to sketch the religious implications which believers, at any rate, draw from such acknowledgment. That is, the account of moral discovery may be related both to a judgment about irreducible value and a reference to God by virtue of such a judgment. Farrer at least seems unwilling to split them apart. In distinguishing the difficult notions of "reading off" and "reading into" he argues that our moral life (and especially our coming to acknowledge that equal regard is due other persons) carries the sort of significance "*off* which ordinary believers read the action of God." [18] One must be careful here, for his case is not readily assimilable into traditional options. There is for instance no assurance that it will compel all to come to a common mind about it. He attempts only to persuade on behalf of a moral claim which implies providential backing, rather than purporting to argue demonstrably for such backing. But he does affirm manifest continuities between native moral insight and religious belief.

> We persuade men of the importance of so contemplating their fellows that they may regard them. We persuade them that regard should acknowledge no limits but those set by the conditions of our life. We persuade them that this regard should be at once so pure and so entire as to find its frustration in the imperfections of men. We persuade them that the frustration is due to an incomplete definition of the object of regard — that what claims our regard is not simply our neighbour, but God in our neighbour and our neighbour in God. Here are four stages of persuasion, and at any stage the persuasion may fail. We shall

17. Ibid., p. 28.
18. Ibid., p. 13.

probably have to be content, like Gideon, to reduce our following step by step as we advance.[19]

Even the last admission — that the further one advances, the less persuasive he will seem to others — still allows native moral insight and religious beliefs positively to bear upon each other.

It is not feasible to give an account of Farrer's major doctrinal proposals. All I wish to suggest here is that in the case of some theological schemes any strict dichotomy between judgments based entirely either on religious belief or on autonomous human nature appears simplistic and misleading. Theologically one is not forbidden to appeal to relevant factual data and common moral judgments. Yet one is likewise not forced to treat distinctively religious beliefs as a mere addendum to moral insights equally at home in a non-theistic outlook. The following statement by Mitchell refers to some basic ingredients in such schemes: where a proper mixture of distinctiveness and continuity is striven for and strict dichotomies excluded.

> Such traditional Christian conceptions as the doctrine of marriage as a sacrament or as an "order of creation" . . . are theological concepts which cannot be discovered in "nature" (unless "nature" is thought of as divinely ordered) and which cannot be derived from the law of love alone. They presuppose a whole theology. . . . But such a theology is not something that we can "posit" or not as we choose. It is a complex conceptual scheme which can, to some extent at least, be judged by its internal consistency and explanatory force. To talk, as Christians commonly do, of "the purpose of marriage" or the "function of sex" is to invoke a teleological theory of ethics based upon a theistic metaphysic, which is not shared by the humanist. This way of thinking cannot be maintained in complete independence of the observed facts of human life as studied by psychologists and sociologists nor, on its own terms, is there

19. Ibid., pp. 25–26.

any reason why it should be. For the God of revelation is also the God of creation.[20]

I shall briefly list some of the reasons why certain schemes (most notably Protestant ones such as Nygren's) seem more disposed toward dichotomies. Within such schemes it will often be natural to think in terms of bestowal as ascription-of-a-status.

Before beginning such a list, however, I should observe that here again one must avoid as far as possible drawing the contrasts between bestowal and appraisal in a crude and flattened-out way. Apart from certain notions of creative fiction, bestowal need not be taken, as we have seen, as a matter of pure agent-commitment. The evaluation in question is one about which the believer is not at liberty to please himself. Virtually everyone agrees, of course (irrespective of any given theological scheme which supports either appraisal or bestowal), that agent-commitment as such is crucial and involves among other things a declaration of policy or the taking up of an attitude. But even among those who talk of bestowal, few will allow that such commitment, even if a free decision on the agent's part, is also an arbitrary one. Bestowal as ascription-of-a-status is held to be more than the agent's self-imposed choice. The principle of irreducible value is taken to be somehow valid in itself; whatever validity it has does not simply depend on agent-espousal, and is not created by the agent from scratch. For the neighbor's status is not assigned on one's own authority; it is conferred by God. It would naturally be difficult to find a believer who holds that the agent chooses to endow the neighbor with irreducible value as a matter of pure resolution or agent-legislation, if this implies that the universe is seen as wholly alien or indifferent and that the agent's choice is based on strictly personal fiat. Clearly most traditional claims about a "revealed theology" have been thought to refer to more than the speaker's own emotions or subjective commitments. At the very least, religious beliefs enter in to furnish some background of intelligibility. Even those theologians who stress the points of discontinuity between the life of love and any surrounding structure of empirically known reality (either natural or social or both) rarely

20. Mitchell, "Ideals, Roles, and Rules," pp. 364–65.

if ever imply that the neighbor's value is a mere fiction. Justifying reasons for ascribing value may be purely theological, and the theology altogether revelational, without severing every connection with some "ultimate" state of affairs. So even if the agent wishes to call his commitment a decision, he is prepared to give reasons for it; reasons he believes are connected to what is ultimately the case.

What then are reasons for preferring bestowal to appraisal? I think I can practically cite now only some general theological concepts which appear to stand behind a case for bestowal: preponderant pressures, if you like, which certain schemes exert. The three reasons I shall identify will remain regrettably vague. I shall try to suggest links and trace implications often not clearly marked out in the literature.

1. Bestowal may seem more appropriate to those who contend that men's knowledge of good and evil is recurrently and fundamentally obfuscated by sin. So they regard the justification of agape as less dependent (if dependent at all) on what can be established by strictly philosophical argument or founded on empirical observation and research. They may find few theological warrants for taking an interest in the outcome of such argument or the results of such research. Because of the "conditions of existential estrangement" they may be inclined to argue that any alleged native moral insight is too indeterminate and ambiguous to furnish by itself decisive backing for any one moral outlook. Consequently they may question, not simply whether there can be solutions to moral dilemmas which everyone will come to accept, but also whether any basic normative standard may be justified by sufficiently compelling argument and evidence to have final interpersonal validity for believer and non-believer alike. Justifying reasons for agape will not prove compelling in the sense that all will agree that they are sound, or even that they are susceptible in this life to universal certification. Those who are convinced that sin has rendered moral uncertainty unavoidable may see themselves forced explicitly to give theological reasons only. And they may take such reasons to be discontinuous in principle with anything natively accessible to all men. Therefore to speak of worth always in relation to God will mean to restrict what is objectively valuable about the neighbor, and knowledge of

that value, to what God has revealed in some distinctly authoritative act such as the life of Jesus. Native moral insight is too deeply flawed to avoid limiting markedly the justifying reasons for agape. Perhaps the most convincing case for equality, on this view, is our "solidarity in sin" or disvalue.

2. The status ascribed may be based largely on a relation before God, without clear continuity to any temporal state of affairs. Kierkegaard states, for instance, that "differences are like an enormous net in which the temporal is held." [21] In this life one cannot destroy the net; one can only lift oneself above it.[22] Equality before God is also held to differ qualitatively from all "worldly likeness." And to abolish temporal differences completely is seen in any event as a practical impossibility. Here and now it appears formally that one imparts value or bestows worth more than one attends to observable characteristics antecedently present which in themselves suffice to evoke agape. In brief, the less equality is linked to observable characteristics and the less the religious state of affairs is held to be generally demonstrable, the more any definite evaluation seems like a bestowal, even though not a purely fictitious one. The evaluation might be called an obedient bestowal, a bestowal which is indeed a confessional recognition (ascription or whatever) based on (or obedient to, or authorized by) God's bestowal.

The relevance of observable characteristics for an agapeic evaluation appears frequently as an issue on which proponents of appraisal and bestowal go separate ways. The issue however is not always very clearly stated. Those who speak of appraisal will normally treat observable characteristics as a persuasive part of a claim to be acknowledged. Perceived uniformities between persons are stressed accordingly. What persons demonstrably share is of essential moral relevance; how they differ is inessential. (At least differences which form the basis of unequal consideration are ruled out. Allowance may still be made for any uniqueness which does not erode the case for equal consideration). Among those who employ a concept of obedient bestowal, I think it is usually assumed that empirical characteristics constitute at least part of the object of evaluation. Otherwise one

21. Kierkegaard, *Works of Love*, p. 82.
22. Ibid., p. 83.

would lack any material basis for distinguishing between agape toward, for example, a human being and a tree. The characteristics themselves, however, it is often argued, are an inseparable blend of common and disparate elements.[23] Admittedly there are salient facts, such as a common bodily structure, which make the evaluation intelligible, with some perceived uniformities. The precise boundaries are sometimes a matter of dispute (e.g., are mental defectives human or subhuman?).[24] Yet it makes sense to identify the human species as having a certain determinate nature with a number of shared empirical characteristics. Nonetheless, it makes sense as well to stress the differences and inequalities among human beings. Some are born without limbs, or eyes, or normal rational powers. One confronts also differences in rank, talent, profundity, and moral goodness among various persons. They seem to follow different stars; their behavior ranges from sainthood to depravity, and they commend rival visions of the good life. The mixture of equality and inequality makes for moral inconclusiveness (or, incompatible moral principles may be linked with similar plausibility to perceivable data) and requires a definite evaluation. The evaluation has then to do with empirical characteristics, including a certain determinate nature, but it is not decisively justified by them. Equality and inequality remain so inextricable that to give priority to what is observably shared seems unpersuasive. One may not avoid going beyond empirical characteristics to justify attaching equal value to the well-being of each person.[25] Once more, for many the case has to rest on a status revealed decisively in an event such as the life of Jesus.

23. See, e.g., the account by Brunner, *Justice and the Social Order*, pp. 25–45.

24. Probably those who want some version of obedient bestowal will be particularly disposed to extend the boundaries of the human as widely as possible. It is better always to err in the direction of inclusiveness, they will typically hold, even in the absence of rationality or potential rationality. But as I shall note in chapter 8, the question of boundaries has received surprisingly little specific attention in the literature.

25. "Let us admit that it was the Christian view of life blended with the Stoic which created the European idea of justice, the conception of the equal dignity of all human beings. . . . But Christian or Stoic, one thing is beyond question. The conviction of the equality of the rights of man derived and still derives its force from a religious or metaphysical *faith*" (ibid., p. 35).

3. Restriction of justifying reasons is not always thought to be
forced upon certain schemes only because of the alleged ambiguity
and diversity of moral judgments which appeal to observable characteristics. One can find more positive, aggressive reasons for refusing to throw open the epistemological gates even partway to what
is generally demonstrable or persuasive to believer and nonbeliever
alike. The reasons are roughly as follows. Theologians are free to
utilize whatever concepts are culturally at hand in the task of
specifying the message of grace. Certainly such general concepts as
"humanity" and "love" will be employed. But employment may
require that they be radically revised and altered. For they must
finally be incorporated into or derive from a theological scheme
which itself depends on divine self-attestation. Such attestation is not
a fixed, constant datum subject to empirical proof or disproof. Indeed,
it is free and sovereign in relation to all general conditions of human
knowledge. It brings its own credentials for intelligible reference.
The believer should only follow after and govern his thought and
language accordingly. Concepts should be elucidated in strict fidelity
to the message of grace. This may involve taking over certain notions
in ordinary morality, e.g., human interests or wants or happiness,
and giving them meanings which reflect doctrinal control. Our
ordinary perceptions of what we should seek in order to be happy
are not just diverse; they are bound to go wrong until they are
grafted on to the message. So it will seem natural to refer to the
neighbor's value not as an immanent quality which calls in itself
for correct appraisal, but as a status conferred by God. Otherwise
one risks loss of governance by grace.

Barth is the most influential proponent of such positive, aggressive
reasons, as I shall show later. There may be a somewhat ironic
alliance between a demand for governance by grace and skepticism
about any other non-empirical alternative. Someone who takes a
position like Barth's may be inclined to press the skeptical case
against any natural knowledge of an elusive, mysterious person not
to be identified with bodily behavior. He may think it better to
maintain from the outset that such a concept of the person is part
of a general reference to realities not observable in ordinary experience, or at least to realities which can be made the objects of

empirical science only at the price of misunderstanding them. Yet he also suspects other sorts of appeals to "natural" knowledge, whether they stem from intellectual intuition, or affective-conative experiences between persons, or what is ascertainable by the deepest introspection. Once one enters the theological circle, the only solid ground he has to stand on is revealed ground. Ethical concepts inside the circle must survive scrutiny by what is already fixed and governing: contingent truths about the grace of God.

Those who prefer some notion of appraisal may think that these three reasons do not escape the charge of crude dichotomization. The neighbor's objectively valuable characteristics need not be so narrowly conceived or contingently known. I shall return to some of the points above. Before doing so, however, I must further identify schemes which support the other major features distinguished in chapter 1.

Justifying Reasons for Self-Sacrifice and/or Mutuality

Several doctrines have been noted above which in Niebuhr's case provide backing for self-sacrifice. He seems preoccupied with a doctrine of sin where pride and self-love are often used interchangeably; and where pride more than unbelief or sloth is the primal character of sin. He also accepts a theory of human nature which holds that the self is able to rise in "indefinite transcendence" over its natural and historical conditions, and believes this ability points to its final longing for God. The self may envisage devotions and gains, and nuances of personal meaning, far richer and more complicated than anything required for societal viability, for tolerable peace and justice. (Hence, "the whole of modern culture tries too desperately to contain the ultimate within the fragmentary tasks and possibilities of history.")

I said that for Niebuhr the ideal content of agape, considered apart from involvement with the claims and counterclaims of historical existence, is frictionless harmony. But in a world of vying interests the purest expression of agape becomes self-sacrifice. In this life agape and prudential self-interest do not always coalesce in at least the following senses: from the point of view of discernible effects upon others, and particularly as this refers to a response of love in kind, the agent who loves agapeistically may fail; and the requirements of collective life include participation in the claims and counterclaims of historical society and likewise admit the claims of self-interest. Agape presupposes the resolution of conflict of life with life. Therefore it cannot be a simple final court of appeal for adjudicating conflicts. And because the sin of pride is so recalcitrant and so varied in its exemplifications, to insist on the claims of self-interest seems redundant at best and usually distortive. What can be insisted on is the paradox of self-realization through self-giving. Yet the sequence must remain intact. And the content of self-realization is construed in large part as trust in divine grace which liberates one from anxiety about both the eventual outcome of a life of love and the present significance (however opaque to oneself) of one's striving.

Let me consider in slightly more detail the beliefs most supportive of this characterization of agape. The theological scheme Niebuhr defends is by his own admission rather unsystematically set out in his writings. On occasion he stresses the continuities between what is disclosed by special historical events such as the life of Jesus and more general experience. Earlier, for example, in referring to frictionless harmony, we saw how he sometimes appeals rather sweepingly to scripture, reason, and a more elemental and diffuse sense of what he thinks we are bound to agree are our deepest and most worthy aspirations. But when he relates agape to what is required for societal viability or for personal expediency, discontinuities prevail. For "the ethic of Jesus," a love which ends in forgiveness must appeal to grace alone and not to any resultant personal benefits in this life.

> Emulation of the character of God is advanced as the only motive of forgiving enemies. Nothing is said about the possibility of transmuting their enmity to friendship through the practice of forgiveness. That social and prudential possibility has been read into the admonition of Jesus by liberal Christianity.[26]

26. Reinhold Niebuhr, *An Interpretation of Christian Ethics* (New York: Living Age Books, 1958), p. 46.

So far as the ideal content is concerned, Niebuhr will relinquish no part of what he takes its radical character to be (or at least the character it must assume in historical society). He thinks for instance that in the ethic of Jesus, love enjoins not simply nonviolent resistance to evil, but rather nonresistance. To safeguard this content, he is willing at many points to restrict justifying appeals to Jesus' teachings about the character of God. We also noted earlier how "the perfect disinterestedness of the divine love can have a counterpart in history only in a life which ends tragically, because it refuses to participate in the claims and counterclaims of historical existence."

If Niebuhr appeals finally to the character of God to justify the content of agape, he appeals to the mercy of God to forgive men for never realizing it perfectly. Usually he doubts whether any difference in the degree of realization between believers and nonbelievers can be clearly demonstrated. At any rate most historical "evidence" he considers leaves him largely unimpressed by doctrines of individual sanctification and the establishment of a collective kingdom of God on earth. Often disagreements between Niebuhr and his critics center on grace as enabling power more than grace as the basis of content.

Niebuhr has failed to reckon with the fact that God is actively present and available, forwarding his kingly rule and bringing it to consummation, and that this has the effect of opening possibilities which simply are not calculable by sinful man as being options under history's conditions of sin.[27]

Disputes about enabling power may affect nonetheless the content of agape in historical society. For if a historical state of affairs is promised in which human relations are qualitatively enhanced beyond anything we presently realize, the effective meaning of love may alter. Agape will refer less to the sacrifice and suffering which deter inordinate self-assertion from its worst excesses, and rather to frictionless harmony and unimpeded communion.

27. Vernard Eller, *The Promise Ethics in the Kingdom of God* (Garden City, N.Y.: Doubleday and Company, Inc., 1970), p. 87.

Two other major beliefs also bear directly on Niebuhr's account. There is what can be called an essentialist strain in Niebuhr's theory of human nature. He would probably argue that some such strain is unavoidable if (among other reasons) one wishes to adhere to the most minimal assumptions concerning original sin. These assumptions need not include in his view belief in a past fall from innocence at a fixed point in space and time. But they do include some version of the following. While there may not be much that is strictly immutable in human nature, what there is prompts inevitable anxiety over and abortive attempts to deny one's finitude. The anxiety and denial find expression in patterns of nearly infinite variety. But they all dispose the self to claim inordinate significance for its own case, for the tasks in which it is engaged and the causes and collectives with which it identifies. Some of the inordinance is merely touching and pathetic. Too much of it is pernicious and will always be so. For the sake of genuinely important differences in degrees of human good attainable, we must harness and beguile it in ourselves and others so far as we can. Yet no interests men might acquire will ever remove this fixed datum as a reality with which we must reckon.

There is certainly more to Niebuhr's theory of human nature than this. As we saw, he does not simply propound psychological egoism. Creativity, for example, and the capacity for "indefinite transcendence," as well as inordinate self-seeking, connect with the same immutable nature. All I wish to observe now is that he views human nature as in some sense beyond the flux of historical society and as conditioning finally what may occur within it. A perspective is thereby afforded for assessing the appropriateness of socio-political action. One aspect of this perspective is the inevitability of inordinate self-seeking. We may safely expect that prior to history's final consummation love's works will be affected accordingly and will never be able to extrude self-seeking altogether.

A final belief concerns history and the *eschata* or "last things." The distinctive background of intelligibility for agape is in part located here. Niebuhr accepts that the purposes of agape and its outcome generally will not be finally frustrated. Yet his own theological scheme requires that the life of love be vindicated unambiguously only at the "end" of history. Consider his discussion of the *parousia*.

> To believe that the suffering Messiah will return at the end of history as a triumphant judge and redeemer is to express the faith that existence cannot ultimately defy its own norm. Love may have to live in history as suffering love because the power of sin makes a simple triumph of love impossible. But if this were the ultimate situation it would be necessary either to worship the power of sin as the final power in the world or to regard it as a kind of second God, not able to triumph, but also strong enough to avoid defeat.
>
> The vindication of Christ and his triumphant return is therefore an expression of faith in the sufficiency of God's sovereignty over the world and history, and in the final supremacy of love over all the forces of self-love which defy, for the moment, the inclusive harmony of all things under the will of God.[28]

Niebuhr wishes to combat what he takes to be two distortions. On the one side, conflicts between good and evil in history are regarded as utterly meaningless. The eschatological consummation, then, annuls rather than sublimates the entire historical process. A related distortion involves destroying any social and historical meaning of life by regarding individual existence as wholly an end in itself. "Eternity" stands only "above" and not also at the "end" of history. Niebuhr thinks that both some mystic doctrines of individual fulfillment and Protestant doctrines of eschatology are open to the charge of such destruction.[29]

On the other side, the consummation is taken as a triumph *in* history: temporality itself is redeemed. By virtue of its own evolu-

---

28. Niebuhr, *Nature and Destiny of Man*, 2:290.

29. "Reformation theology is on the whole defective in failing to preserve the Biblical conception of the end; and modern Barthian eschatology accentuates this defect. It pays little attention to a possible meaning of history as a continuum and speaks of eschatology in terms of the eternity which impinges upon every moment of time" (ibid., p. 298).

tion and development the historical process emancipates men from sin and guilt. Conflicts between good and evil are more than meaningful; they are unambiguous here and now.

Niebuhr tries to avoid both distortions. The following statements suggest how he does so.

> Against utopianism the Christian faith insists that the final consummation of history lies beyond the conditions of the temporal process. Against other-worldliness it asserts that the consummation fulfills rather than negates, the historical process. There is no way of expressing this dialectical concept without running the danger of its dissolution. The dissolution has, in fact, taken place again and again in Christian history.[30]

> The hope of the resurrection . . . on the one hand . . . implies that eternity will fulfill and not annul the richness and variety which the temporal process has elaborated. On the other it implies that the condition of finiteness and freedom, which lies at the basis of historical existence, is a problem for which there is no solution by any human power. Only God can solve this problem. From the human perspective it can only be solved by faith.[31]

Though some of the formulations remain admittedly imprecise, the general lines seem clear enough for my illustrative purposes now. The treatment of agape in this life is affected by wider beliefs about (including differing estimates of) the character and effects of providential action, the degree of plasticity of human nature, and the historical limits and possibilities of relations between collectives.

In chapter 1 a sketch of the feature of mutuality was also attempted, and contrasted explicitly with a characterization like Niebuhr's. I said that in the case of mutuality, some notion of communication and sharing is involved. Love refers, in part or altogether,

30. Ibid., p. 291.
31. Ibid., p. 295.

to a quality of relation *between* persons and/or groups. Those attitudes and actions are loving which establish or enhance some sort of exchange between the parties, community and perhaps friendship. One may observe three things initially. First, disagreement need not always focus on the ideal content of agape. It was pointed out before that when Niebuhr speaks of frictionless harmony he shifts the center of gravity somewhat from sacrifice as a property of the self's own attitudes and actions to sacrifice as a concordant relation between selves. The issue is often whether and to what extent such an ideal is realizable in this life, hence what the purest and most perfect expression of agape can be. Second, while frictionless harmony points to a broad substantive overlap between Niebuhr and the proponents of mutuality, the phrase may not be the most felicitous for what the latter have chiefly in mind. "Harmony" immediately evokes "conflict" as its opposite. What needs stressing is not harmony-conflict, but communication and "between-ness." Third, important differences in nuance sometimes exist between theological schemes backing mutuality as a characteristic of personal relations and those backing it as a characteristic of social relations. I shall consider them in turn.

Mutuality as a characteristic of personal relations is often supported by the following sort of account of grace. It is held to be misleading at best to regard the content of grace as centrally forgiveness or perfect disinterestedness. To be preoccupied with suffering and forgiveness, and with the agent's freedom from all acquisitive interests, may be to obscure the ultimate purpose of providential action. For what is always sought is an increasingly conscious relation between God and man as an end in itself, and in conformance, between human creature and human creature as related to God. Thus Burnaby holds that the "serious, perhaps . . . fatal defect" in Nygren's scheme (applicable to Niebuhr as well) is neglect of philia, the Greek word signifying a mutual relation, "a bond which links two centres of consciousness in one." [32] The final objective of divine love is "the mutual 'inherence' of persons, life in one another." [33]

---

32. Burnaby, *Amor Dei*, p. 18.
33. *Ibid.*, p. 306.

The love which endures, which offers itself to the unloving, is always the servant of its own high purpose — not to rest till the sundered fellowship is restored, till rejection is changed to response. Calvary is for the sake of Pentecost: *It is expedient for you that I go away*. . . . The "mercifulness" which is literally *com*passion is the way in which we are called to imitate the divine perfection in a world still to be redeemed. Yet suffering can be the end neither for God nor man. . . . Charity believeth all things, hopeth all things; and its faith and hope no less than its endurance are creative of that unity of the Spirit which is its end.[34]

To restrict justifying appeals to Jesus' teachings about the character of God is thus to beg a pivotal question. For the issue concerns this very character. If one understands the work of grace to be in this life a concordant relation between two persons — where both are human and where one is human and one divine — then to safeguard a self-sacrificial content enjoining nonresistance rather than nonviolent resistance seems beside the point. Nonresistance should be practiced only if and when it enhances a mutual relation. The final criterion is always the quality of the relation. If we distill from the teachings and life of Jesus, and the experience of the community led by the Spirit, we arrive at "the holy of holies": mutual relations of a personal kind are the highest value. Sometimes, though not necessarily, appeal is made to the experience of human relatedness as a general phenomenon. Wherever people meet in openness and mutual help, they do more than experience only private emotion or talk only to each other; they put themselves in a context which leads to an awareness of God. Wherever persons are related to each other in the right way they open themselves to a disclosure of the Spirit, and their relation may be a medium for such disclosure.

One should note also that this sort of scheme, at least as elucidated by those (like Burnaby) who wish to remain within a broadly orthodox tradition, need not depart formally from the general eschatological

34. Ibid., p. 307. See also pp. 367–68, and John McIntyre, *On the Love of God,* p. 30.

lines laid down by Niebuhr. Imitation of the divine perfection takes place in a world still to be redeemed. Here men see only in part; they await a consummation beyond anything attainable via internal historical evolution. What Burnaby holds out for, in a way Niebuhr does not, is what one may call material continuity between love in this world and the next. "The mutual inherence of persons" refers both to the standard by which we ought to assess present attitudes and actions and to the character of life beyond the consummation. But this likewise means that love is greater than faith and hope: it alone will not cease. One may cite Augustine, whom Burnaby takes book-length pains to treat sympathetically.

> For to faith and hope shall succeed at once the very substance itself, no longer to be believed in and hoped for, but to be seen and grasped. Love, however, which is the greatest among the three, is not to be superseded but increased and fulfilled, — contemplating in full vision what it used to see by faith, and acquiring in actual fruition what it once only embraced in hope.[35]

Finally, in chapter 1 mutuality was also identified as a characteristic of social relations; agape furnishes a comprehensive ideal of social cooperativeness. Men are reciprocally connected with larger groups and attention must be given to collective welfare. Those actions are loving which create and sustain community. Within and between groups, and in the social order as a whole, one ought to struggle for a progressive realization of harmony and brotherhood.

Unlike Niebuhr, proponents of mutuality in this sense often assume that groups are capable of suspending their collective self-interest to the extent desirable. The aim is seen as realistically one of fostering cooperativeness and not simply balancing interests. Conflict is not so much of a fixed datum as Niebuhr appears to believe. Our sociopolitical life may constitute more than important, but finally limited, variations on well-established themes.

---

35. *On the Perfection of Man's Righteousness*, from *The Works of Aurelius Augustine*, ed. Marcus Dods, 15 vols. (Edinburgh: T. and T. Clark, 1871–1876), vol. IV, trans. Peter Holmes, pp. 327–28.

Support and backing for a standard of social cooperativeness need
not differ very widely in many cases from justification of a general
notion of mutuality. So we find one writer, for example, complaining
that Niebuhr re-introduces a Reformation (and allegedly "semi-Mani-
chean") stress on self-sacrifice as a "deterrent good" rather than the
"essential good" of harmony and brotherhood.[36] Phrases used interchangeably in referring to such essential good include "the total in-
terrelatedness of man with man," "personal communion," "Christian
love as friendship," "friendship as the ultimate value of human life,"
and "a holy community of love in this world." No distinction seems
forthcoming between others to whom one may refer only in the third
person and others whom one may address as "you" or "thou." Personal communion and social community alike are supported by typical
beliefs concerning "the power of divine unity working in all things
to reconcile . . . ideological conflict."

But the above clearly does not take one very far. There is more to
be said about the connection between friendship as the ultimate value
of human life and more impersonal exchanges between wider communities; one may also find schemes which support a content not so
centered on philia. Moltmann writes:

> Love does not snatch us from the pain of time, but takes the
> pain of the temporal upon itself. Hope makes us ready to bear
> the 'cross of the present'. It can hold to what is dead, and hope
> for the unexpected. It can approve of movement and be glad of
> history. . . . Where in faith and hope we begin to live in the
> the light of the possibilities and promises of this God, the whole
> fullness of life discloses itself as a life of history and therefore a
> life to be loved. Only in the perspective of this God can there
> possibly be a love that is more than *philia,* love to the existent
> and the like — namely, *agape,* love to the non-existent, love to the
> unlike, the unworthy, the worthless, to the lost, the transient and
> the dead; a love that can take upon it the annihilating effects of

36. Herbert Warren Richardson, "Martin Luther King — Unsung Theologian,"
Commonweal 88 (1968): 201–03; reprinted in Martin E. Marty and Dean G.
Peerman, eds., *New Theology No. 6* (New York: The Macmillan Company,
1969), pp. 178–84.

pain and renunciation because it receives its power from hope of a *creatio ex nihilo*.[37]

It may be of course that philia here, as love to the existent and the like, differs from what was earlier meant by friendship. I noted some of the conceptual ambiguities surrounding mutuality in much of the literature. In the final chapter I shall say something more about points of possible clarification. In any event, agape has been held to have direct socio-political relevance, often in schemes where hope is a socio-political virtue. If the agent believes he may act cooperatively with others to bring about changes in the social order beyond anything that has gone before, then agape may become the standard by which the status quo is critically assessed and the definer of those future arrangements which defeat at last the multiple alienations experienced among men to the present. Again, I cannot examine here secular versions of such a hope, as that in Marxist thought. But I can note a particular theological support, and its effects upon agape. Here is perhaps a classic instance of how "rival theologies within the same religion can sometimes express rival political visions of the world." [38]

I have remarked already on the way disputes about grace as enabling power can affect the content of agape in historical society. One may expect a future which is more than a repetition of the past, and where belief in providence includes anticipation of the "ultimately new." [39] Sometimes it is unclear whether such power is available to believer and non-believer alike and what the criteria are for distinguishing divine promise and human hope. But it is clear that claims about what is immutable in human nature tend to drop away. Messianic and

37. Moltmann, *Theology of Hope*, pp. 31–32. While agape seems not explicitly at the center of a scheme like Moltmann's having to do with the eschatological category of hope, sufficient references exist to warrant looking tentatively at the effects incorporation sometimes brings. See also, e.g., pp. 24, 26, 30–36, 91–92, 208, 212–13, 225, and 338.

38. Alasdair MacIntyre, *Marxism and Christianity* (London: Gerald Duckworth, 1969), p. 3.

39. Jürgen Moltmann, *Religion, Revolution and Future*, trans. M. Douglas Meeks (New York: Charles Scribner's Sons, 1969), p. 61.

eschatological imagery largely replace any essentialist strains thought to be beyond the flux of historical society and conditioning finally what may occur within it. And an eschatological horizon of promise is taken to govern situations of moral choice. So Barth's "transcendental eschatology" comes in for similar but far more elaborate criticism than (as noted earlier) Niebuhr provides. Barth is held to concentrate on the "epiphany of the eternal present" rather than the "apocalypse of the promised future." [40] God's revelation is for Barth self-vindicating, and every moment in time may be its bearer. "End" comes to be equivalent with "origin" and the eschaton nothing else than "the transcendental boundary of time and eternity." [41] On the other side, Moltmann insists in a way Niebuhr never does on the prospects of revolutionary change beyond important but finally limited variations on well-established themes. A radical hope in and striving for God's promised reign anticipates transformation and newness uncalculable by present experience.

A nest of issues connected with the above must be largely set aside now. Among other things, one faces the basic question, notoriously difficult and many-sided as it is, of how theological disputes such as these cannot be simply understood, but must be adjudicated as well. Yet for my purposes, two points are worth noting in conclusion. First, while often the virtue of hope seems nearly to displace love, at least in emphasis, it is still the case that sometimes (though not as clearly as with Burnaby) love refers to the character of what is hoped for. One reads for instance: "It was a student in Tübingen who transformed the saying of Che Guevara: 'The vocation of every lover is to bring about revolution' into 'The duty of every revolution is to bring about love.' " [42] In any event the content of agape remains vague. Moltmann's contrast between agape and philia suggests a content closer to equal regard than to mutuality. Perhaps the assumption is that since they need not be incompatible, one may simply commend them both, with mutuality as internal ideal fruition.

The most distinctive effect of such an eschatological scheme appears then to lie in another place. The scheme warrants struggle, possibly

40. Moltmann, Theology of Hope, p. 57.
41. Ibid., p. 51.
42. Moltmann, Religion, Revolution and the Future, p. 147.

violent struggle, to bring historical society into greater conformity with what is on the normative eschatological horizon. So one need not insist with Kierkegaard that differences are like an enormous net in which the temporal is held. One's only alternative to admitting that *some* differences will remain is surely not just to lift oneself above all of those one happens to find. The point is *praxis*: one ought to expend one's energies on behalf of those social and personal arrangements in which the well-being of each is — de facto — equally valued. Justification is located more in the hoped-for future. Reliance on the divine promise makes it less urgent to demonstrate empirical equalities between men in advance. The human agent ought to appraise his neighbors in light of God's bestowal of irreducible value on them not by leaving the world to its own devices, but by accepting responsibility for changing it toward greater demonstrable congruity with such bestowal. Human life here and now should mirror increasingly its status before God, a status it is destined one day to display unambiguously. And one practical outcome of such an effort is likely to be a rectifying bias toward those who suffer most from unequal consideration. Kierkegaard could reply that equality before God is distinguishable from a program to abolish even some temporal differences. I think one can acknowledge unexamined logical difficulties in the passage from one sort of equality to another,[43] and still recognize that such passages often occur in fact. Distinctive moral perspectives and energies may then be galvanized out of such eschatological beliefs, and these may influence both the content and application of agape.

Some General Considerations at Stake

The comparisons thus far have necessarily been piecemeal. But they do illustrate how the status and justification of agape may vary within different theological schemes; and they also suggest some of the possible moves and restrictions different schemes actually afford. I shall now point to certain more general considerations.

43. Of course there are also different sorts of "temporal" equality; liberalism for instance is frequently held to foster economic inequality as well as political equality.

Often justification is determined largely by the distinctive structure of a specific theological scheme. Some see themselves obliged — for theological reasons at least in part — to pursue the case for agape from commonly available insight as far as they can, because they do not wish too radically to separate creation and redemption, and so on. There may be complementary appeals in the confidence that there cannot be ultimate sundering. Many Roman Catholic thinkers have reflected confidence in what can be commonly acknowledged as morally relevant and perhaps binding apart from any explicit religious associations it may have. Gilleman appeals inclusively for instance to affective and mystical as well as cognitive elements, and also to "the gratuitous order of providence." These several elements when rightly apprehended make one aware that the profound, essentialist tendency of man is love.[44] It would seem misleading to say that the agent *decides* to adopt this tendency as the basic principle for the guidance of life. Rather, the tendency characterizes the agent who chooses. One is free only to live in accordance with it and attend to its implications; or to try — with consequences which are ultimately self-defeating — to deny it. Finally the tendency does not produce discordant evidence. Any de facto plurality of basic, incompatible principles is accounted for by concepts such as "blindness," "corruption," "mistake," and by alleged differences in "moral maturity," "perception," "insight." The raw material of a human life possesses a definite *telos;* it is neither egoistic nor morally neutral.

> If our profound tendency, instead of being love, were a force seeking realization through domination or a blind creative energy channeled by rigid laws, then the scale of moral value would be overturned: the prevailing ideal would be the morality of superman or sheer legalism.[45]

44. Gilleman, *Primacy of Charity*, e.g., p. 160.
45. Ibid., p. 99. This is a major claim and Gilleman does not always defend it with persistence. Occasionally he seems to doubt, for instance, whether the tendency is known, even fragmentarily, apart from the incarnation (e.g., p. xxii). But I am more concerned now to distinguish some formal lines of authority than to trace the nuances (and obscurities) of individual treatments.

In traditional Catholic fashion one *knows* the tendency by virtue of one's own reason and experience (phenomenologically described, in Gilleman's case) as well as by virtue of Jesus as the norm or paradigm, by scripture, and by tradition. All of these are in continuity with one another and will prove finally not to be conflicting. What is "natural" is to be approached openly and positively,[46] with prior assurance that at least eventual continuity will be demonstrated. The treatment of agape must reflect this assurance, as well as the admission that reason and experience, while congruent, are not enough — that supernatural help is required if the complete reality and the goal of final communion with God are to be adequately realized.

Gilleman brings then to his case for the primacy of charity or agape distinctive doctrinal assumptions. While he attempts important internal reform within moral theology, his doctrinal scheme in its essentials remains Roman Catholic and Thomist, just as Nygren's remains Lutheran. The effects in both cases are far-reaching. For Nygren and for many other essentially Reformation schemes, there is less certainty about continuities in this life, or at least less confidence in their general demonstrability. Such lack of confidence fosters insistence that here and now one is unable to connect different ways of life with unambiguous gains and losses. Certain general reasons were suggested earlier for a chastened moral epistemology. I do not mean to imply of course that Nygren is representative of all Protestant schemes. It has been argued in the case of Calvin, for instance, that some "ethical universals" may be partly legitimated on natural or empirical grounds in a fashion complementary with revealed

46. Nygren's lack of such an attitude is one of the points criticized by Gilleman in his review of the French edition of Nygren's work in *Nouvelle Revue Théologique* 3 (May-June, 1946): 347–49. Recently in writings by Catholics the question has been re-examined of whether there is a distinctively Christian morality beyond "generally valid natural morality." Some wish now to hold that "human morality" and "Christian morality" are "materially identical." See the summary and bibliographical references in Richard A. McCormick, S.J., "Notes on Moral Theology: April-September, 1970," *Theological Studies* 32 (March 1971): 71–78.

knowledge. "Calvin's notion of humanity was never . . . simply derived from theological assertions. It had a very strong empirical ingredient, and it made room for moral reflection on the basis of reason and nature." [47] And despite Niebuhr's preoccupation with sin, one finds him arguing (occasionally at any rate) that the love Christ reveals on the cross is required only to "complete," "clarify," and "correct" the account of a standard which men in general know fragmentarily and realize imperfectly.[48] Niebuhr appears more pessimistic about the prospects of justifying love partly via native moral insight than Gilleman and less so than Nygren. Certainly many Protestants have thought that arguments from generalized self-interest (as the golden rule is sometimes interpreted) may persuade a sufficient number to allow for societal viability. While such arguments have often seemed to fall under the principle of justice more than love, morally permitted disagreements on issues of "civic righteousness" may be, as it were, cut down in an other-regarding direction.

Perhaps it is the case that the structures of specific schemes are often distinguished according to which of two very general doctrines is given prominence. The doctrines are: (1) human existence in general "cannot ultimately defy its own norm"; (2) some special authoritative event such as the life of Jesus cannot be rendered superfluous. Many will try to maintain them both in rough balance. Others will be willing at least to pay a considerable price in one direction or the other. Gilleman for example endeavors to steer between regarding "natural love" as so corrupted that charity is an alien intrusion and regarding it as so unambiguous as to make any link to the historical Jesus an accidental aid to a way of life otherwise known. He seems concerned especially to treat natural love, however diluted its present condition, as complementary with what is revealed and capable of gratuitous elevation. Others concentrate on the exemplarity of Jesus in contrast to what they regard as the bewildering variety of contradictory motives, standards, and actions of men. The alleged ambiguity of native moral insight and failure

47. Little, "Calvin and . . . Natural Law," pp. 196–97.
48. Niebuhr, *Nature and Destiny of Man*, 1:70, 81–90.

in execution makes an authoritative event anything but superfluous. And an interest to assure the decisive moral authority of the event disposes them to insist on ambiguity.

In addition to such internal differences between schemes, I think one should try to suggest some more general effects of religious belief on the justification of agape. One should attend, that is, not only to the ways schemes may differ between themselves, but also to assumptions more widely shared which mark off religious grounds from non-religious ones. Many of these assumptions have already been anticipated. Let me specify further at least three kinds of broad and compatible connections between religious beliefs and agape frequently put forward. Such beliefs may provide a background of intelligibility; furnish explicit backing; or have effects upon the content of agape itself.

Religious beliefs may provide in the first instance a *background of intelligibility* for agape. They serve to define the total arena within which actions are viewed and assessed. A certain sort of world is seen to lie behind the life of love, a world which will finally not prove indifferent, unsupportive, or hostile to such a life. Whether the support is held to be verified in this life or in a future eschatological consummation (or partly now and fully then) depends in part on the theological scheme in question. But one lives with a confidence and expectation that the purposes of agape and its outcome generally will not be finally frustrated. Beliefs about the ultimate facts of human existence, then, form this sort of background.

That such a background or frame of reference is often assumed seems obvious enough. Yet one should pause briefly to note some of the issues implied and claims made. References to "ultimate facts" point for example to a series of questions widely canvassed by philosophers but unfortunately largely neglected by theologians (irrespective of whether they treat agape extensively), namely, questions connected with an alleged logical gap between "is" and "ought." [49] The gap, it is claimed, prevents one from deriving an

---

49. The issue of the logical relationship between is and ought has been called "the central problem of moral philosophy." A mere sample of the enormous literature includes: Arthur N. Prior, *Logic and the Basis of Ethics* (Oxford:

evaluation from a premise containing no such element. If the premise is descriptive, the conclusion cannot be evaluative. So ethical principles cannot rest upon purely descriptive facts of experience. Unless one adds an evaluative element to the premise, a logical gap remains; and all connections between factual statements and ethical principles must likewise remain contingent ones. Sometimes it is said that the history of ethical theorizing is replete with instances of this fallacy. Attention to the gap would, as Hume believed, "subvert all the vulgar systems of morality." Consider for example the reasoning of the psychological hedonist held to be fallacious:

> Pleasure is that to which all men aspire
> Therefore pleasure is good

The fallacy is commonly supposed to subvert much of religious ethics as well. From a factual statement such as "God is love" one cannot logically conclude, "therefore one ought to love one's neighbor."

This troublesome gap is one, as I said, to which theologians have devoted comparatively little attention.[50] Certainly in the literature

---

Clarendon Press, 1965); G. E. Moore, *Principia Ethica* (Cambridge: Cambridge University Press, 1960); W. K. Frankena, "The Naturalistic Fallacy," *Mind* 48 (1939): 464–77; R. M. Hare, *The Language of Morals* (Oxford: Clarendon Press, 1961), "The Promising Game," *Revue Internationale de Philosophie* 70 (1964): 398–412; John R. Searle, "How to Derive 'Ought' from 'Is,' " *Philosophical Review* 73 (1964): pp. 43–58. The articles mentioned (plus others) have been collected in Philippa Foot, ed., *Theories of Ethics* (Oxford: Oxford University Press, 1967). Another helpful collection of recent articles is W. D. Hudson, ed., *The Is/Ought Question* (London: Macmillan, 1969).

50. Many of the issues relevant to religious ethics are surveyed in Burton F. Porter, *Deity and Morality* (London: George Allen and Unwin Ltd., 1968). Other discussions include essays in *Christian Ethics and Contemporary Philosophy*, pp. 15–180, and in *Religious Studies* 5 (December, 1969): 129–79; Ninian Smart, *Reasons and Faiths* (London: Routledge and Kegan Paul, 1958), pp. 179–96; W. W. Bartley III, *Morality and Religion* (New York: St. Martin's Press, 1971). See also Basil Mitchell, "Ethics and the Will of God," *Sophia* 1 (July, 1962): 1–7, and a forthcoming volume on morality and religion; and one other forthcoming volume: Gene Outka and John P. Reeder, Jr., eds., *Religion and Morality* (Garden City, N.Y.: Doubleday).

before us it is largely ignored. Thus I would digress unduly were I to examine it in very much detail. But it may be worth noting briefly three of the possible kinds of relation between religious beliefs and ethical principles that can be extrapolated from the general discussion concerning is-ought. This should help to characterize further the general background often assumed.

One may call the three kinds of relation the *psychological,* the *logical,* and the *reasonable.*[51] The psychological can simply be mentioned now and then set aside, for it was considered briefly in chapter 5 and in any case, no logical objections need arise. Many theologians hold that religious beliefs and experiences furnish an adequate (sometimes the only fully adequate) psychological motivation to practice the life of love. The agent then is empowered to display the requisite attitudes and actions.

When we reflect on the question of a logical relation, objections abound, as indicated above. While a vast number of theological writings simply reflect no awareness of logical difficulties in (say) moving from the "indicative" to the "imperative," those that do are often prepared to grant some variant of the following: "If a statement does not contain some element of evaluation or jurisdiction then no evaluative/regulative principle may be derived from it without the addition of another premise which does contain such an element."[52] Such a formulation admits the logical gap to be un-

---

51. Another kind of relation is also sometimes distinguished: the *genetic* or *casual.* So it might be claimed that out of the historical matrix of religious communities commandments have arisen, such as, you shall love your neighbor as yourself. Yet unless the ethical principle in question has religious features built into it, the connection need not be a necessary one. The principle might have emerged in some other way as well. Moreover, to give an account of the origin is distinguishable from establishing its truth. And one may try to show that the principle is susceptible to universal certification without having to demonstrate that it has had, de facto, universal acceptance. Cf. William K. Frankena, "Public Eucation and the Good Life," *Harvard Education Review* 22 (Fall, 1961): 411–26.

52. A. D. Galloway, "Fact and Value in Theological Ethics," *Religious Studies* 5 (December, 1969): 173. See Hare, *The Language of Morals,* p. 28: *"No imperative conclusion can be validly drawn from a set of premises which does not contain at least one imperative."*

bridgeable, while leaving open the issue of whether any factual statement is utterly devoid of an evaluative element. No logical fallacy may be committed and the autonomy of ethics is not impugned if one can throw substantial doubts upon the enterprise of finding a purely factual statement. "An articulate naturalist position will be something like this: Perhaps you cannot get an 'ought' from a bare 'is', but you so seldom find a bare 'is' that it hardly matters." [53] A tough-minded theological naturalism might then attempt this sort of program:

> Among the many facts which are not 'value-free' are the basic doctrines of Christianity. . . . To affirm it is clearly no platitude but involves at least two substantial assumptions: that the basic doctrines of Christianity can indeed be called 'facts'; and that it is indeed possible for facts not to be neutral but to involve claims, for 'is' to have 'ought' built into it. . . . I do take Christianity to be concerned with 'matter of fact', true or false, not only with outlooks on life or perspectives which refuse to compete with ordinary empirical statements.[54]

Presumably Gilleman has some such program in view when he refers to charity-love as a profound spiritual tendency. Whatever one may think about the cogency of his demonstration of such a tendency in human nature, he does not have in mind a fact which contains no element of evaluation.

For a variety of reasons, including crucial epistemological ones, many theologians would hardly wish to indicate a willingness for religious beliefs to compete with ordinary empirical statements. Religious existentialists, for example, might insist that faith involves affirming some event to be an act of God which is susceptible — and in principle must emphatically be susceptible — to an alternative explanation by empirically verifiable criteria. Others argue at least that statements about God are factual in a different sense than are statements about trees and birds. Speaking roughly, the former refer to

53. Oppenheimer, "Christian Flourishing," p. 164.
54. Ibid., p. 165.

realities, such as the will of God for men, often taken as objective (something is thought to obtain independent of the agent's decision) and non-natural (the facts are not about the natural world and a claim to belief in them need not always be tested by the types of procedure which lead to empirical verification or falsification). In any event, many contend that the comprehensive set of assertions about God in the Judeo-Christian tradition include moral values built in as part of the meaning.

Some however, are inclined to allow more than a pro forma acceptance of the distinction between description and evaluation. That is, the distinction is not largely honored in the breach by casting doubt upon the frequency of bare neutral "is-es." The distinction may be taken seriously by arguing that the relation between religious beliefs and ethical principles is reasonable rather than logical.

> Theologians may also contend . . . that the law of love or benevolence may be rationally justified on theological grounds, even if it cannot rest on such grounds logically. They may argue, for instance, that if one fully believes or unquestionably experiences that God is love, then one must, if he is rational, conclude that he, too, should love. They may say that although this conclusion does not follow logically, it would be unreasonable for one to draw any other or to refrain from drawing it. In this belief they may well be right. For all that I have said, I am inclined to think they are right; however it does not follow that the principle of benevolence . . . *depends* on religion for its justification even in this non-logical sense. It still may be that it can also be justified in some other way.[55]

Two comments here. First, the central contrast between a logical and a reasonable relation is one which is, respectively, deducible and practically intelligible. It would not be logically self-contradictory or nonsensical but it would be patently bizarre and unintelligible for the believer to hold that God is love and then to judge that he ought to hate his neighbor. One recognizes the connections — between state-

55. Frankena, *Ethics*, p. 85.

ments such as God is love and judgments that one ought to love one's neighbor — as justified in the sense that they strike one as intelligible and appropriate for a believer to bring forward. But the connections are not strictly proved inductively or deductively; the judgments are not entailed in the sense of being self-evident and necessary inferences. Second, given his premises, Frankena appears correct in saying that the principle of benevolence can possibly be justified in ways *independent* of religion, perhaps in an analogous non-logical or practically reasonable way. But let us recall from chapter 3 that for Frankena, benevolence is the principle which enjoins us to do good and to prevent, and avoid doing, harm. Clearly this content overlaps with but does not exhaust what agape has meant for many in a religious context. So it would seem that the question of a possible reasonable, non-theological justification of benevolence or agape must be left open. The answer in any particular case may depend on both the substantive content given to the principle and the cogency of the precise justification offered.

Even if one takes the distinction between description and evaluation seriously, then, one can still argue that religious beliefs and experiences provide a practically intelligible framework for agape. The connections are subtle and complex. What is often claimed in general is that conceptions of normative standards such as agape are intelligible in light of and integrally tied to wider conceptions of human nature and the world. Sometimes it is contended that such ties characterize non-religious as well as religious accounts of morality.

> The integral relation of metaphysics and morality is not peculiar to theists or Christians. Some (like Camus) see human life as a heroic gesture of nobility in an uncaring universe, others (like Nietzsche) see it as the survival of the strongest; as the theatre of ephemeral happiness or the predetermined interplay of atoms. All such visions of life offer a particular metaphysical interpretation of morality. One may refuse to adopt any such vision; but that can be seen as the denial of one of reason's most insistent demands, to 'see life whole'.[56]

56. Keith Ward, *Ethics and Christianity* (London: George Allen and Unwin Ltd., 1970), p. 35.

It is also often claimed however, especially among those who display a greater restiveness with any distinction between factual statements and evaluative judgments, that one discovers the framework more than one chooses it. Differing interpretations may be in fact interminable among men, but this does not mean that they are all simply projections on a neutral screen or outlooks on life or perspectives. Theologians usually believe that a life of love somehow goes with the grain of the universe and will not be unsupported. On the question of "existential anxiety" rather than "works righteousness," they deny that whatever each person does or thinks or feels is "finally" of no consequence. Here again, in a wider context, some of these assumptions are shared by certain groups of believers and nonbelievers (whatever the decisive differences which may separate them at other points), by Thomists, Hegelians, and Marxists, for instance, who are all placed by Iris Murdoch under the title of "Natural Law Moralists."

On the Liberal view we picture the individual as able to attain by reflection to complete consciousness of his situation. He is entirely free to choose and responsible for his choice, whereby he shows which things he regards as valuable. The most systematic exposition of modern liberal morality is existentialism. Contrast the Natural Law picture. Here the individual is seen as moving tentatively *vis-à-vis* a reality which transcends him. To discover what is morally good is to discover that reality, and to become good is to integrate himself with it. He is ruled by laws which he can only partly understand. He is not fully conscious of what he is. His freedom is not an open freedom of choice in a clear situation; it lies rather in an increasing knowledge of his own real being, and in the conduct which naturally springs from such knowledge.[57]

Barth's theological vision is also directed substantively along these lines, despite his strenuous rejection of natural law on other grounds.

57. Iris Murdoch, "Metaphysics and Ethics," *The Nature of Metaphysics,* ed. D. F. Pears (London: Macmillan, 1966), pp. 114–15.

However narrow the basis of our certain knowledge of the reality which transcends the individual, the reality is inescapable. And for Barth, to discover the graciousness of divine activity is to discover what is morally good.

Religious beliefs may also furnish intelligibility in the sense of *explicit backing.* In chapter 1 it was observed that love for God is sometimes the originative and justificatory reason for neighbor-love. The latter is one appropriate test of one's love for God. It was also pointed out that beliefs concerning God's action in creation and redemption are invoked to emphasize that the neighbor is the object of divine love. Love for God thus provides backing explicitly by requiring conformity in loving what He loves. As we shall see in Barth's case as well, there is particular attention to the way in which neighbor-love shares in the seriousness of a divine command. It is anything but a self-imposed, arbitrary human decision. Again, explicit backing involving an injunction *to love* the neighbor (rather than specifying *what* in detail the agent must do so to love) is often seen as the most serious sort of religious commonplace.

The notion of explicit backing poses certain difficulties and contains various nuances, none of which can be examined in detail here. References to an explicit divine command to love may for instance similarly encounter is-and-ought difficulties. Those who take the gap seriously often attempt to allow for certain kinds of psychological and logical autonomy and hold that such autonomy is compatible with beliefs about a divine command to love. So they may maintain that to believe the divine will is thus-and-so is not to deny that the agent must himself *assent* to such a will as having supreme moral authority for him. They may also deny that they are offering a descriptive account of what everyone (believer and non-believer alike) means in the very use of moral words such as right and good. They may contend only that right and good consist for them (and many others who accept as authoritative Judeo-Christian moral discourse) in those attitudes and actions which are loving, and that such love is commanded by God. They may go on to argue that in any case in moral discourse generally, when two people disagree, one looks in vain for some prior determining rule which establishes which judgment is wrong. No single normative standard is already definitely fixed in the meaning of the moral words used.

There are also nuances in the account of explicit backing within a given scheme and between schemes. Some, for instance, rely largely on political imagery. God commands the human agent to love and it is the duty of the agent as servant to obey. In others, familial imagery predominates. It is the will of the heavenly Father that His children obey Him by loving each other. Men should out of gratitude accept their status as children of God and think and act accordingly.[58] Or again: men should love God by conforming to or imitating on their own level and with their own capacities the character of His action. A life of love is consistent with the final purpose of such action, just as non-love frustrates it. "Backing" refers then to a justifying reason which the believer may self-consciously cite for his own adherence and to the support and blessing (as he supposes) given by God to every act of love anywhere by anyone.

Finally, religious beliefs may have *effects on the content* of agape itself. We saw how Kierkegaard believes that love for God throws up certain limits around the character and intensity of neighbor-love. Another more general example has to do with the very notion of the "neighbor" and what counts in loving him in conformity to God's loving him. Descriptive and evaluative elements are often combined in the "neighbor" to be loved, built in as constitutive features specifying who he is and how he ought to be treated.

I suspect that religious views differ from 'humanist' views . . . by incorporating very different beliefs as to what really is good or bad for human beings. The religious believer finds in a supernatural order a whole extra dimension of preeminently important gains and losses, benefits and harm; his difference from

58. Some hold however that gratitude as the sole reason is not enough. One reads for example that "gratitude for God's benefits would not be a sufficient ground for *unreserved* obedience if it were severed from fear of God's irresistible power" (Peter Geach, *God and the Soul* [London: Routledge and Kegan Paul, 1969], p. 129).

the non-believer is . . . simply on the question of whether they are real or chimerical.[59]

Sometimes then distinctive assessments of what is good-making in itself, i.e., intrinsically good (for instance, communion with God), are superimposed upon more ordinary assessments, with the addition of correspondingly fitting treatments (for instance, witnessing in Barth's sense).

Some thinkers wish to go beyond superimposition, to say more than that religious beliefs may intelligibly *modify* what it means to love the neighbor. They treat any agreement between humanist and Christian in advocating neighbor-love as primarily a verbal one. Neighbor-love in a Christian context retains unavoidably a unique meaning, to be characterized always with reference to Jesus as the moral paradigm and perhaps to the cumulative moral reflection within the community of faith about the sorts of attitudes and actions which such love enjoins. Most crucially, Jesus' love is the criterion of what shall count as neighbor-love. His love is not to be tested by some "master-concept" of love in general; rather, it is itself the final test. He is the exemplar and all other notions of love must await assessment as compatible, or be revised or renounced. While this criterion is normally not understood as requiring literal conformity, the distinctive attitudes and patterns of action exemplified in the story of Jesus are to be applied to everything else. Two major assertions are frequently regarded as essential to maintain the exemplarity of Jesus.

59. G. J. Warnock, *Contemporary Moral Philosophy* (London: Macmillan, 1967), p. 79. Humanist views are also often professed to be significantly less "essentialist" than religious ones. See, e.g., H. J. Blackham, "Humanism: The Subject of the Objections," *Objections to Humanism,* ed. H. J. Blackham (Hamondsworth: Penguin Books, 1967), p. 18: "There is no supreme exemplar of humanist ethics, because, on humanist assumptions, there is no *summum bonum,* no chief end of all action, no far-off crowning event to which all things move and for which all things exist, no teleology, no definitive human nature even. Instead there are many possibilities, better and worse, and ways of avoiding the worse and realizing and increasing the better. Thus there are many patterns of good living, which can be exemplified, and none that is best or comprehensively or exhaustively good."

They are, first, that most or all men are unable to discern the moral demand for themselves; and second, that Jesus was unique in possessing that ability. . . . If they are granted, it would be reasonable to accept the life of Jesus as exemplary — not an example of what can be known, in a logically prior way, to be right, but as the revelation of what is right. Yet if either assertion is rejected, then either Jesus becomes simply an example of what we can know for ourselves to be right, or there is no reason why one should select Jesus as defining the ideal for man.[60]

Some wish in addition to grant a certain authority to the community entrusted with (among other things) deliberation on what Jesus' love implies in various situations. Within the community, it is alleged, distinctive accounts of moral problems are often forthcoming and particular reasons taken to count as moral ones.[61]

Certain believers and non-believers do not wish to see the justificatory case for agape stand or fall altogether on explicitly religious or theological grounds, or to defer even prima facie to the moral reflection of any special community. Before ending I shall look briefly at several non-theological accounts of moral principles in general and agape in particular.

Possible Non-Theological Grounds

Having identified some of the various and complex patterns of incorporation, I shall now turn aside from such theological schemes to attend cryptically to some relevant philosophical discussion, returning in part to a large question referred to earlier: is there some common core of native moral insight which all persons are held to

60. Ward, *Ethics and Christianity*, p. 97. Ward's book as a whole is a valuable attempt to state the necessary conditions for a distinctively Christian ethic.

61. See the discussion by R. W. Beardsmore, *Moral Reasoning* (London: Routledge and Kegan Paul, 1969). He cites, as an instance of the diversity in what people count as moral reasons and the determinative effects of different communities on such counting, the comparative attitudes toward suicide of a Catholic and a Japanese Samurai (p. 137).

share, or are there common standards to which all may appeal, and if so, what is their relation to agape? Many theologians have accorded moral authority to a variety of experiences and standards accessible to and binding upon all men, independent of religious belief. As I have said, the issue of an ultimate non-religious justification of agape is not at the center of the theological literature. Yet it is often assumed in that same literature that some moral principles may be so justified. As I have also remarked, there are a welter of justificatory appeals, to natural law, phenomenology, the golden rule, and so on. Perhaps references are made most often to justice, however ambiguous and sometimes incommensurable its meanings. And despite neglect in the theological literature, what of cases within "mere morality" put forward by philosophers for much of the content of agape itself (apart from built-in religious features to which attention was called previously)? Are there alternative non-religious grounds for judging that the well-being of others ought to be considered as well as one's own, that each person is irreducibly valuable and one person's well-being is as valuable as another's?

I shall first sketch the contemporary philosophical context in which these and related questions arise. I shall offer as we proceed some commentary on the relation of proposed non-religious cases to agape.

To begin with, what are some of the most frequently-invoked conditions which must be fulfilled in order for a principle to be a moral principle of any kind? Let us proceed from the less to the more controverted in recent discussion. The first three are often taken as necessary conditions, but whether they are jointly sufficient as well as severally necessary is an issue on which widespread disagreement exists. Virtually everyone agrees that the subject-matter of ethics is action-guidance (including those attitudes, intentions, feelings, and so on, tied directly to such guidance). The aim of moral principles is to function as practical directives concerning what persons ought to do and be and/or what the agent ought to do and be.

1. A moral action-guide (an AG) must be *prescriptive*. Moral principles not only concern action; they lead to action. The agent commits himself to the sorts of action enjoined by whatever principles he holds. Moral judgments and actions are, it is argued, con-

nected logically: in saying that one ought to do X, the agent is pre-
scribing to himself. The adage that "actions speak louder than
words" expresses in a crude way what is meant in part by this condition. For principles to be moral principles, then, one must be
willing to act on them. The agent ought to live by them; further,
he ought to will that others do so, a move that involves what is
sometimes called reversibility. Hare, the best-known modern ex-
ponent of the first two conditions I have noted, makes this point as
follows.

> It is necessary, not merely that this principle should be produced,
> but that the person who produces it should actually hold it. It is
> necessary not merely to *quote* a maxim, but (in Kantian lan-
> guage) to *will* it to be a universal law. It is here that prescrip-
> tivity . . . makes its most decisive appearance. For willing it
> to be a universal law involves willing it to apply even when the
> roles played by the parties are reversed.[62]

2. In order to establish reversibility, and in his ethical theory
generally, Hare relies on a combination of prescriptivity and *universalizability*. In chapter 4 I said that universalizability requires
that in a particular situation of moral choice one logically commits
himself or someone else to making the same judgment in any other
situation which is similar in the morally relevant respects. Moral
judgments must have "general application" or at least must be
capable of being made of general application. Such application requires coherence and consistency.

3. A moral action-guide must be *overriding, final,* and *supremely
authoritative*. This condition is not as widely discussed as the first
two, but it seems often assumed.[63] A moral obligation is overriding,
though to be overridingly motivated to follow it is another matter.
Nothing can override a moral obligation, and other obligations,
e.g., political and legal ones, derive what force they have from

62. Hare, *Freedom and Reason,* p. 219; see also p. 73, and *The Language of
Morals,* pp. 68–69.
63. See, e.g., Downie and Telfer, *Respect for Persons,* pp. 115–22.

moral ones. I note this condition only in passing, for while it poses interesting and important issues, they are too far afield from our present interests. I shall now list some more relevant and controversial conditions sometimes put forward.

4. Consider the following two conditions proposed by Frankena:

x has a morality or moral AG only if it includes judgments, rules, principles, ideals, etc., which (d) concern the relations of one individual (e.g. x) to others, (e) involve or call for a consideration of the effects of his actions on others (not necessarily all others), not from the point of view of his own interests or aesthetic enjoyments, but from their own point of view.[64]

Here are conditions for moral principles which are trans-individual: they involve sociality inherently. Hence they also involve a material content which overlaps more obviously with agape as a normative principle. The contention is that any moral principle should be more than the agent's supreme action-guide; it should make possible various sorts of cooperation between men.[65] Yet one should notice also that these conditions are still fairly noncommittal in comparison with agape as regard for the neighbor qua human existent. For admitted as moralities are "nationalistic and class ideologies as well as universalistic ones, justice as well as benevolence, inequalitarian as well as equalitarian theories of justice, etc." [66] Taken as non-moral are such AG's as in-principled egoism or prudentialism and aestheticism. The criteria do not even exclude the possibility of a Nazi AG for example, assuming this required an individual at least to consider the interests of other Nazis.[67]

5. One can find cases going beyond Frankena's rather minimal kind of sociality. In addition to the first three conditions set out a moment ago, some accept a social definition of morality (often under

64. William K. Frankena, "The Concept of Morality," *The University of Colorado Series in Philosophy* 3 (January, 1967): 9.

65. Ibid., p. 11.
66. Ibid., p. 9.
67. Ibid., p. 10.

the heading of "the moral point of view") which on occasion seems closer to an ideal of universal brotherhood as a condition for reasoning morally. Here is a summary of two such conditions:

A moral agent must adopt rules to which not only he and his friends conform as a matter of principle, but rules to which everyone can conform as a matter of principle. Moral rules are meant for everybody.

Moral rules must be rules which are adopted for the good of everyone alike. The principle of impartiality or justice is involved here, since the interests of all people must be furthered, or at least given equal consideration when some moral rule has to be overridden.[68]

How is agape to be located in relation to these conditions? It seems obvious that the more the conditions are universalistic, the greater the overlap. Then one must decide how cogent the case is for each condition from the vantage point of "common moral reasoning." One should not overestimate the philosophical consensus even on the minimal level of the first two conditions. MacIntyre has argued, for example, that even the universalizability requirement (which is objected to by many as nearly vacuous) is more than a neutral logical analysis of what is constitutive of any moral principle.[69] It prescribes a meaning for moral words and so implicitly a morality. MacIntyre prefers to be more inclusive even than Hare and allow the word "moral" to characterize decisions in which the agent does not legislate for all relevantly similar situations. Certain existentialists, then, are not just moral doubters; they may appropriately employ moral discourse even when they hold that decisions are arbitrary as well as free, that normative moral disputes are in prin-

68. Kai Nielsen, "On Moral Truth," *Studies in Moral Philosophy, American Philosophical Quarterly* Monograph No. 1, p. 13. See Baier, *The Moral Point of View*, esp. pp. 187–213

69. Alasdair MacIntyre, "What Morality is Not," *Philosophy* 23 (October, 1957): 325–34.

ciple interminable, and that moral principles are in no sense valid in themselves but are created by agent-espousal.

Yet suppose that some formal conception of universalizability or justice can be justified on publicly accessible non-religious grounds, perhaps on grounds of generalized self-interest, perhaps as embedded in the logic of moral words. Even so, the two further trans-individual conditions proposed by Frankena remain, as we have seen, fairly noncommittal in comparison with agape. And it is interesting to note that the last conditions I mentioned, and similar universalistic ones, have been regularly attacked for enshrining a particular normative code — "liberal Western morality" — and making it impossible to say of a society which overtly treats women as inferior or contains an explicitly defined caste system that it has a genuine morality.[70]

It is also interesting to note that defenses of such conditions have sometimes attempted to construe them as formal ones.[71] Thus the criterion of reversibility may be invoked in the fashion of Hare to reduce the number of those who would be willing to ascribe an inferior status if they were on the receiving rather than the giving end. But whoever is willing to be a recipient is reasoning morally after all. Thus, such universalistic conditions are held not to determine the content of any moral judgment.

The wisdom of characterizing such conditions as formal ones is widely disputed. Whether or not the agapist agrees that they are formal, he may welcome them as enabling a significant reduction in the variety of consistently held de facto moral disagreements. If people are willing to universalize and so give equal weight to the interests of others, agreements of a basic, minimal sort may be reached. But he may still ask whether such formal conditions continue to provide logical room for principles of substance other than agape and not easily reconcilable with it. In chapter 8 I shall further discuss this question and certain others which have to do with the relation between universalizability and agape.

70. E.g., Paul Edwards, "The Ethnocentric Fallacy," *The Monist* 47 (1963): 563–84.

71. E.g., Nielsen, "On Moral Truth," pp. 9–25.

I will now consider two recent cases of non-religious reasons which specify still further in an other-regarding direction. The first case is Maclagan's. In a penetrating article he characterizes the normative content of agape along the lines of equal regard. He then asks about its justification. He acknowledges that there is a theological answer to the question of justification, but holds that theological beliefs in this case are at most correlative and not prior. The relation between such beliefs and the principle may be genetic or casual in that, however agape "may first have entered into our spiritual tradition, it is capable of sustaining the absence and surviving the loss of the theistic faith that is so often appealed to in justification of it." [72] Maclagan also discards any case for "intellectual intuition." Yet he refuses to conclude that there is no justification beyond agent-espousal. So he is left with the following account:

> What in this predicament *can* we say but that the recognition of the worth or importance of persons is actually integrated with the Agape-response itself, is a constitutive moment in it, response and recognition being only different facets of a single experience? On this view it is *in* Agape that we *see* the significance of persons, and we could say with equal truth and, so long as we attend carefully to our meaning, with equal safety that Agape is warranted by the apprehended worth of its object or that Agape provides its own warrant.[73]

Apparently the "Agape-commitment" is very like a Kantian concept of the categorical imperative: it is a fundamental and inescapable element in our moral thinking, even if not universally and unfailingly experienced. While I cannot stay to explore the point now, it can be asked whether Maclagan's account of agape is not part and parcel of much that is Kantian in his ethical thory as a whole. He characterizes the moral law or moral demand as a categorical requirement, the absoluteness of which we *cannot* doubt.[74] So "the

72. Maclagan, "Respect for Persons as a Moral Principle — I," p. 208.
73. Ibid., pp. 208–09.
74. Maclagan, *Theological Frontier of Ethics*, e.g., pp. 53, 62. Maclagan may go beyond Kant in positing an ontological order of values neither as inexplicable nor as inscrutable as Kant might suppose.

claim of acknowledged duty, whatever may be its nature and origin, neither requires nor admits of *justification* by reference to what is other than itself." [75] Among other things, one may observe here another kind of incorporation: agape is affected by Maclagan's ethical theory as a whole. Determinative issues relate to the cogency of his theory and the legitimacy of the incorporation of agape into that. Theologians will agree or disagree depending on their assessment of both.

The second case concerns an account of equalitarian justice which overlaps significantly with agape. The account by a number of philosophers is often linked to a doctrine of universal human rights. Vlastos provides one such account. He offers a rationale for equalitarian justice without appealing directly to theological or metaphysical doctrines. Points of normative overlap with agape are plain enough. For instance, "everything other than a person can only have value for a person." [76] Even those things such as musical compositions and courageous deeds which may be valued for their own sakes nonetheless fall into "an entirely different category from that of the *valuers,* who do not need to be valued as 'ends' by someone else in order to have value." [77] The valuers, persons, are in a unique sense "ends in themselves." They have irreducible value. Moreover, there is no way of grading persons as such. There "can be strictly and literally superior or inferior poets, teachers, bankers, garage-mechanics, actresses, statesmen; but there can strictly and literally be no superior or inferior persons, individuals, men." [78] We incur a "category mistake" if we praise a man as a man. Hence we may say that one person's well-being is as valuable as another's. So one can reply to a hypothetical visitor from Mars who hearkens from a strict meritarian society:

> You would weigh the welfare of members of the elite more highly than that of "riff-raff," as you call them. We would not.

75. Ibid., p. 57.
76. Vlastos, "Justice and Equality," p. 48.
77. Ibid., p. 49.
78. Ibid., p. 70.

If A were a statesman, and giving him relief from pain enabled him to conclude an agreement that would benefit millions, while B, an unskilled laborer, was himself the sole beneficiary of the like relief, we would, of course, agree that the *instrumental* value of the two experiences would be vastly different — but not their *intrinsic* value. In all cases where human beings are capable of enjoying the same goods, we feel that the intrinsic value of their enjoyment is the same.[79]

Reference to capacity indicates one sort of justification Vlastos offers. While not all persons are capable of experiencing all values equally, many cases exist where all persons are so capable. "Thus, to take a perfectly clear case, no matter how A and B might differ in taste and style of life, they would both crave relief from acute physical pain."[80] In such a case the same value is accorded to such relief, regardless of whether the recipient is talented or mediocre. Such equal intrinsic value affords the ground for equal human rights. In short, it seems that a whole set of important situations exist where men experience the same values. Any natural equality ought to be mirrored in equality of consideration, with one man's well-being accorded the same weight as another's. We *find* such intrinsic value, i.e., we appraise it correctly, where such appraisal is tied to one or more shared characteristics.

Vlastos' account has not escaped skeptical challenge. He is said to be far clearer about normative content than about justification. Nielsen, for example, while a professed socialist in politics and an egalitarian in normative ethics, remains unconvinced that universal human rights have ever been rationally justified by way of compelling argument and sufficient evidence. He takes Vlastos explicitly to task. For one thing, Nielsen denies that there is any conceptual impropriety in praising a man as a man. Why should one not say

79. Ibid., p. 51.
80. Ibid. See also John Wilson, *Equality* (London: Hutchinson, 1966); W. T. Blackstone, "On the Meaning and Justification of the Equality Principle," *Ethics* 77 (July, 1967): 239–53.

that Hamlet, Othello, and Cordelia are superior to Richard III, Iago, and Goneril? To praise a man as a man seems often enough a working concept.

> When Vlastos will not allow us to grade men as men, it is not because there is any conceptual impropriety in doing so or any category mistake involved. Rather what Nietzsche would regard as the stench of Christian moralism is overpowering Vlastos' judgment here. Put more neutrally . . . it is Vlastos's own distinctive Christian moral commitments and not anything in the logic of moral discourse or any kind of conceptual necessity that leads him to this conclusion and that gives it whatever 'justification' it has. There are perfectly intelligible, and *perhaps* even superior moral conceptions, that would instead be committed to the idea that there are superior and inferior human beings. Certainly a Master Morality would be one of these.[81]

Furthermore, to say that a whole set of important situations exists where men experience the same values does not strictly imply that the intrinsic value of their experiences is the same. One person may, for example, enjoy relief from acute physical pain far more than another. It can even be asked: are there any wants all men may be said to have?[82] Finally, even if we assume (as we have no good reason for doing) that one person's well-being has as much intrinsic value as another's, it does not follow that the *total* value of one life is equal to another. One might argue that a world of Hamlets would conduce to far more human happiness than a world of Richard IIIs. We may fittingly judge all that persons do and are, including the effects of their lives upon others.[83]

81. Kai Nielsen, "Skepticism and Human Rights," *The Monist* 52 (October, 1968): 586.

82. "Even if we take that supposedly basic want, the proper use of one's limbs, for instance, we find cases, such as that of St. Paul, where men, though they may begin by not wanting their thorn in the flesh, end by cherishing it for the sake of the side effects which it produces" (W. D. Hudson, "Fact and Moral Value," *Religious Studies* 5 [December, 1969]: 137).

83. Nielsen, "Skepticism and Human Rights," pp. 590–91.

I do not propose here to explore the intricacies of Vlastos' formulations and Nielsen's challenge.[84] Those theologians who are skeptical, for reasons given earlier, of appeals to what can be established by strictly philosophical argument or founded on empirical observation and research may regard a challenge such as Nielsen's as confirmatory. They may see it as one more indication that such appeals will always remain inconclusive, with new disagreements constantly erupting. Those who do not believe they are theologically forbidden to appeal to common moral reasoning and relevant factual data may welcome cases offered on non-theological grounds. They may see themselves as susceptible to Nielsen's challenge; required to specify as clearly as they can the conception of the person they wish to defend. It may include references to capacities held to be universally available (such as the possession of a rational will, the ability to make an effort, to engage in moral inquiry, and so on) and important situations where persons experience the same values.

Those who appeal to common moral reasoning, and yet do not regard religious belief as a mere addendum, may wish to say something like the following about non-religious or humanist cases for agape. First, agape as a full-dress concept in the theological literature has features built into it and beliefs backing it which by definition a humanist version could not include (e.g., the intrinsic good-

84. I shall only observe that it appears that Nielsen misleadingly widens the case he attacks beyond the case Vlastos actually offers. To show this in detail would be again to digress. But it is germane to observe in passing that Vlastos seems concerned to elucidate the principle of equalitarian justice and a distinctive conception of the person tied to it. For all he has said, he could agree with Nielsen that there are intelligible alternative conceptions. Indeed, Vlastos indicates how *im*moral an equalitarian polity would seem to a person who recognizes only merit-values and denies irreducible "human worth." Vlastos does not suggest that such a person would be making a logical or factual mistake in taking equalitarian arrangements to be all wrong; they *would* be all wrong from his, alternative, conception of the value of the human person. So the conception Vlastos considers may well be closer to a Christian and a Stoic one than to (say) the Platonic. In any case he wants a conception which allows unequal as well as equal distribution to be consistently joined on premises which are solely equalitarian. Such a conception may admittedly not be the only intelligible one when sweeping appeal is made to the "logic of moral discourse" as such.

ness of communion with God and the correlative treatment of witness, the belief that each man's irreducible value connects with his being a creature of God, and so on). Second, the question of whether a humanist version may be compatible or simply identifiable with parts of agape is still left open. Likewise undetermined is whether one can formulate a humanist scheme in which it makes sense to speak of each man as irreducibly valuable and where one person's well-being is as valuable as another's. Certainly the agapist need never deny that the life of agape is, in most of its features, *realized* among non-believers as well as believers. And it is hard to see why he should not be glad for non-theological schemes that attribute to each man the irreducible worth and dignity which he commends. What he can argue for are intelligible links between the several parts of his own scheme. And a possible difference he might find lies in the extent of a *guarantee* that the needs of others are to be assessed with care and met with diligence. On this injunction, at any rate, the agapist himself has virtually no room for substantive maneuver. Disagreements and discriminatory judgments are reserved mainly to the working out of its implications for different sorts of cases where stresses and strains appear and interests clash.

7

Karl Barth on Agape

I want now to break off direct concentration on claims in the literature as a whole and consider an individual treatment at greater
length. I shall examine the views of Barth both because he has
illuminating things to say on this subject in particular and because he
seems now to be at the very least the most significant Christian
theologian in the first half of the twentieth century. In so doing, I do
not wish to imply that in every instance he resolves the problems and
clarifies the ambiguities so far exposed. Indeed, Barth does not discuss all of the major topics already set out and it would in any case
prove unworkable to treat each one in the same detail. Moreover,
Barth's treatment has ambiguities of its own. But I think a chapter
devoted separately to him is nonetheless of value because he is very
instructive on a variety of issues I have taken up (whatever one thinks
about his general position on revelation), he considers some important
issues not yet discussed (e.g., whether agape quite includes the
feature of universality), and there is point in supplementing what has
necessarily been a selective sketch of particular thinkers. I shall follow
roughly the same order of topics as before on the questions he does
consider.

Barth on Equal Regard, Self-Sacrifice, and Mutuality

I will start, then, by asking what normative content Barth accords
to agape. Two features are stressed at a variety of points: equal regard and self-sacrifice. His account of agape as equal regard reflects
the centrality of the feature in most of the literature. He often seems
to assume it nearly as a matter of course. So we read that agape as
neighbor-love means

identification with his interests in utter independence of the
question of his attractiveness, of what he has to offer, of the
reciprocity of the relationship, or repayment in the form of a
similar self-giving. In *agape*-love a man gives himself to another
with no expectation of a return, in a pure venture, even at the
risk of ingratitude, of his refusal to make a response of love.[1]

Here again agape is not dependent on a response and involves simply
caring about the other for his own sake. "Christian love turns to the
other purely for the sake of the other. It does not desire it for itself.
It loves it simply because it is there as this other." [2] A favorite word
in this connection is "interposition" (*Einsatz*); I love the neighbor
as myself when I "stand surety for him," when I make myself responsible for him, when I become his "guarantor" and seek "nothing
else but to be this." [3] One ought to make oneself responsible for him
whether one finds him comparatively more interesting than other
persons or whether one is able to elicit a response from him.

But sometimes Barth construes neighbor-regard in a sense which
risks eliminating any distinction (as discussed in chapter 1) between
identification and permissiveness. In agape, "the loving subject gives
to the other, the object of love, that which it has, which is its own,
which belongs to it." [4] This gift precedes any consideration of the
right or claim the other may have and even the actual use of the
gift. Such radical liberality confirms that the self is not controlled by
private ambition. And this brings in the feature of self-sacrifice, or as
Barth prefers, self-giving (*Hingabe*).[5]

For in Christian love the loving subject reaches back, as it were,
behind itself to that which at the first it denies and from which it
turns away, namely, itself: to give itself . . . away; to give up

---

1. Barth, *Dogmatics*, IV/2:745.
2. Ibid., p. 733.
3. Ibid., p. 819. See also Barth, *Die Kirchliche Dogmatik*, (Zollikon-Zürich:
Evangelischer Verlag A.G. 1955), IV/2:390: "Sie besteht darin, dass Einer für
den Anderen . . . sich selbst einsetzt, sich selbst zu seinem Bürgen macht:
nichts von ihm und mit ihm will als eben: ihm Bürge sein."
4. Ibid.
5. Ibid., p. 730. See Barth, *Die Kirchliche Dogmatik*, IV/2:828.

itself to the one to whom it turns for the sake of this object. To do this the loving man has given up control of himself to place himself under the control of the other, the object of his love. He is free to do this.[6]

Barth does not discuss in this context the difficulties falling under what I have called the question about the blank check. I think however that his preference for "self-giving" rather than "self-sacrifice" is more than fortuitous. Perhaps, unlike Niebuhr, he is preoccupied not so much with loss to the self as with gain for the other. At least references to self-giving seem always explicitly linked to other-regard; one gives by virtue of making oneself the other's guarantor rather than by virtue of abandoning one's own interests. These are close of course and here possibly no more than a nuance separates Barth and Niebuhr. Yet as I shall try to show in the last chapter, it can make an important difference in avoiding certain objections if self-giving is justified only derivatively from other-regard.

What of the feature of mutuality? So far as this refers to relations based on "liking" and "disliking" particular neighbors for reasons having to do solely with their particularity, then it is deliberately contrasted with agape. Liking can prompt many laudable actions toward the other. But it is from the standpoint of agape always flawed because it is never really free from possessiveness. The self finds the other attractive or interesting as an object finally of private enjoyment and perhaps reassurance. This is very different from the second great commandment, identified as interposition.

Christian love for the neighbour and brother does not guarantee that the one will make himself "lovable" to the other in the shallower sense of the term. It begins as such at the very point where the pleasure which men have in one another, and the favours which they may show in consequence, do not necessarily cease, but may very well do so, or for various reasons find no place.[7]

6. Ibid., p. 733.
7. Ibid. Cf. Barth, *Church Dogmatics,* II/2, trans. G. W. Bromiley, J. C. Campbell, Iain Wilson, J. Strathearn McNab, Harold Knight, R. D. Stewart (Edinburgh: T. & T. Clark, 1957), p. 719.

Yet while Barth distinguishes agape and friendship, he does not just oppose them as Kierkegaard is inclined to do. All of us clearly "like" some persons more than others and may be prepared because of this to be kind and generous toward them. It is unnecessary and actually unwise to denounce in the strongest possible terms all such bonds. One must simply be concerned with agape's independence from, not its condemnation of, every relation presupposing liking.

But although Christian love for the neighbour and brother does not exclude this presupposition — it may indeed be realised on this presupposition — it is not in any way tied to it. It does not really depend upon the fact that the one likes another nor does it find realization necessarily in what the one usually does for the other on this presupposition. It may also be realised in an action in which he does not earn his favour or win him to himself.[8]

There may however be another sense of mutuality for Barth, distinctive from "liking" or the other senses discussed in chapter 1, though reappearing with some frequency in the tradition. Agape operates independently of attractiveness but not of religious belief. And belief provides a context of meaning within which agape may be exercised among those *in* the confessing community in a fashion impossible to extend toward those outside it. Agape is not identifiable with a "universal love of humanity."[9] "But — however irksome this may be to those who regard Christian love as a human virtue — it is still a closed circle."[10] Barth qualifies such a statement in several respects. Agape is practiced *for the sake of everyone* just as the community lives for the sake of the world. The restriction to the believing community is "practical" and "provisional" rather than "theoretical" and "definitive." Nevertheless Barth does not quite wish to hold that agape includes the feature of universality.

Two central reasons appear to lie behind the restriction placed on

8. Barth, *Dogmatics*, IV/2:819.
9. Ibid., p. 802.
10. Ibid., p. 804.

agape. The first is scriptural. Barth believes such a conclusion follows unambiguously from biblical exegesis. The second reason has to do with his treatment of agape as a definite action or event in the histories of certain men, a subject to which I shall turn in more detail presently. Precisely as a distinctive event, agape is inextricably linked with faith, and both are *new* actions appropriating the one action of God's grace. Faith as reception is man's response to God's "justifying sentence"; love as self-giving is man's response to God's "direction." [11] They are two different aspects of one event and hence are inseparable. The faith-love correlation places agape in the community as that circle where meaningful communication is possible.

Neither reason seems to me devoid of crucial difficulties. To start with, many exegetical treatments differ from Barth's. The New Testament may not speak with a single voice at this juncture as Barth confidently supposes. At a minimum, a progressive narrowing is often identified, beginning with an implied universalism in Jesus' teaching about the neighbor and finishing with a practical restriction to believers by an early church struggling for its identity in hostile social conditions.[12] And for the bulk of literature I am examining, agape

11. Barth, *Church Dogmatics,* IV/1, trans. G. W. Bromiley (Edinburgh: T. & T. Clark, 1961), pp. 102–03. For a formal statement on the relation between justification and sanctification, see Barth, *Dogmatics,* IV/2: esp. 499–511.

12. The exegetical arguments pro and con are complex and go beyond my concerns here. Among those who trace a change from the universalism implied in Jesus' teaching about the "neighbor" as "man" or "anyone in need" to the narrowing of the conception of "neighbor" in many of the epistles and in the fourth gospel until it was equivalent to "member of the Christian community," see C. Spicq, *Agapé dans le Nouveau Testament,* 3 vols. (Paris: Librairie Lecoffre, 1958–59), English translation (without the extensive footnotes); *Agape in the New Testament,* trans. Sister Marie Aquinas McNamara, O.P. and Sister Mary Honoria Richter, O.P., 3 vols. (St. Louis: B. Herder Book Co., 1963, 1965, 1966); Hugh Montefiore, "Thou Shalt Love thy Neighbour as Thyself," *Novum Testamentum* 5 (1962): 157–70. Cf. also Viktor Warnach, *Agape* (Düsseldorf: Patmos-Verlag, 1951), especially pp. 33–179. For an interesting discussion which proceeds on quite different lines, cf. Krister Stendahl, "Hate, Non-Retaliation, and Love," *Harvard Theological Review* 55 (1962): 343–55. Stendahl concentrates largely on love for those in the community of the faithful as found in both Qumran and biblical texts, but he acknowledges at the end that Matthew 5:44–48 appears to transcend this restriction.

is taken to be universal in its range. Nygren, for instance, accepts that agape plainly includes this feature.[13]

So far as the faith-love correlation is concerned, Barth's point seems to be largely descriptive rather than normative. Agape *can* only flourish in the community: "As it cannot be practised by all, it cannot be meaningfully addressed to all." [14] Here then is a sense of mutuality in which the exchange involves shared meaning; believers address each other within a context of intelligibility not in the first instance public. To be sure, they ought to exemplify "friendliness" to those outside and a readiness to love everyone. But they cannot honestly say that such intelligibility exists or that agape can be practiced apart from faith. Yet difficulties remain, in part because several claims are not always distinguished. It is one thing to say that a life of agape makes sense to believers in that a theological scheme gives it its only, or at least its most adequate, context of intelligibility and justification. It is another to say, however implausibly, that the de facto *exercise* of agape (or an appreciable part of it) is possible only for believers. It is still another to say that the objects of agape should be limited to co-believers. All three claims of course are disputable, but in any event they do not necessarily follow from one another.

The last claim is perhaps the most problematical of all. Ought a definite faith-state, unlike attractiveness, to condition whether and not only how the agent loves? One would have thought that in Barth's view the believer, on his own level and with his own capacities, ought to correspond to God's love, which is surely universal. Furthermore, what is to be made of those passages where Barth takes pains to avoid tacitly condemning erotic man when warrantably rejecting eros?

> But if he is in the hands of God, even erotic man must and will be affirmed in and with the love which is from God. . . . His

13. Nygren, *Agape and Eros*, pp. 63–64. While he does not construe universality in scope as agape's most distinctive feature, it is clearly part of the content. He cites in support not only the synoptic gospels but also Galatians 3:28. See also Häring, *Law of Christ*, 2:360–73.

14. Barth, *Dogmatics*, IV/2:805.

erotic love will not be affirmed. But he himself will be affirmed as the man which he does not cease to be even as he loves erotically. . . . And this affirmation proclaims his reconciliation; the fact that God has loved, and loves, and will love even him.[15]

Barth seems here to refer not just to the erotic man who also is in some sense a believer. Several pages earlier, moreover, Barth speaks of the representatives of eros-love and the *caritas*-synthesis as objects of a Christian love which has both "ecumenical and missionary power."[16] So one may be forced to conclude either that Barth is on occasion internally inconsistent about whether believers ought to love those outside the community or that the practical restriction of agape to the community is entirely descriptive and not at all normative. Clearly passages exist which support the former reading. And even if one takes the latter reading as more typical, some difficulties still are not easily met. I shall note here the difficulties which bear most directly on the normative features of agape identified previously.

If one says that agape as independent self-giving ought to guide each believer's actions, but that in fact such self-giving is never realized except between believers, then "ought implies can" in only a restricted sense. One ought to "stand surety" for every neighbor with whom one has to do, but one can only when special conditions obtain so far as the recipient is concerned. A more likely reading is that two different meanings have simply attached themselves to the same word. The first was set out earlier: agape as neighbor-love means "identification with his interests in utter independence of the question of his

15. Ibid., p. 748.
16. Ibid., p. 738. See also his discussion of what the believing community owes to the world in *Church Dogmatics*, III/4, trans. A. T. MacKay, *et al.* (Edinburgh: T. & T. Clark, 1961). For example: "It is the circle of love directed towards the neighbour as such, i.e., the fellow-man as he is without the Gospel, namely, the stranger, the non-Christian, the enemy perhaps, the man who is openly or secretly godless. If this neighbour experiences opposition, hatred, contempt, or even indifference from this circle . . . , if a different wind from that of genuine human freedom blows on him, how can he attend and listen to the testimony of the freedom of the Spirit, of the kingdom and grace, which is supposedly borne to him?" (p. 503).

attractiveness, of what he has to offer, of the reciprocity of the relationship. . . ." A second meaning has to do with the particular sense
of mutuality as shared meaning within a context of communal intelligibility. One should note again the difference between this sense
and the more common ones considered in the first chapter. The response which interests the agent is not pursued for the sake of some
personal reassurance or other private benefit. No, the reciprocity now
envisaged involves confirmation of one's existence as a believer by the
other, and vice versa. Even after one grants this distinctive sense of
mutuality, however, some of the same general questions apply about
the relation between the features of independent self-giving and mutuality. Mutuality may, in Barth's sense as well, supplement independent self-giving as appropriate, internal fruition. It simply happens
that a full disclosure of meaning occurs only between believers. Agape
positively requires regard for everyone affected by one's actions, but
allowance is made for a special richness in that particular disclosure of
meaning to which the agent may appropriately aspire yet which happens solely within the community. To say more may occasion conceptual incompatibility. For agape as equal regard enjoins the agent
to attend to those characteristics all men share, apart from what
differentiates men from one another. When faith is understood as a
particular historical event which occurs only to certain men, then its
presence in the recipient cannot constitute a condition for agape's
presence in the agent, or else such agape is not independent after all.
The special richness of shared meaning which faith affords cannot
therefore — without conceptual confusion — be taken as a condition
in the strict sense for agape's presence or absence in the agent.

The notion of faith and love as definite events happening to certain
men will become clearer as I examine Barth's treatment of self-love,
especially in relation to eros. I shall also mention in the last chapter
one other plausible way to construe the faith-love correlation, though
it is not very explicitly considered by Barth.

Love for God and Neighbor-Love

To the question of whether there is anything in the phrase
"love for God" that is not more adequately treated either as faith or

as neighbor-love, Barth responds in the affirmative. In so doing he seems to agree at least partly with Catholic formulations. Unlike Nygren, he is not disposed to prohibit anything but passivity. Barth affirms a distinctive creaturely freedom in relation to God that is more than pure reception and yet not a matter of nefarious human spontaneity. A man "makes use of" such creaturely freedom by giving himself to God, by (a phrase Barth continually uses) putting himself at God's disposal. When Barth speaks of this self-giving, his affirmations seem not unlike those in the Catholic tradition concerning the final referral of all things to God. However banal it may sound, loving God is being supremely and finally interested in Him.

> He is this not merely peripherally but centrally; not merely momentarily but — no matter how often he may forget or deny it — in the continuity of his existence, of his life-act. . . . And the basic note in the life of the Christian as the man who loves God is that . . . everywhere and constantly and repeatedly, with a definiteness which cannot be excelled, in a way which cannot be said of the other things and factors which interest and claim and gladden and trouble him, or of other men or the whole world or even himself, He has significance as the axiom of all axioms.[17]

In terms of human conduct, moreover, Barth denies that neighbor-love exhaustively defines love for God. Here he shifts deliberately from an earlier period in his own thought. In a comparatively recent *excursus* he attests to joining forces with a group (including Nygren) during that period which regarded all direct love for God as an "erotico-religious" aberration.

> The only thing is that we were a little late with our protest, since the final and true epogee of the type of love rejected was long since past. It lived on only in the form of reminiscences and repristinations. There was no obvious superfluity of living mystics

17. Barth, *Dogmatics,* IV/2:793–94.

and pietists of the first rank, and therefore no acute danger from this angle.[18]

The opposite aberration manifested itself in such protest by "identifying the Christian act of love on practice *only* with obedience in love for one's neighbour." [19]

> We imagined that we had freed ourselves from Mysticism, Pietism and Romanticism and their dangerous off-shoots. But were we not on the point of subscribing to a no less dubious antithesis (that of A. Ritschl and his disciples and successors), according to which the work of the Holy Spirit must be reduced to the management of an eternal working-day, and with the abolition of a true and direct love for God and Jesus there is basically no place for prayer? There was scope for better instruction at this point.[20]

In his own way, then, Barth concludes against Brunner that there are human actions which properly refer to love for God and cannot be translated without loss into neighbor-love. He repudiates explicitly Brunner's contention that two sets of duties divide hopelessly the object of human action between God and man so that denigration of ordinary earthly life inevitably follows.

> Though a man cannot for a moment withdraw from his obligation to his neighbour by fleeing to a special religious sphere, and though there exist neither general human undertakings nor particular pious practices by which he could and should gain, augment or preserve the divine good-pleasure, yet only on the basis of a very strained exegesis of Mk. 12:29f., and its parallels could we say that the commandment to love our neighbour in some sense absorbs that to love God and takes away its independent quality. The truth is rather that the double command to

18. Ibid., p. 795.
19. Ibid. Italics mine.
20. Ibid.

love points us to two spheres of activity which are relatively — no more, but very clearly so — distinct.[21]

What are examples of activities within these two spheres each of which constitutes a legitimate part of Christian ethics? Barth enumerates them:

Alongside work there is also prayer; alongside practical love for one's brother there is also divine service in the narrower sense; alongside activity in state and community there is also that in the congregation; alongside the other sciences there is also theology. And obviously all these and similar activities are to be regarded also as command and duty, as a matter of human action.[22]

Neither sort of activity, in short, totally coincides with the other nor is to be depreciated in relation to the other. Love of neighbor does not completely absorb the concrete activities involved in love for God. On the other hand, the practice of contemplation, meditation, oblation, and the like, never justifies indifference, evasion or injustice toward the neighbor.[23]

Barth is not unaware of another sort of question which can be addressed particularly to those who distinguish faith and love for God and who thereby refer to two separable kinds of activity. In stressing the distinction between love for God and love for neighbor (or at least their non-identity in terms of specifiable creaturely actions) is one dividing his devotion inconsistently in two directions? Can he love at the same time two such qualitatively different objects? This is a perennial question and has been posed recently by Charles Hartshorne with reference to the two great commandments.

One hundred per cent of our interest (mind), devotion (heart), energy (strength), and whatever else is in us (soul) is to have

21. Barth, *Dogmatics*, III/4:48–49.
22. Ibid., p. 49.
23. Cf. Barth, *Church Dogmatics*, I/2, trans. G. T. Thomson and Harold Knight (Edinburgh: T. & T. Clark, 1956), p. 434.

God as its object. It follows that if there be anything additional
to God, it must receive zero attention! Yet we are to love ourselves
and our fellows. A contradiction? Yes, save upon one assumption,
that there cannot be anything "additional to God." Rather, all
actuality must be included in His actuality, and all possibility in
His potential actuality.[24]

I cannot of course consider here Hartshorne's own way of treating
the problem through the metaphysics of God's actuality, including the
actuality of the neighbor. But Barth addresses himself to the question in his own way. He contends that the first commandment is
the commandment of and in all others. If there is to be a second
expressly distinct from it only three explanations concerning the relation between them appear to Barth to be possible. First, the second
commandment is *another* demand also absolute "in the strict and
proper sense." [25] Second, the two commandments are to be *identified;*
each is to be construed as the other. Third, the second is *subordinated*
to the first; it is simply "the first and most important of the particular, relative and subordinate commands, within which . . . the
commandment to love God forms the real nerve and content." [26]

Each of these three explanations is considered in turn, rejected in
the form in which it was initially stated, and then reformulated to
agree in part with the others. The first explanation is objected to
for exegetical reasons. The very brevity of the second commandment,
Barth maintains, rules out any transfer of what is contained in the
first. There are not two Gods to be loved exclusively and totally and
therefore the same love cannot be demanded in both cases. The truth
in this first explanation is that in reacting to both commandments
one is reacting to God's command; they share a common source. Each
commandment claims man absolutely, "and absolutely for God." [27]

24. Charles Hartshorne, *The Logic of Perfection and Other Essays in Neo-
classical Metaphysics* (Lasalle, Illinois: Open Court Publishing Company, 1962),
pp. 40–41.
25. Barth, *Dogmatics,* I/2:402.
26. Ibid.
27. Ibid., p. 409.

But man stands in and between "two times and worlds" and exists before and for God in two distinguishable ways.

> It is the same God speaking to the same man. He speaks to him in two ways, because he exists in two ways. But because it is the same God who speaks and the same man who listens, in both cases an absolute obedience is demanded. Two absolute commandments? No, but two commandments of the one absolute Lord, so that they both have absolute significance for the same man as God has determined and without competing the one with the other.[28]

The second explanation may imply a crude equation of God and neighbor which Barth regards as blasphemous. He believes that the explanation may have a milder and more sophisticated version where identity is founded upon the experience of human love. According to this version, since love for God is known and "necessarily determined" by love between men, it can at the very most be the "supreme norm" or the "hypostasised expression" of such human love. Barth is aware that such a milder view does not intend systematically to reduce love for God to an illusory projection, but he believes that it is nonetheless embarrassingly vulnerable to purely projectionist conclusions. Yet in this second explanation too one may see the entirely acceptable interest in affirming the final unity of these two loves. But such unity is a matter of revelation rather than general knowledge or experience; in this life it may be believed but it cannot be perceived. Man cannot escape the "two-foldness" of his existence; neither, therefore, can he ignore the twofold nature of the command given to him. The identification of the two loves must always remain a matter of deontological passion.

> If we try to love God as the neighbour, it will not be the God whom we are commanded to love. And if we try to love the neighbour as God, it will not be the neighbour whom we are commanded to love. If we are not to deviate from the divine

28. Ibid.

revelation, if we really want to obey the one commandment of God, we can only love God and our neighbour. The desire to experience the unity of these commandments, and corresponding speculation about that unity, must be suppressed for the sake of the true unity of the commandment and of obedience to it.[29]

From all that has been said, it is not surprising that Barth treats the third explanation (where the second commandment is subordinate to the first) as more adequate than the first two. But even this explanation must not be clumsily formulated. Subordination must not be taken to signify, according to Barth, a slackening of divine seriousness, as if neighbor-love were a purely secondary decision. In this sense there is no subordination. Neighbor-love no less than love for God is the opposite of human caprice; each is on the same level of seriousness. But the third explanation is correct in pointing to the distinction between "the two times and worlds."

> The two times and worlds are not symmetrical. They do not balance each other. The one prevails over the other. That which comes and remains has the priority and superiority over that which now is and passes. . . . It is therefore quite right that in the text of Matthew the commandment to love God should be described not only as the first, but also as the "great" commandment. It is in fact the basic and comprehensive commandment, the greater circle which includes in itself the lesser commandment of love to the neighbour.[30]

The conclusion which must not be drawn from this, however, is that love of neighbor allows for a greater degree of arbitrary human decision. Neighbor-love is admittedly less permanent; it is a "sign" rather than "a completed and eternal work." But it is contained within the total divine commandment to love and, while subordinate, participates in its absoluteness.[31] Man's response to God is embodied necessarily if not exhaustively in his regard for the neighbor.

29. Ibid., p. 410.
30. Ibid.
31. Ibid., p. 411.

Self-Love

Barth has grave misgivings about even using the term "self-love."
"Love must always have an opposite, an object. . . . What we love
— if we love at all — is always something else or someone else." [32]
It is therefore hardly surprising that he does not find in the self-love
referred to in the second great commandment something independently laudable. At most self-love is not blameworthy; it does not
need to be especially encouraged. People have more than enough
unreflective attachment to it. "God will never think of blowing on
this fire, which is bright enough already." [33]

> It is true that this self-love is the visible and tangible reality of
> the one who loves his neighbour. The commandment itself recog-
> nises and establishes it to be true. But the commandment:
> Thou shalt love thy neighbour, is not a legitimation but a limi-
> tation of this reality.[34]

Such an assessment seems often close to Nygren's, as when Barth
writes "When I love my neighbor, I confess that my self-love is not
a good thing, that it is not love at all. I begin to love at all only
when I love my neighbor." [35]

Yet Barth occasionally appreciates more than Nygren the positive
need for natural self-identity and dignity. Though normally Barth
does not refer to such identity as self-love, it clearly possesses some
of the characteristics which others have described by that name. This
is particularly the case in his treatment of personal relations, relations which he thinks do not deny but rather require individual
responsibility and liberty. "On both sides . . . the being has its own
validity, dignity and self-certainty." [36] The I and the Thou are not

32. Ibid., p. 388.
33. Ibid.
34. Ibid.
35. Ibid., p. 450.
36. Barth, *Church Dogmatics*, III/2, trans. G. W. Bromiley, R. H. Fuller,
Harold Knight, and J. K. S. Reid (Edinburgh: T. & T. Clark, 1960), p. 248.

interchangeable; reciprocity involves meeting but not union. Each must receive the other's speech and assistance. Neither can neglect or abandon his own task and life. The bond between them must not become a matter of belonging in which one is the other's property.[37] Independent identification with another's interests should not be confused with total loss of self in the other. Another context in which some positive valuation occurs is more directly theological. It makes sense to talk of a dignity applicable to all men, including oneself, which depends on grace and not on individual merit. So we read, for example, on the general subject of "respect for life": "The freedom for life to which man is summoned by the command of God is the freedom to treat as a loan both the life of all men with his own and his own with that of all men." [38] Life in oneself as well as others ought to be assessed as a gift to be valued wholly apart from idiosyncratic successes and failures.

Such self-identity and dignity are acknowledged to be necessary, but rarely extolled. This is even more the case with the explicit account of agape. The normative content always involves self-giving; agape is opposed, if not to natural self-assertion as such, at least to the — seemingly inevitable — "uncritical intensification and strengthening" of this assertion. Only in a realm transcending the agent's own causes and possessions can one speak of unintended "exaltation, gain and joy" for the one who loves agapeistically.[39]

Barth elaborates on self-love in his consideration of eros. This is another point where reconciliation of individual statements within the corpus is difficult if not impossible. I shall mention two senses of eros important for Barth, but then set them largely on one side. The first concerns eros as an expression of something characteristic of human nature. Barth believes that the "secret of humanity," its indestructible nature, is the primordial bond *between* men, the state of being *for* others.

> Properly and at its deepest level, which is also its highest, human nature is not isolated but dual. It does not consist in the freedom

37. Ibid., p. 269.
38. Barth, *Dogmatics,* III/4:335.
39. Barth, *Dogmatics,* IV/2:788.

of a heart closed to the fellow-man, but in that of a heart open to the fellow-man. It does not consist in the refusal of man to see the fellow-man and to be seen by him, to speak with him and listen to him, to receive his assistance and render assistance to him. It does not consist in an indifference in which he might just as well be disposed for these things as not. But it consists in an unequivocal inclination for them. Man is human in the fact that he is with his fellow-man gladly.[40]

In the eros of ancient Hellenism the element of *gladness* was stressed unforgettably. "The Greeks with their eros . . . grasped the fact that the being of man is free, radically open, willing, spontaneous, joyful, cheerful, and gregarious." [41]

A second sense refers to the particular love between a particular man and woman and encompasses "understanding, self-giving and desire." [12] Here again the value judgment is positive in that the life-partnership of marriage is based on eros-love in this sense. Barth argues that de Rougemont neglects such eros-love and so must found marriage merely on decision and resolution.[43] To sever eros-love from marriage has for Barth no compelling theological or other warrant. In the context then of considering the indispensable basis for marriage, Barth commends a "sanctified eros." [44]

The question of the relation between the two senses above and the third seems one of almost impenetrable obscurity. I think one may fairly say that Barth attaches distinct (and sometimes incompatible) meanings to the same word without always stopping to acknowledge it. His treatment of eros seems a classic example of how a single word may drift uncertainly between distinct experiences and different concepts. The third sense of eros carries a negative valuation. He depicts it (in a way vaguely reminiscent of the "aesthetic stage" in Kierkegaard) as wholly confined to a melancholy cycle of enthusiasm

40. Barth, *Dogmatics*, III/2:278.
41. Ibid., p. 283.
42. Barth, *Dogmatics*, III/4: e.g., 219.
43. Ibid., p. 201.
44. Ibid., p. 220.

and disenchantment, acquisition and loss.[45] Yet the third sense is especially interesting because it is most explicitly compared and contrasted with agape. Perhaps it also reflects the influence of Nygren. In any event, the contrast between eros and agape is strongest here, whereas one could argue that the first two senses of eros are completely compatible with agape.

Eros in this third sense is distinguished above all by acquisitiveness.

> It does not have its origin in self-denial, but in a distinctively uncritical intensification and strengthening of natural self-assertion. It is in this that the loving subject finds itself summoned and stirred to turn to another. It is hungry, and demands the food that the other seems to hold out. This is the reason for its interest in the other. It needs it because of its intrinsic value and in pursuance of an end. As this other promises something — itself in one of its properties — there is the desire to possess and control and enjoy it. Man wants it for himself: for the upholding, magnifying, deepening, broadening, illuminating or enriching of his own existence: or perhaps simply in a need to express himself: or perhaps even more simply in the desire to find satisfaction in all his unrest.[46]

However much such a man may appear to forget or transcend himself, his governing interest is some prospective state of his own. Various objects may be used and consumed, ranging from the sensual to the religious. In relation to every object eros "will always be a grasping, taking, possessive love . . . and in some way and at some point it will always betray itself as such."[47] All the attitudes and actions of someone effectively controlled by eros will be tainted by efforts to realize "his own entelechy, i.e., in needing and therefore in seeking, desiring and successfully finding and enjoying himself in his particularity."[48]

45. Barth, *Dogmatics*, IV/2: e.g., 788.
46. Ibid., p. 734.
47. Ibid., pp. 734–35.
48. Ibid., p. 739.

How then are eros and agape compared and contrasted? Barth
proceeds through seven "steps." First, one is dealing with man as
such in either case so that however much the two loves are distinct
in direction and determination, they have to do with one kind of
human being rather than two.[49] This signifies, secondly, a denial by
Barth that agape and eros are properties of human nature. Neither
kind of love refers simply to the raw material. Both loves are "historical determinations of human nature." [50] The same human being may
love in one way or the other so that agape and eros are matters of
personal history. It simply turns out that man *does* always love in
these two ways.

Third, both loves are self-expressive in a basic and determinative
sense: they effectively govern an entire personal history.

Fourth, and this really amplifies Barth's initial observation, the
same man expresses the same nature in both agape and eros, but in
contrary patterns. Man's particular existence rather than his nature
is altered.

> The only thing is that, as man loves in one way or the other,
> it comes upon him that the one unchangeable, perennial human
> nature is put by him to a very different use and given a very
> different character.[51]

This leads Barth to a fifth and formal statement. Though agape
and eros only affect human nature in terms of use and character
they do in this manner have a "distinctive relationship" to it. In
human nature they share a common point of departure and accordingly they may be legitimately compared. "They are both new in
relation to this human nature, but they both take place in connexion
with it." [52]

> *Agape*-love takes place in correspondence and *eros*-love in con-
> tradiction to this nature; the one as its "analogue" and the

49. Barth, *Dogmatics,* IV/2:741.
50. Ibid.
51. Ibid., p. 742.
52. Ibid., p. 743.

other as its "catalogue"; the one as man does that which is right
in relation to it, and the other as he does that which is not right
in relation to it. *Agape*-love takes place in affinity, *eros*-love in
opposition to human nature.[53]

Barth next undertakes material substantiation of such a statement.
His sixth step is to affirm that man essentially, naturally, and originally belongs to God. "Man cannot escape or destroy or lose or alter
the fact that it is only in this that he is truly and naturally and
essentially a man." [54] In the personal history of each man there must
be a decision whether and to what degree he will conform to this
original relationship.

> *Agape*-love consists in the fact that he accepts God as his eternal
> Counterpart. . . . *Agape* consists in the orientation of human
> nature on God in a movement which does not merely express
> it but means that it is transcended, since in it man gives himself
> up to be genuinely freed by and for God, and therefore to be
> free from self-concern and free for the service of God. *Eros*-love
> consists in this respect in the new thing (which is absurd in
> relation to human nature) that man shuts off himself against
> this freedom.[55]

The seventh and final step is to affirm that it is also essential,
natural, and original for man to be with the fellow-man. I have already alluded to this "secret of humanity."

> In *agape*-love the essential fellow-humanity of man is respected.
> For the one who loves in this way there can be no opposition or
> neutrality in relation to the other. In his love there takes place
> the encounter of I and Thou, the open perception of the other
> and self-disclosure to him, conversation with him, the offering

53. Ibid.
54. Ibid.
55. Ibid., pp. 743–44.

and receiving of assistance, and all this with joy. . . . The same cannot be said of *eros*-love. In most cases this does, of course, consist in an address to one's fellow, and perhaps with considerable warmth and intensity. But as in relation to God, so also to his fellow, the man who loves erotically is not really thinking of the other but of himself. His fellow is envisaged only as an expected increase and gain for his own existence, as an acquisition, a booty, a prey, to be used by him in the pursuance of some purpose.[56]

In chapter 2 I distinguished between the claim that acquisitive self-love is a discriminable set of attitudes and actions which has reappeared with depressing persistence throughout human history, and the claim that acquisitive self-love constitutes the sole spring of behavior, identical for every man. The latter is tantamount to psychological egoism where men pursue their own individual and private satisfaction and cannot help pursuing it. At the deepest level all aims are genetically derived from and may be reductively analyzed into one and only one. Barth's treatment of eros as acquisitive self-love seems clearly to fall under the first claim. It turns out that men always do love either in the fashion of eros or agape. But both are new in relation to human nature rather than being properties of it. Thus Barth in stressing eros as acquisitive self-love does not propound a version of psychological egoism. He distinguishes a characterization of "human nature" and a characterization of eros. The former has to do with the primordial bond between men.

The conceptual distinction between human nature and eros separates Barth and Nygren at this juncture. Barth believes his position reflects a substantive theological difference from that of Nygren which is subject, in Barth's view, to some "strangely manichean tendencies." "If it is really God who rules the world and not the devil, does not every abyss — without ceasing to be such, and as such to be dangerous — have a bottom somewhere?" [57] Agape would be curiously at odds with itself if its own character were assured only through in-

56. Ibid., pp. 745–46.
57. Ibid., p. 741.

sisting on the antithesis.[58] Thus Barth's final stress — representative of his entire theology — is on the sense in which agape lives in but not by the opposition to eros. Moreover, Barth goes on to admit that both loves are experientially present in the believer and that one must take care not to be condescending in his denunciations. The believer moves between the two loves; he lives always in the tension on the way from eros toward agape.

It is difficult to make entirely precise Barth's claims in his treatment of agape and eros. On the one side, he seems to hold that in every historical period all of the actions of all men are effectively governed by *either* agape or eros. On the other side, as we have seen, he appears to hold that in every historical period all of the actions of all men reflect the influence of *both* agape and eros, the former as laudably other-regarding, the latter constantly corrupting. That is, Barth seems formally to distinguish between agape and eros in accordance with the first claim. Yet he also acknowledges an experiential co-presence between acquisitiveness and other-regard which seems closer to the second. But nothing very definite is forthcoming about how these claims might conceivably connect. In the case of the first, an important assumption appears to be that at the most basic level a single, determining ground of attitudes and actions obtains and that this ground is either agape or eros. Which ground governs the actions of particular persons may not perhaps be ascertainable by men, but only by God. Nevertheless a single ground is affirmed as characteristic of every man. However impure the appearances and however inscrutable the ground, no intermediate state of affairs exists. Each man loves in one way or the other and thereby gives a distinctive character to his perennial human nature. He incorporates either agape or eros as the supreme standard governing his own personal history. In the second claim above, no such single ground is affirmed to exist as the sole determining spring of action. Any notion of two absolutely discrete kinds of personal history, at whatever hidden recess of motivation, is rejected. Agape and eros refer to kinds of influences to which all men are alternately susceptible and whose comparative governance is a matter of degree. One may admit the

58. Ibid., pp. 746–47.

importance of distinguishing conceptually agape and eros as in the
first claim, but insist that so far as experience is concerned, the second
sets the boundaries. Probably Barth is closer to my account of the
second, though it is not easy always to be certain. The general point
then is that in the case of agape as well as eros, claims about effective
governance may differ, such differences are often glossed over (by
Barth and many others as well), and questions of possible incompat-
ability between claims are raised all too infrequently.

Subsidiary Rules

Barth has been repeatedly grouped with men like Brunner, Dietrich
Bonhoeffer, and Paul Lehmann, all of whom are thought to propound what I shall call theological contextualism. There are affinities
and differences between this position and situation ethics as espoused
by Fletcher which it is well to identify. Generally Barth and others
hold that the divine sovereignty is fundamentally infringed upon unless there is a final sense in which it is *God* who commands in the
present moment. To quote Brunner:

> The fact that the holiness of God must be remembered when
> we dwell on His love means that we cannot have His love at our
> disposal, that it cannot ever be perceived as a universal principle,
> but only in the act in which He speaks to us Himself.[59]

God's loving command is *His* command and we can never anticipate
it or formulate a rule to express it. The event of hearing the command
sometimes appears to connote an immediacy of a staggering kind,
where human deliberative or interpretive processes are seemingly suspended:

> Casuistical ethics makes the objectively untenable assumption that
> the command of God is a universal rule, an empty form, or
> rather a tissue of such rules and forms. As in the case of human
> law, it thus requires to be filled out by concrete and specific ap-

59. Brunner, *Divine Imperative*, pp. 117–18.

plication to come into force as a command. Now this may well
be necessary for the "form of the good" and similar philosophical
epitomes of the moral law. But the case is very different with
the command of the living God. This is given to man not only
universally and formally but in concrete fullness and with definite-
ness of content. . . . It is always an individual command for
the conduct of this man, at this moment and in this situation; a
prescription for this case of his; a prescription for the choice of
a definite possibility of human intention, decision and action. It
commands not only how man is to think and act here and now,
but also quite specifically what is to take place inwardly in his
mind and thoughts and outwardly in what he does or refrains
from doing. It leaves nothing to human choice or preference. It
thus requires no interpretation to come into force. To the last and
smallest detail it is self-interpreted.[60]

On the human side, the alternatives tend to be reduced to an either/or,
to a matter of someone's final loyalty. Nothing must interfere with the
ultimately decisive issue in every human life: whether a person perceives his life as a divine gift which at the same time claims his
supreme devotion. The preoccupation on the part of Barth and others
is, *that* a person love and that a person love in *definite* ways attesting
to a fundamental seriousness (Barth polemicizes against a "mere"
attitude or inner disposition), but *not* that a person love in ways which
can be definitively specified in advance.

It is this latter endeavor which Barth and others find objectionable
and which make them highly suspicious of "casuistry" (I shall not
discuss whether their understanding is really a caricature of such an
enterprise). For there must be nothing finally obstructing the relation between the One who commands in love and the human response
of agape in which the self qua self is engaged. But "code morality,"
it is alleged, is *religiously* perilous because it may provide just such a

60. Barth, *Dogmatics,* III/4:11–12. Cf. Brunner, *Divine Imperative,* p. 117;
Dietrich Bonhoeffer, *Ethics,* ed. Eberhard Bethge (New York: The Macmillan
Company, 1955), pp. 161–62; Paul Lehmann, *Ethics in a Christian Context*
(New York: Harper and Row, 1963), p. 77; H. Richard Niebuhr, *The Responsi-
ble Self* (New York: Harper & Row, 1963), p. 67.

diversionary occasion. However praiseworthy specific rules and laws might be in themselves, they may furnish a sublime opportunity for corruption on the highest level. They may prompt a fatal shift in priorities, where the self turns away from the God who commands in order to deliberate in advance on what ought to happen to the loving man, what specifically he must do. This may in turn encourage human presumption by at least implying that man has the immanental capacity to perceive God's command, that this perception *pertains* to man as such (rather than continually *accruing* to him). Whenever such an implication is drawn, the basis for confidence will have disastrously shifted. Thus there must be no doubt, in Barth's view, about the most essential task of ethical reflection:

> [E]thical theory is not meant to provide man with a program the implementation of which would be his life's goal. Nor is it meant to present man with principles to be interpreted, applied, and put into practice. . . . Ethics exists to remind man of his confrontation with God, who is the light illuminating all his actions.[61]

Barth and others do not deny that there is also "constancy and continuity" in God's command. Definite relationships and structures are admitted to be more or less permanently present, whether these be "spheres" (Barth), "orders" (Brunner), or "mandates" (Bonhoeffer), to which love applies and in reference to which most of the standard moral questions can be considered (e.g., sexuality, war, euthanasia, etc.). Indeed, when Barth considers particular moral issues he is often surprisingly (and I think inconsistently) definite about attitudes and actions expressly enjoined or forbidden. There are, it turns out, rather pronounced constancies or continuities in God's command. To cite but one example:

> The command of God shows him irrefutably — in clear contradiction to his own theories — that as a man he can only be

61. Karl Barth, *The Humanity of God,* trans. Thomas Wieser (Richmond: John Knox Press, 1963), p. 86.

genuinely human with woman, or as a woman with man. In proportion as he accepts this insight, homosexuality can have no place in his life, whether in its more refined or cruder forms.[62]

Such a judgment appears binding in every relevant situation. It seems virtually exceptionless.

Which of these sides predominates in Barth's corpus, the contextual or the constant, is a matter of legitimate dispute. I am mainly interested now, however, in Barth's opposition to a legalism which he believes extrinsic to the fundamental purposes of his theology. Barth wishes to consider (whether he does so consistently or successfully is another matter) special moral issues without jeopardizing the claim that it is really God who commands and is to be obeyed at every moment. In relation to the legalism he opposes, he is content to grant the possibility of "conditional imperatives," "signposts," or "approximate criteria" which provide directions for individuals and groups.[63] Even the biblical injunctions such as those found in the Decalogue and the Sermon on the Mount are, for Brunner, unsystematic and "casual" examples of the infinitely varied life of love. They are not generalized "cases" or "instances" which anticipate particular decisions.[64]

Certainly there are some obvious affinities between Barth, Brunner, Bonhoeffer, and Lehmann, on the one hand, and a situationist like Fletcher on the other. The references to "conditional imperatives" and the like are in some respects akin to illuminative maxims. Yet there is a determinative difference, however much the former group may have influenced the latter. This difference is illustrated by Fletcher's criticism of the view of the conscience found in Lehmann as "pretentious, pride-prone," and "non-rational," a "guidance theory, at-

62. Barth, *Dogmatics,* III/4:166.
63. Ibid., pp. 86–88; John C. Godsey, ed., *Karl Barth's Table Talk* (Edinburgh: Oliver & Boyd, 1963), p. 82. See also Barth, *Against the Stream,* ed. Ronald Gregor Smith (New York: Philosophical Library, 1954), esp. p. 29.
64. Brunner, *Divine Imperative,* pp. 135–39. See also Joseph Sittler, *The Structure of Christian Ethics* (Baton Rouge: Louisiana State University Press, 1958), pp. 48–57.

tributing moral choices to God's guidance in some unspecified way." [65]
For Fletcher conscience is not a power "either innate or ambient" but
is more like a "function." It is basically an "emotionally untied" rational judgment. The rationality Fletcher has in mind is thoroughly
empirical and "data-centered." There is a suspicion of any claim that
the divine command leaves nothing to human choice or preference,
expressed as follows: "[M]en have to decide for themselves what the
loving will of God, known in principle by faith, can and shall mean
in any concrete situation." [66] On the other side, one can imagine
that someone like Barth would be wary of Fletcher's apparently total
reliance on human judgments for the content of every moral decision.
Barth might see here the figure of the human titan who stands at the
crossroads and decides whether and how he will obey and love. (It
is interesting to note that each side might accuse the other of being
"pride-prone"; one is too certain about God's command and the
other too confident that men can decide for themselves.) This difference may be summarized in the distinction between theological
contextualism and empirical situationism.

Virtue

Barth reflects the Protestant suspicion described in chapter 5 about
independent attention to the subject of virtue. He too extols repetition
rather than growth. Grace is to be seen as new every morning. Men
cannot hope to lessen their dependence on it. And every moment
offers a new occasion for disobedience. Barth is skeptical of the
motives of those who devote much of their time and effort to the
discussion of virtue. In a theological context at least, there is the opportunity for the same kind of corruption referred to earlier. A shift in
priorities may occur, where the agent gazes fixedly at himself, concentrates on what *he* ought to do, or what interior state *he* should
foster. Such a shift carries enormous risks. Whenever these seem
lightly taken, it may be because human exemplifications of love are

65. Fletcher, "What's in a Rule?", pp. 340–41.
66. Fletcher, "Situation Ethics Under Fire," p. 167.

fatally preferred. In practice if not in formal organization, sanctification may absorb justification and sanctification itself pass into the praise of human nobility.

Given this skepticism, it is hardly surprising that Barth does not address many questions noted in chapter 5. In most of his references to human agape he talks in general of doing rather than being. For example, I also said earlier that he polemicizes against a "mere" attitude or inner disposition. He prefers to stress overt actions and utterances. Consider this statement.

> The . . . idea that we have to reject is that in the human response to God's love we have only a correspondence in disposition or in thought and emotion. This is false because in the love of God we do not have to do primarily with a disposition or with thought and emotion but with an act which God has willed and executed with all the energy of the crucifixion. It is this act which is the basis, the creative model, of true human love. If the latter is its imitation, it too is an act, and not merely an internal but an external act, the act of the whole man.[67]

The account of imitation is thus incorporated into dominant strands in his theology. Human agape as act is imitative of divine love which is likewise "act" rather than "being"; a reality which, because it is an event, never "is" but only "occurs." [68]

But this preference is expressed in very general terms. The relations between judgments of character and conduct identified in chapter 5 are not closely considered. However, Barth has interesting and more specific things to say on issues discussed in that chapter under the heading of grace and personal agency. There I anticipated by observing that Barth appears to want his own version of elicitation, where grace frees man to do what he cannot do by himself and where the creaturely response, while genuinely a response, is never considered in itself more than creaturely.

Barth rejects most of the account of agape as an instrument of in-

67. Barth, *Dogmatics,* IV/2:786. See also p. 742.
68. Barth, *Dogmatics,* II/2:548.

vading grace. He agrees with Nygren that there is no consequent accretion of power in the agent which is then at his disposal, proper to him as such. And he also claims with Nygren that grace intervenes decisively and awakens effectively.[69] But he repudiates Nygren's references to the creature as the tube or channel through which grace flows. Barth labels as "theomonistic" the conception of human agape as a prolongation or continuation of God's love. Such a conception does justice, he thinks, neither to the qualitative difference between Creator and creature nor to the free character of human love for God. The object of the divine initiative must be a correspondingly free act.

> At the climax of his book . . . Nygren has the following train of thought under the heading: "The Christian as the Channel of God's Downstreaming Love." Not man, but God Himself, is the subject of Christian love. But He is so in such a way that divine love uses the Christian as its tool and instrument. . . . It is the view of Luther . . . that the Christian is set between God and his neighbor as an "instrument" "which receives from above and gives out below, like a vessel or pipe through which the stream of divine bounty should flow unceasingly to others." Now, with due respect to Luther, this is the view which I must set aside at the very outset and carefully avoid in all my future deliberations. Have we been released from *eros* only to say the more pietistically about *agape* that which effaces all clear contours and destroys all healthy distances? It seems to me that if we are to say anything really worth while at this point we must say much less than this.[70]

Barth also assesses critically the Catholic account of infused and acquired virtue. He has some hard things to say of Peter Lombard for

69. Occasionally these claims seem nearly as unreserved as Nygren's. He maintains at one point for instance that God creates new and different loving men (*Dogmatics*, IV/2:776–77). Yet on the other side he argues that the reason human agape is in fact so infinitesimal is that the Holy Spirit only liberates man for his own action, and man is responsible for an all-too-conspicuous frailty. Such frailty should be openly acknowledged.

70. Ibid., p. 752.

example, who, he believes, identifies love for God and neighbor with
the Holy Spirit: "In the Christian life of man the Holy Spirit Himself
replaces the human *motus animi*." [71] Barth believes that such a view
verges on the magical and he endorses some of the criticism by
Thomas Aquinas against Lombard. Acquinas contends, according to
Barth, that human love can only participate in divine love and in itself is a creaturely act of reason and will. Yet he cannot accept Aquinas'
own further step, which Barth takes to be a supernatural quality added
to the natural power disposing the agent to acts of charity (an alternative perpetuated by Gilleman). This alternative introduces a third
factor which operates uncertainly between God and man.

> If we stress its divine character, we are involved in the same
> difficulties as those which Thomas himself raised against Lom-
> bard: where is the real man in this *forma habitualis,* who is, of
> course, supposed to be the subject of love? But if we stress its
> human character, where is the mystery of the origin of love, the
> miracle of the Holy Spirit? And with what right or consistency
> dare we introduce into the debate a third factor in the strict
> sense? [72]

Barth thus sets aside both alternatives.

> If we want to find an answer to the question of the human pos-
> sibility of love, i.e., a possibility in the sphere of man, we can-
> not take refuge either in the "docetic" anthropology of a Lombard
> or the "Ebionitism" of a Thomas. We can only point to the fact
> that we live in the sphere of the Church, that we are therefore
> baptised and look to the fulfilment of the promise, that Jesus
> Christ died and rose again for us. This is the true *forma habitualis
> superaddita,* which does not ascribe to us either a miraculous ex-
> tension of our own capacity, nor under the guise of this superna-
> tural quality a liberty which abolishes grace *qua* grace. If . . .

71. Barth, *Dogmatics,* I/2:374.
72. Ibid., p. 375.

we do trust in the promise, how can we doubt that man as he is, real man without deduction or addition, can participate in the promise, and that the miracle of the outpouring of the Holy Spirit consists in the fact that this man with his natural capacity . . . does in faith participate in the promise and in faith begin to love?[73]

Acquirement is also unacceptable for obvious reasons in light of the above. Barth wants to retain the freedom of a corresponding human act, but the love in question is evoked and sustained from without; it is not simply self-activated or self-directed. One may take it as interpersonal, but it is likewise asymmetrical.

The version of elicitation offered by Barth is once more in accordance with his whole theology. And here he takes more terminological care. He prefers deliberately for instance to speak of God's love as the basis (*Grund*) rather than the origin (*Ursprung*).[74] The latter term is not used because it connotes some point of identity between divine and human love. There is similarity but nothing more. Barth does not intend to disparage this similarity; it is more than coincidence, in his view, that the Bible uses "love" for both divine and human action. But such similarity must be restricted or else one claims for human agape an unwarranted kind of divinized power bridging heaven and earth.

The first and evocative love is not the same as the love which is evoked. The relationship between them is that of a word and answer, of permission and the use made of it, of command and obedience; not of the beginning and continuation of one and the same movement.[75]

Moreover, Barth does not use grace and love interchangeably except in reference to God's love. We saw that for Nygren the subject is actually God in all genuine neighbor-love. In Barth's case, God's love

73. Ibid.
74. Barth, *Die Kirchliche Dogmatik*, IV/2:853.
75. Barth, *Dogmatics*, IV/2:752.

is synonymous with grace and man's love with a gratitude that does not destroy "all healthy distances."

> The love of God always takes precedence. It always has the character of grace, and that of man the character of gratitude. There always remains a great difference in the order, nature and significance of divine and human love. The latter cannot repeat or represent the former. It cannot attain equality with it. It can only follow it and therefore be analogous to it. It can only correspond to it as a likeness and copy.[76]

So Barth avoids words like "elevate" and "divinize." Instead, God's love "elects," "purifies," and "creates," and human love "imitates," "corresponds," "reflects." A man loves in correspondence to God's love because he is genuinely empowered to love, but always only as a creature.

Affirmations about grace as enabling power cannot then be converted into anthropological statements. Love cannot be predicated in the same sense of God and the creature. Yet grace is not without effect; it really liberates man for fellowship on his own level and with his own capacities.

Status and Justification

To determine how agape is supported, justified, or defended, one must venture into the thick of Barth's theology.[77] Of the issues posed

76. Ibid., p. 754.

77. The following treatments of Barth's theology are especially helpful: G. C. Berkouwer, *The Triumph of Grace in the Theology of Karl Barth,* trans. Harry R. Boer (Grand Rapids: Wm. B. Eerdmans Publishing Company, 1956); Henri Bouillard, *Karl Barth,* 3 vols. (Aubier: Editions Montaigne, 1957); Hans Frei, "Niebuhr's Theological Background," *Faith and Ethics,* ed. Paul Ramsey (New York: Harper and Brothers, 1957), esp. pp. 40–53; Robert W. Jenson, *Alpha and Omega* (New York: Thomas Nelson & Sons, 1963); Hans Küng, *Justification,* trans. Thomas Collins, Edmund E. Tolk, and David Granskou (New York: Thomas Nelson & Sons, 1964); H. U. von Balthasar, *Karl Barth: Darstellung und Deutung seiner Theologie* (Kohn: Verlag Jakob Hegner, 1962); James M. Gustafson, *Christ and the Moral Life* (New York: Harper & Row, 1968), esp. pp. 11–60; Donald Evans, "Barth on Talk about God," *Canadian Journal of Theology* 16 (1970): 175–92.

in chapter 6, I shall consider the following: the content of grace to
which human agape should correspond; the more general background
or framework of intelligibility for agape, which in Barth's case is
pre-eminently the covenant; some additional effects on the content
itself (I noted instances of explicit backing when the relation of the
two great commandments was considered); and his attitude toward
non-theological grounds.

To establish the context for this discussion, let me offer one preliminary remark. Barth takes with monolithic seriousness the God-
relation as the alpha and omega of all things, including ethics. He
has been called a God-intoxicated man. Above and in everything else,
persons should affirm in practice that they do not belong to themselves. Despite his inescapable influence, many regard the theology
Barth thinks appropriate to such seriousness to be unrepresentative and
in crucial respects mistaken. Others take it as the boldest and most
consistent instance of what theology must be, if grace is really to be
central. I cannot try to decide that large question here. I must content myself with second-order exposition and commentary on Barth's
scheme. Above all I want to illustrate what aggressive theological
incorporation of agape may mean in a given case. Indeed, "incorporation" may not fit Barth's intentions. At least he does not wish
to find a meaning of love already functioning in a non-theological
context and merely modify it for theological purposes. He wants the
latter purposes to control totally. They must provide at a minimum
the normative or paradigmatic meaning. One's understanding of
human agape must be governed by one's understanding of God's love.
If discontinuity with kinds of love in non-theological usage accom-
panies such control, one must pay that price. Otherwise one may fail
to let grace be prior and determining.

Regarding the content of God's love for which human agape is the
practical corollary, Barth in certain passages supports the four features
Nygren distinguishes. Grace is both "spontaneous" and "unmotivated," and "indifferent to value," in the sense that no extrinsic
reason outside God's own nature determines whether He loves.

God's loving is concerned with a seeking and creation of fellowship without any reference to an existing aptitude or worthi-

ness on the part of the loved. God's love is not merely not conditioned by any reciprocity of love. It is also not conditioned by any worthiness to be loved on the part of the loved, by any existing capacity for union or fellowship on his side. If he has such a thing, it is itself the prior creation of the love of God. It is not and does not become the condition of that love. It is the object of the divine pleasure which follows the preceding love.[78]

Likewise grace is "creative" or "value-creating." Some inalienable value in the soul is not simply uncovered and extolled. Whatever generic worth the creature has reflects the prior love of God. So, finally, God's love is the "initiator of fellowship." Barth stresses more than Nygren that such fellowship is an end in itself. While Nygren certainly acknowledges that fellowship is the final good, he concentrates on the divine initiative. Barth acknowledges such initiative in turn. But he affirms untiringly that God has nothing higher than Himself to give. To seek and create fellowship with men is to express His love decisively.

> God's loving is concerned with a seeking and creation of fellowship for its own sake . . . God is the One who loves, and as such the blessing and the sum of all good things. . . . Loving us, God does not give us something, but Himself; and giving us Himself . . . He gives us everything. The love of God has only to be His love to be everything for us.[79]

The preoccupation with fellowship allows room for Barth to include a part of the feature of mutuality. Certainly what is sought is an increasingly conscious relation between God and man as an end in itself, and in conformance, between human creature and human creature as related to God. Barth is only concerned to safeguard once more the recognition of healthy distances. And so he does not say that wherever people meet in openness and mutual help of any kind, they put themselves in a context which leads to an awareness of God. Relations be-

78. Barth, *Dogmatics*, II/1:278.
79. Ibid., p. 276.

tween persons are clearly a medium for a disclosure of the Spirit only in the restricted sense of witness. Persons can tell one another about something; their human relations as such cannot produce the thing itself. Here too Barth wishes to preclude unnecessary vulnerability to projectionist interpretations. I shall return to his account of witness.

Finally, Barth does not eschew all talk of self-sacrifice or self-giving in his depiction of grace. He writes at one point that "this self-sacrifice of God in His Son is in fact the love of God to us." [80] Yet if one reads beyond this sentence it is clear that the emphasis on fellowship places the treatment of sacrificial love in a context not identical to Nygren's or Niebuhr's. Self-sacrifice is characterized as part of the gift "into our existence," the message of Emmanuel, with human guilt and sin borne and borne away. Barth is not preoccupied with the lostness of divine love, betrayal and failure, its utter heterogeneity with the "world." Triumph and happiness outdistance suffering and sin. But of that, more will also be said later.

It seems obvious in Barth's case as well as Nygren's that if the believer is to correspond, he must set no limits to his love by virtue of the particular worth of particular men. His love is imitative when it is independent of the limits set by idiosyncratic character and conduct. Yet the account of the neighbor as irreducibly valuable, where worth is acquired by being loved by God, reflects Barth's distinctive theology. Some effects of that theology were anticipated in chapter 6. The preponderant pressures exerted are toward a confessional recognition of worth bestowed by God. Empirical characteristics admittedly constitute at least part of the object of evaluation.[81] Nonetheless one cannot avoid going beyond such characteristics to justify equal value attached to the well-being of each person. And for Barth especially, worth is worth only in relation to God. I shall examine in more general terms his version of this belief.

We have seen how religious beliefs often serve to define the total arena within which actions are viewed and assessed. The total arena

80. Barth, Dogmatics, I/2:378.

81. In another context, "man is man and not a cat." See his famous reply to Brunner, "No!" in Natural Theology, trans. Peter Fraenkel (London: Geoffrey Bles, 1946), p. 88.

in Barth's case is the covenant. His characterization of agape is indeed integrally tied to and intelligible in light of this central theological concept. Barth is radically serious about its centrality. Clearly for him the neighbor's status is not assigned on one's own authority. The status is conferred by God in unmerited grace. While subordinate to Him, it is taken as one shared by all persons equally in relation to each other. Conferral occurs as a part of the destiny of man which God has willed from eternity by virtue of making man His covenant partner. The covenant is God's all-inclusive, even pre-temporal Yes to man. God decides before all time to love man. "The covenant fulfilled in time is a covenant resolved and established in God Himself before all time." [82] From beginning to end the covenant is sheerly a matter of grace, that to which God has freely and sovereignly bound Himself. It is the final word about the nature and destiny of every man.

In being elected, man is objectively determined. The creation itself is simply the "external basis" of the covenant, just as the covenant is the "internal basis" of the creation.[83] The neighbor's irreplaceable value in relation to God, his very existence *as* covenant partner, is hardly something about which any creature is at liberty to please himself. We are to acknowledge a status which is valid irrespective of that acknowledgment. We do not have to do only with an outlook on life, a perspective, a *"Weltanschauung* among *Weltanschauungen."*

Yet for Barth this reality is revealed in one particular history. It is a history which God in His free and sovereign will has chosen. Statements about a special disclosure of God's love must precede, in the most radically irreducible fashion, whatever is said about the nature and content of that love. "We cannot speak of a love of God the Creator *in abstracto,* supposedly active and manifest in nature and history as such." [84] What is finally authoritative for Barth's scheme is confined to a particular set of revealed events. The divinely elected

---

82. Barth, *Dogmatics,* III/2:218.

83. See Karl Barth, *Church Dogmatics,* III/1, trans. J. W. Edwards, *et al.* (Edinburgh: T. & T. Clark, 1958). Jenson, *Alpha and Omega,* offers a perceptive study of some of Barth's central theological concepts, including the covenant and creation.

84. Barth, *Dogmatics,* I/2:379.

events are the history of Israel, and the man of Israel, Jesus Christ, as attested to in scripture. Every instance of language about God must be understood as a predicate of this one authoritative subject.

What is involved in the act of God's love to us we learn decisively, centrally, and comprehensively . . . from the Old Testament witness to the covenant of Yahweh with Israel and the New Testament proclamation of the kingdom, of the lordship of God on earth, which has been inaugurated in the existence of the one man Jesus of Nazareth. . . . The covenant is the divinely inaugurated and directed history of a nation in which His will is at work to unite with all nations and all men, and to unite all nations and all men with Himself. The kingdom is the divinely inaugurated and directed history of a man of this one nation as the representative of all others in which God has united with this One in the accomplishment of His will, and in this One has united all nations and all men with Himself.[85]

In chapter 6 I said that the structures of specific schemes are often distinguished by which of two very general doctrines is given prominence: (1) human existence "cannot ultimately defy its own norm"; (2) some special authoritative event such as the life of Jesus cannot be rendered superfluous. Barth, characteristically, undertakes to affirm both. The norm of human nature consists, as we have seen, in the following: man essentially, naturally, and originally belongs to God and with his fellow-man. One may in his own personal history violate this norm through a life governed by acquisitiveness. Yet such sinful violation is finally defeated violation. God is and will remain man's eternal Counterpart. Man cannot abrogate the covenant.[86]

85. Barth, *Dogmatics*, IV/2:760.
86. Note the way in which Barth describes sinful violation in light of the covenant of grace, in *Dogmatics*, II/1:371: "Arrogance is seen as pitiable folly, the usurpation of freedom as rigorous bondage, evil lust as bitter torment. It is again true that man by his own fault has plunged himself and is continually plunging himself into these ills, and in view of this we shall have to speak . . . of the righteousness of God. But it is also true that this resistance of the

Barth wants with equal energy to guarantee a link to the historical
Jesus which is far, far more than an accidental aid to a way of life
otherwise known. He opposes every appeal centered in general
anthropology on the basis of which one does theology and ethics.
Instead he turns "to a stringent Realism, in which God, his reality
and nature are to be understood as being the independent ground of
all relation of God with creatures." [87] Only such Realism can, it seems
to Barth, avoid the perils of subjectivism or "immanentism."

> Moreover, Barth had to reject the temptation to transcend the
> Realism of revelation in the direction of idealistic metaphysics,
> i.e., in the overcoming of history through ideal essence. The
> latter task made Barth insist that there be no division between
> ontology and Christology. All ontic statements are made on the
> basis of the historical revelation in Jesus Christ.[88]

It follows that no theologically warranted judgment about the neighbor's irreducible value can appeal to some fixed anthropological
datum, construed as lying behind and knowable apart from these
divinely elected events, and to which Jesus simply testifies. On the
contrary: Jesus' love is the criterion of agape, of what shall count as
neighbor-love. Barth goes so far as to maintain that our very knowledge of human nature as essentially, naturally, and originally belonging to God and with the fellow-man depends on Jesus. "The nature
of human possibilities rests upon and is knowable by the fact that
they are realised in Him." [89] It is Jesus who is definitively "man for

---

creature, this sinfulness of man, has in itself and as such the simple meaning
of folly, bondage and torment. And as such it is the object of God's compassion."

87. Frei, "Niebuhr's Theological Background," p. 42.
88. Ibid.
89. Barth, *Dogmatics,* III/2:59. Further: "As the nature of Jesus, human
nature with all its possibilities is not a presupposition which is valid for Him
too and controls and explains Him, but His being as a man is as such that
which posits and therefore reveals and explains human nature with all its
possibilities."

God" and "man for other men," [90] and thus the paradigm of what agape means.

A typical way for Barth to formulate the relation between the two very general doctrines is to distinguish between a de jure state of affairs and de facto knowledge of it.[91] The covenant obtains for all men. No creaturely resistance can finally succeed in defiance of this norm of human nature. Yet only some persons know de facto what obtains for all. I referred earlier to the faith-love correlation as new actions in the personal histories of certain persons. They appropriate the one action of God's grace and thus depend on that "historical point of departure" where such grace is disclosed. So the life of Jesus cannot be rendered superfluous.

Barth's particular attempt to affirm both doctrines draws criticism from very different quarters. Some are unhappy with his account of the de jure state of affairs; others with the de facto knowledge of it. This chapter is not the place to pursue these controversies.[92] To sum-

90. Ibid., esp. pp. 55–71, 203–22.
91. E.g., Barth, *Dogmatics,* IV/2:511.
92. Any attempt to do so would be rash, because such controversies have to do with doctrines which predominate throughout Barth's massive writings. I shall only pause now to mention in passing sample points at issue, in order to identify further some complex questions tied to justification. But this excursion into central problems in theology and philosophy of religion must be of short duration.

Let me take the de jure side first. Certain Lutherans, for instance, hold that Barth's thought tends toward monism (see, e.g., Thielicke, *Theological Ethics,* esp. pp. 98–117). The de jure state of God's all-inclusive, pre-temporal Yes is so complete as to appear fixed and static. Divinely elected events in history only "actualize" the covenant will. Therefore what is recorded in the New Testament itself "carries with it noetic but not ontic-historical progress" (ibid., p. 110). "The incarnation is no new event, it is not the inauguration of a new covenant; it cannot be the historical juncture of two aeons; but simply recapitulates, clarifies, and reveals events which, as enacted and completed facts, belong to the perfect tense of Old Testament salvation history, or even to the pluperfect tense of pretemporality" (ibid., p. 109). Several things follow from this approach, it is argued. History dissolves in several respects. It is hard to see, first of all, what remains of eschatology. The "end" seems indeed wholly transmuted from the "apocalypse of the promised future" into the "epiphany of the eternal present." It is also hard to see how sin and moral evil can be anything other than "priva-

marize, Barth wants what I shall call *the widest possible referential expanse within the narrowest epistemological brackets*. Truths about the love of God are truths applicable to all persons prior to their doing anything in particular. The status of irreducible value is finally a

---

tion" and "unreality," or a possibility "superseded" and "left behind." The tenacity of even penultimate corruption is not given its due. Finally, the allegedly fixed and static de jure state means that the agent "merely" knows. Human de facto knowledge seems to lack some vital quality of *decisional* drama. The sting in struggle and suffering and risk is withdrawn.

Barth would not regard all of the above as criticism. Certainly he wants to attest to the "triumph of grace." God's covenant will is first and foremost an intratrinitarian occurence. Prior to the creation, man and man's entire world was loved as the Son stood before the Father. And however difficult it may be for persons to perceive in successive moments of their lives, grace does not fluctuate. Censure and condemnation clearly occur, but their *telos* is the restoration of communion. We can even say: sin is not *necessary* for grace. In order for the covenant to be willed, men need not have sinned. So if grace is really to govern, and "strangely manichean tendencies" avoided, every abyss must have a bottom somewhere. Yet it would be a mistake to suppose that Barth thus means to endorse a facile optimism or deny divine judgment. Every abyss continues to be dangerous. Barth takes as perhaps the quintessence of corruption any attempt to obscure the distinction between Creator and creature. To speak of the triumph of grace is part of the adoration of God and only *derivatively* to extol the dignity of the creature. Consider this austere passage (Barth, *Dogmatics,* II/2:555): "The question arises whether the Greek tragedians did not see deeper than Plato and all the Platonists. Their characters are all portrayed in an impotent desire for godlikeness and attempt to attain it. And they are coldly directed back to their own limits by the gods. But this opposition of man to the absolute superiority of the eternally good and his desire to master it on the one side and the wrath of God against this undertaking on the other, are changed by Plato and his followers into a mutual *methexis* (or participation), in which the originally existent good is as clearly reflected and recognized in the finite as the finitely good in the infinite." God initiates and governs our knowledge of Him. He will only be known where and when He wills to be known. Judgment falls on the presumption of the creature. Moreover, to charge that faith and love are de facto actions having the status of the "merely noetic" is to disparage unfairly. Faith as reception and love as self-giving are to affect every level of the psyche. They involve far more than an intellectual act cut off from feeling and moral commitment. It should be noted that disputes about the de jure state of affairs may have subtle effects on the definition of the good life and what one seeks for the neighbor. As I shall show later, Barth wants, for example, to build into the notion of the good life some dominant strain of rejoicing.

status before God. Yet the truths are contingently known in Jesus Christ. Only believers know what is the case for *all* persons, and they really do know it.

What, more specifically, is the effect of the above on the content of agape? Barth proceeds largely as one would expect. The account of

---

On the de facto side, it is also charged that Barth does not execute successfully his basic epistemological intention. His claim to begin and end with a single history of revealed events appears to some ruinously abstract. So much is introduced which is not convincingly derived from or governed by Christology. Others accuse him of a flat contradiction in his account of language as applied to God and as applied to men (see for instance the excellent article by Evans, "Barth on Talk about God," esp. pp. 188–91). Barth appears both to opt for sheer equivocity (the meanings of words such as love in human discourse do not contribute even provisionally to meanings as applied to God) and to reject equivocity (human words are used by God to make knowledge of Him possible). Such issues go back to Barth's first decisive break with liberalism. He thinks his critics are forced to hold some version of what he calls "the two cardinal propositions in philosophy of religion in the 19th and 20th centuries": "1. Man's meeting with God to be regarded as a human religious experience historically and psychologically fixable; and 2. This experience to be regarded as the realisation of a religious potentiality in man generally demonstrable" (Karl Barth, *Church Dogmatics*, I/1. trans. G. T. Thomson [Edinburgh: T. & T. Clark, 1960] p. 219). If one begins with these two propositions, Barth thinks projectionist interpretations (such as Feuerbach's) are waiting in the wings. Without a stringent Realism of revelation, such interpretations will seem disarmingly plausible. It is better to rule out from the start in-principled appeals to general anthropological data. One must not begin, as the liberals do, with an immediate "religious relation" in which the human subject, by virtue of some account of the general conditions of human knowledge, *modifies* the content of grace given to it. If we even accept provisional human meanings of words when we speak of God, we will, he argues, inevitably end in idolatry. Is Barth right? Is his program logically self-contradictory? If we refer to any pre-existing human capacity whatever, will we finish if we are rigorous in projectionism and idolatry? Is it possible to avoid referring to some capacity? Again, this chapter is not the place to try to settle such questions. But if one agrees that some provisional human meaning of love is allowable as an initial basis for understanding, he can still insist that when applied to God, love acquires a paradigmatic or standard-setting use. Some such claim, furthermore, as discussed in chapter 6, is part of what is required for Jesus to be the exemplar. If Barth cannot cogently have more, one must see that he will not have less.

the covenant stands behind the descriptive and evaluative elements built into the notion of the neighbor, specifying not only who he is but also how he should be treated. Barth holds that the vantage point of the covenant furnishes a distinctive assessment of what is good-making in itself or intrinsically good, namely, communion with God and being with the fellow-man gladly. The corresponding treatment which Barth thinks most fitting is witness. For him, this concept above all is involved in any really serious characterization of neighbor-love. A person should not withhold from another the proclamation of grace because in the creaturely event of witness is present the one essential element in genuine mutual love between them.

> To be sure, there are other relationships between them as well. Apart from many that are unimportant, or only externally and technically important, there are those that involve a very inward and profound and significant and meaningful intercourse and exchange. These, too, may be a means of love. But in them they may withhold the witness which they owe to one another. In them they may still be isolated and left to their own devices.[93]

It is preferable, Barth argues, not to link the concept of witness to any end beyond confession. There should be no project the agent imposes. "Therefore in my testimony I cannot follow out the plan of trying to invade and alter the life of my neighbor. A witness is neither a guardian nor a teacher." [94]

Such witness has three indispensable "forms." The first may be called explicit declaration. At this point in particular Barth is unashamedly scriptural and churchly.[95] The agent should point to and tell about a divine love which he can never personify or reproduce directly. And it is grace which should be stressed, rather than one's sin or need or individual experience.

The second form of witness is to assist within the terms of the other's "psycho-physical existence." It is notable that Barth very

93. Barth, *Dogmatics*, IV/2:816.
94. Barth, *Dogmatics*, I/2:441.
95. Ibid., p. 443.

quickly criticizes any single-minded attention to this assistance. One should construe it "as a sign of the promised help of God." [96] He remains wary of a false temporal seriousness. Suppose one takes the instance of a man who gives his life in place of another (certainly central in a scripture passage such as I John 3:16). The act as such, Barth argues, is not spared from ambiguity and disparate interpretations. A "miracle" of divine self-attestation is required if the act is to be a genuine witness.

> Can he really help him by doing this? No, he has not saved him from death; for sooner or later death will overtake the one who is saved. . . . Can he give to this expressive act the effect that the one who is saved does, in fact, recognise the sign of real help in face of death, the witness to Jesus Christ which is given him by it? Again: No, he cannot do that. Many a person has been saved from death by another without receiving and accepting in that event the witness of the one who saves him. He cannot really make the one who is saved see what there is to see in the act. Even, then, in this simplest and clearest instance of one man assisting or acting for another there has to be . . . a divine miracle if witness is to be borne by the service of the one to the other and if that witness is to be real assistance.[97]

Finally there is the form of witness displayed in the set of a person's life. In this context Barth employs a word which he usually consigns to his list of pejoratives: *attitude.* It would be a mistake to regard this as a recurrent theme in Barth's writings. We have seen how he normally commends actions rather than attitudes. Yet he does allow that the quality of a life seen in its entirety may have effect as a witness.[98] It is even arguable that some of the older concern about virtue re-emerges here, though not in traditional terms. Barth wants, at least in a wide sense, the theological virtues of faith, hope, and love. They are not to be taken of course as divinized properties. And

96. Ibid., p. 444.
97. Ibid., p. 446.
98. Ibid., p. 449.

one must not attempt to specify in elaborate detail in advance which definite actions correlate with them. But faith, hope, and love ought to form part of a constant state of interior agent-dedication, exemplified in long-term patterns. There should, for instance, be continuity in the agent's absolutely all-engrossing interest in God. And the neighbor may be helped thereby on his way.

I do not mean to imply that Barth ignores the strictly mundane needs of the neighbor. It is obvious to him that they fall as well within the scope of neighbor-love. In a volume on "special ethics," he is willing to devote the better part of 704 pages to their elucidation, including some of the hardest cases where interests clash.[99] But the most distinctive impact of his scheme on the meaning of agape lies in his relentlessly tying it to the God-relation. Let us note several final results of this impact.

First, if one attends to grace, Barth thinks one will be wary of making the concept of agape very self-contained. One should not try to capture "the bird in flight." The agent ought to remain open to the free movements of grace from situation to situation. He should not become self-preoccupied via the details of his own conduct. I have alluded already to Barth's theological contextualism. Yet just as there is also constancy and continuity in the movements of grace, there is some substantive content which imitative human agape possesses as well, regardless of circumstances. Barth takes agape to be "the essential and enduring Christian act."[100] It is distinguished from "nonessential and transitory activities" and is the final criterion in deciding among them. He goes so far as to hold that under agape, for example, the "whole conduct which Paul requires of Christians is included — even what is said about their relation to the state."[101] And the permanent normative content he does accept was described at the beginning of this chapter. It is beyond this content that Barth most often thinks it perilous to specify in advance.

Second, the chief reason that acts of neighbor-love, for Barth, tend so often to be assimilated into expressions of witness is that he simply

99. See Barth, *Dogmatics,* III/4.
100. Barth, *Dogmatics,* IV/2:732.
101. Barth, *Dogmatics,* II/2:719.

believes that the final, most urgent need of the neighbor is God Himself. As I said in chapter 6, our ordinary perceptions of what we should seek in order to be happy are not just diverse. They are bound to go wrong until they are grafted to the message of grace. So one should take the final need with utter seriousness and other needs less seriously. " 'To accept as right' means to lay aside all hostility to God's action — as if we were injured or humiliated by it, as if we had to guard and defend ourselves against it, as if there were some important interests which inclination or even duty compelled us to defend against it." [102] "Love is nothing more and does not wish to be anything more than the obedient erecting of the sign of divine grace." [103]

Lastly, the meaning of the good life for every agent, while not specifiable in detail in advance, is nonetheless dominated by a current of rejoicing. A direction is given to one's life which does permeate thought and action. Human agape confirms and reflects grace by taking nothing as seriously as grace. Certainly sin, flaws, corruption, and so on are there, and not to be superficially considered. Yet the essence of sin is not so much the denial of sin as the denial of reconciliation. Each person is called on to affirm this freely and variously, and encourage others to affirm it. One may perhaps refer appropriately to Barth's well-known devotion to Mozart.

Mozart's center is not like that of the great theologian Schleiermacher, identical with balance, neutralization and finally indifference. What happened in this center is rather a splendid annulment of balance, a *turn* in the strength of which the light rises and the shadow winks but does not disappear; happiness outdistances sorrow without extinguishing it and the "Yes" rings stronger than the still-existing "No." Notice the *reversal* of the great dark and the little bright experiences in Mozart's life! "The rays of the sun *disperse* the night" — that's what you hear at the end of the *Magic Flute*. The play may or must still

102. Ibid., p. 579.
103. Barth, *Dogmatics*, I/2:401.

proceed or start from the very beginning. But it is a play which in some Height or Depth is winning or has already won.[104]

I arrive finally at Barth's view about possible non-theological grounds for justifying agape. He passes over issues concerned with the necessary and sufficient conditions for moral principles of any kind. Nor is he interested in specific cases within "mere morality" for agape. In the present context, he is preoccupied with formal lines of authority. Suppose one says that only believers know the "true" human situation — which is about the covenant — and that they really know it. What is one to conclude about the status of a theological ethic derived from such a starting point? Here Barth is exceptionally aggressive. If there is to be the widest possible referential expanse, then theological ethics cannot acquiesce in a role of isolation. It cannot be content merely to furnish distinctive visions and requirements for those in the believing community, and leave the "world" to its own autonomous moral devices.

> What we have to ask . . . is whether theology can seriously contemplate two things. First, can it really be restricted . . . to a sphere which is no doubt remarkably distinguished by the concepts of religion, revelation, Church, grace, Spirit, etc., but which is characterised as a very narrow and rather obscure sphere by its isolation from the sphere of reason, experience and human self-determination? And secondly, can it really ascribe to reason, experience, human self-determination, etc., an independent content of truth, an autonomous dignity and authority, which in its own preoccupation with revelation and the outpourings of Christian self-consciousness it can safely leave on one side? To put the question differently: Is God's revelation revelation of the truth, or is it only the source of certain religious ideas and obligations, alongside which there are very different ones in other spheres? Outside and alongside the kingdom of Jesus

104. Karl Barth, "Wolfgang Amadeus Mozart," *Religion and Culture Essays in Honor of Paul Tillich,* ed. Walter Leibrecht (New York: Harper & Brothers, 1959), pp. 76–77.

Christ are there other respectable kingdoms? Can and should
theology of all things be content to speak, not with universal
validity, but only esoterically? . . . Does it really believe in its
own themes if it concedes that the other ethics has its source
and subject in reason, experience and self-determination? — as
if all this did not lie from the very outset in its own sphere, the
sphere of theological ethics; as if it could be right to accept all
these quantities as self-evident, to concede autonomy to man's
knowledge of good and evil; as if . . . we could salute the
grace of God, as it were, and then go our own way.[105]

And if the epistemological brackets are to remain narrow, theological ethics cannot count on some native moral insight to supply certain
principles to which all may subscribe and which it at most can only
reinforce and supplement. Any sort of coalition seems to Barth impossible. One is left then with the following contention of what
theological ethics is compelled to do: "From the point of view of
the general history of ethics, it means an annexation of the kind that
took place on the entry of the children of Israel into Palestine." [106]
Other inhabitants, however more ancient their right of domicile and
however attractive their cultus and culture, had to be resisted and
their territory taken over. Barth even uses the following analogy:

Christian ethics . . . is not one disputant in debate with others.
It is the final word of the original chairman — only discussed,
of course, in Christian ethics — which puts an end to the
discussion and involves necessarily a choice and separation.[107]

Barth's dogmatic account distresses many otherwise largely sympathetic readers. They value, for example, the wisdom of his discussions of most specific moral issues. But they refuse to follow him
when he characterizes the formal relation of theological and non-
theological ethics. And unfriendly critics charge him with a kind of

105. Barth, *Dogmatics*, II/2:526.
106. Barth, *Dogmatics*, II/2:518.
107. Ibid., p. 519.

theological imperialism. He obviously thinks he has no consistent alternative other than the one he takes. Again, ethical concepts must
survive scrutiny by what is already fixed and governing: contingently
known truths about grace. The concepts which survive concern the
de jure moral arena of all men, despite the de facto unawareness of
so many.

One must not suppose from the above, however, that Barth endorses a theological imperialism in the sense of asserting that some
persons should seek to dictate other persons' actually held moral or
political views. He does not approve of social arrangements which
encourage intolerance of the standards of others.[108] Nor does he
approve of any theologian taking certain conclusions about specific
moral issues for granted. The history of theological reflection on
such issues affords ample ground for humility.

Still, the case for the formal sovereignty of theological ethics over
the entire range of moral questions is radically argued, perhaps unprecedentedly so. To determine how unprecedented Barth's view is,
and whether it is finally coherent, exceeds my present purposes. I
must be satisfied to have shown certain consequences of his theology
as a whole for many of the questions in earlier chapters. Is there
any conspicuous point at which Barth might profitably have said
more? I think so. As his impassioned defense of the sovereignty of
theological ethics indicates, his overriding concern is to mark off
formal lines of authority. Yet after various effects of such lines have
been duly noted, and because he is obsessed with them, questions
remain, especially about the content of human agape itself. We have
seen that Barth refers to an enduring meaning of agape irrespective
of circumstances. As neighbor-love, it includes "identification with

108. He defends for instance the political values of a pluralistic constitutional
democracy, by way of analogy from Christological premises. See, e.g., Karl
Barth, *Community, State and Church* (Garden City: Doubleday & Company,
1960). His procedure, however formally consistent, has prompted the inevitable
question of whether a theological starting point and the views of a parochial
Swiss citizen do not too happily coincide. However that question is answered,
there are many reasons Barth might consistently offer on behalf of toleration.
For another defense of the compatability of toleration and a conception of moral
objectivity, see Ward, *Ethics and Christianity,* esp. pp. 54–56.

his interests in utter independence of his attractiveness, of what he has to offer." Many important and intricate issues arise here which deserve more extensive discussion than Barth gives them. I propose to concentrate on such issues in the last chapter. Some of them will be treated perhaps in ways other than Barth would wish. What is implied about both justification and application will not be ignored altogether. But I want above all to look further at the normative core.

Summary Comparisons

In the foregoing I have noted the following points of major identity and difference between Barth and the figures examined earlier. (1) Barth stresses with Kierkegaard and many others the centrality of equal regard as the normative content of agape. (2) He also, like Reinhold Niebuhr, stresses self-giving, though with more explicit links to other-regard. (3) Like Kierkegaard, he distinguishes agape and friendship, but unlike Kierkegaard, he does not oppose them. (4) Barth agrees, with much of the Catholic tradition and in contrast to Nygren and Brunner, that "love for God" cannot be translated without loss into either faith or neighbor-love. (5) Usually he finds the self-love in the second great commandment as at most not blameworthy but not a manifest obligation. (6) Much of the time, together with Nygren, he regards the content of eros as acquisitiveness and thus as contrary to agape. (7) But he parts from Nygren to distinguish explicitly between an acquisitive notion of eros and "human nature." (8) Barth correlates agape with faith as new events occurring only to certain men. Sometimes he proceeds to say as well that the objects of agape are confined to co-believers (a move I at least find to be confused). (9) He is suspicious of the enterprise of casuistry and espouses (though not always consistently) a kind of theological contextualism in which the agent must allow God to specify how love is to be applied in very particular situations. (10) He disagrees with Nygren in taking agape as a definite *human* action. God is not the subject of neighbor-love. The action in question, considered in itself, is wholly a creaturely one. But for all that, it depends on grace. (11) Barth's own theological scheme has pronounced effects on the context and content of agape. These are due most of all to the relentless and distinctive way in which he sees the God-relation as the alpha and omega of all things, including ethics. Particular stress on the agapeistic treatment of witness corresponds to the all-important need of the other for God.

8

A Revisit

> Even one who has done me some sort of injury or harm has not shed his humanity on that account or stopped being flesh and blood, a creature of God very much like me; in other words, he does not stop being my neighbor.
>
> Martin Luther

> Act so that you treat humanity, whether in your own person or in that of another, always as an end and never as a means only.
>
> Immanuel Kant

It is time now to try to assess the state of the discussion as a whole and to explore at greater length the major claims centering around agape as a substantive ethical principle.

In the discussion as a whole many of the issues and positions identified suggest a recurrent range not circumscribed to the particular literature under scrutiny. Clearly such literature reflects in some measure distinctive modern preoccupations. But, of course, it also reflects theological and philosophical points at issue which have turned up repeatedly. So it would prove instructive to compare in detail positions identified here with biblical exegesis of relevant texts, with Augustine, Aquinas, Luther, Calvin, Hobbes, Bishop Butler, Jonathan Edwards, et al. And in the case of the golden rule, for instance, one could compare references and commentary in various other religious traditions, including Judaism, Islam, Taoism, Confucianism, and Buddhism. As mentioned at the outset, we have before us issues whose almost obstinate longevity among sophisticated and unsophisticated alike indicates how deeply they are felt and how inescapable they are in ethical reflection.

There is another initial point to note about the discussion as a whole. The meaning ascribed in the literature to love in general and to agape in particular is often characterized by both variance and ambiguity. The variance is obvious enough and yet I think two reasons for it ought to be especially pointed out. First, between writers (even when they are largely self-consistent) particular meanings are frequently incorporated into and reflective of distinctively wider beliefs and entire theological schemes. Sometimes this means that distinctive evaluations have attached themselves to words such as agape, self-love, etc. In saying this, I do not mean to hold that in the literature the words themselves are normally so vague as to be altogether indeterminate, with no generally accepted meanings whatever. Someone who, for instance, proposed that agape was not an other-regarding principle at all could do so only under pain of misunderstanding the minimal meaning ascribed by virtually everyone concerned. I noted in the introduction that in the case of agape one has to do with a principle already set in a tradition so that one is not free simply to stipulate whatever meaning he likes. Moreover, I think it is possible to identify a normative content which does greatest justice to recurrent usage and serves to illuminate the most characteristic problems. This is the main subject to which I shall turn in a moment. Yet on the other hand, there are limits to the degree of determinateness beyond which the choice of a feature for emphasis (at least) reflects different evaluations involving the authors' own views about human nature, human good, and so on. Thus, for example, Niebuhr's preoccupation with self-sacrifice accords with his general estimates of the character and limitations of personal and collective life. Similarly, Barth's objection to Nygren's theology as betraying strangely manichean tendencies is not unrelated to his own attempt to distinguish clearly between "human nature" and acquisitive eros. In short, variance sometimes reflects differences in substantive theological and ethical beliefs and the links between them.

A second and more general reason for variance is this. With a word as common as "love," it is unrealistic to suppose that all of the characteristic meanings could be absorbed into some single point of identity, if only because it is extremely unlikely that there is one homogeneous field to which the word always applies. For this reason if for no other one presumably should not always expect to locate among the multiple meanings a hidden one which could account for them all. Agape and eros do appear then in part as comprehensive terms for differing (and sometimes rival) concepts. A certain kind of ambiguity arises, however, in connection with such presumed unrealism. For it is probably true to say that not everyone in the literature agrees that a quest for some common meaning must prove wholly futile. D'Arcy and Tillich, for instance, offer accounts of agape and eros which purport to do more than adopt and recommend a particular meaning. D'Arcy claims that his account demonstrates a basic pattern inevitably experienced by every person and into which every allegedly one-sided treatment such as Nygren's can be fitted. And Tillich locates "one point of identity" between the several aspects or "qualities" (not "types") of love, namely, the generic "urge toward the reunion of the separated." [1] Again in Tillich's case, the several qualities, agape, eros, philia, and epithymia are all inevitably experienced. D'Arcy and Tillich, then, try to encompass and illumine various characteristic meanings. Generally, however, one is uncertain whether such attempts involve an acceptance of all ordinary meanings and a demonstration of what these "actually" refer to, or whether they dismiss certain things that others refer to as agape and eros as non-existent or as incorrectly described. In the first alternative, a single theoretical notion *assimilates* everything in itself; in the second, it *reduces* everything to itself. Assimilation presumes to do justice to principal meanings, but in a way which comprehends and successfully integrates them all. Reduction usually involves not just explicit exclusion of certain meanings, but a different account of the thing in question, e.g., mutual love. It seems to me that accounts like D'Arcy's and Tillich's, despite what the authors sometimes seem to say, reduce more than they assimilate and that such reduction is often disguised recommendation, though in a misleadingly declarative form.

Taken together these reasons point to at least three sorts of variance found in the literature as a whole. (1) There may be a comparatively straightforward and unambiguous disagreement on points, for instance, of theological substance (such as those between Barth and Nygren). If such points are explicitly linked, as clearly they

1. Tillich, *Systematic Theology*, 3:137. See also Tillich, *Love, Power and Justice*, esp. pp. 27–28; *Morality and Beyond*, pp. 40–41.

sometimes are, to the distinctive content of agape and eros, then conceptual elucidation cannot of course by itself resolve disagreements. (2) There may be verbal differences which are assumed to be disagreements because the same term is defined in varying senses, but which when explicitly compared are found to be not conflicting but simply different. I noted this possibility in the case of some senses of self-love. (3) There may be verbal differences which on examination turn out also to be substantive ones. One of the virtues of clarifying varying and ambiguous usage is that it sometimes allows one to determine whether (2) or (3) obtains.

This study would be far from finished — even as an analytical sketch — if one were content to remark on the variance and ambiguity in the literature. For there are also points which emerge repeatedly and comprise certain dominant patterns. I propose now to explore these, at whatever risk to any uncertain neutrality so far maintained.

Since we have touched on such a variety of the traditional questions in ethics, it is hardly feasible here to say something about them all at proportionate length. Primarily, I want to consider further the normative content most often ascribed to agape and then compare this both with other features commonly put forward and with self-love and justice.

Characteristic Issues for Agape as Equal Regard

The normative content most often ascribed I have called equal regard, involving in Barth's words, "identification with his interests in utter independence of the question of his attractiveness." Agape is, in both its genesis and continuation, an active concern for the neighbor's well-being which is somehow independent of particular actions of the other. To say even as much as I did in chapter 1 raises a number of difficult questions. I shall identify several of the most prominent.

One is that non-exclusiveness must somehow link with uniqueness. That is, attribution to everyone alike of an irreducible worth and dignity does not mean that people are indifferently interchangeable.

Nothing makes good the loss of any single other. Yet many would hold that particular achievements furnish whatever content the notion of uniqueness possesses. Furthermore, do others really *want* to be regarded for reasons other than acquired excellences which allegedly make them the individual personalities they are? The answer to this line of questioning has generally been as follows. An exclusion of comparisons at the most basic level is not tantamount to interchangeability as such. For example, it may be plausibly held that I ought to have an equal affection for all of my children (while perhaps not equal esteem or admiration), but this in no way means that I ought to view them as equally replaceable. Moreover, wholly apart from other sorts of reasons which may or may not be independently sufficient, the believer may hold that uniqueness exists by virtue of what men share together. For a man's relation to God is never established by his individual achievement or merit, but is nevertheless something which all men are affirmed to have, and yet have in a way which accords to each a particular history for which there is no identical replacement. Indeed, this line of questioning might be turned on its head. If my regard for another depends simply and solely on his individual achievements, merit, or desert, in principle anyone who "performs" equally well is interchangeable with him. Then I am ranking people according to a grading concept in reference to which their basic and individual dignity becomes an appropriate subject for praise and blame and where varying scores may be accumulated.

We thus arrive at the point about individual merit and preference which the agapist finds potentially dangerous and against which he wishes to safeguard. He need not deny or discount that one of the wants people have is to be praised for acquired excellences. He may, for instance, connect this to their freedom to live and develop in a distinctive way which, he holds, constitutes part of the well being to be equally weighed (a point to which I shall return). He may likewise accept that uniqueness always connects to particular behavior, though to failures as well as successes. What he does deny is that human dignity ought ever exhaustively to be based on or weighed in proportion to individual merit and preference. For the appeal to merit and preference always carries with it the danger that the differences based on those standards may be confounded with the sameness of human dignity. What the agapist is concerned to prohibit is illustrated in this statement: "At the risk of displeasing innocent ears, I submit that egoism belongs to the essence of a noble soul, I mean the unalterable belief that to a being such as 'we,' other beings must naturally be in subjection, and have to sacrifice themselves to us." [2] Here there are "naturally" and without remainder superior and inferior neighbors, whose respective well-being is valued differently. On the one side, the agapist might argue, those who are highly successful may be deluded into thinking that they belong to a superior "moral caste" and are entitled to a privileged consideration of their own well-being. They suppose that the realization of their own good has some higher value than that of a "mere nobody." [3] Similarly, the unsuccessful may confuse their failures with the worth of their own well-being and thereby acquiesce in being used as means or instruments.

In part, the principle of equal regard enjoins man not to let his basic attitudes toward others be determined by the disparities in talent and achievement and the inequalities in attractiveness and social rank which differentiate men. He is not, for example, to value his neighbor in accordance with the value of that neighbor's social position. He is to attempt to get behind social, political, and technical titles which are the all-too-evident tokens of inequality. He is not to confuse the differences in instrumental value which various titles doubtless often reflect with the irreducible value of the well-being of the holders of these titles. He is enjoined to identify with the neighbor's point

2. Friedrich Nietzsche, *Beyond Good and Evil,* trans. Helen Zimmern (London: George Allen & Unwin, Ltd., 1967), p. 240. See also p. 225: "The essential thing . . . in a good and healthy aristocracy is that it . . . should . . . accept with a good conscience the sacrifice of a legion of individuals, who, *for its sake,* must be suppressed and reduced to imperfect men, to slaves and instruments." I am interested in such views in themselves, whatever Nietzsche may have said elsewhere and whether or not they reflect the dominant strains in his thought. Cf. also Vlastos' citation of these statements, "Justice and Equality," p. 71. Vlastos' discussion as a whole is one to which I am particularly indebted.

3. Vlastos, "Justice and Equality," pp. 51, 70–71.

of view, to try to imagine what it is for him to live the life he does, to occupy the position he holds.[4]

Another question concerns whether any further distinctions ought to be made between certain of the neighbor's generic characteristics, each of which is equally valued in comparison to the same characteristics in others. (Hence we might say, "One neighbor's freedom is as valuable as another's.") The assumption is that implied in any human relation are characteristics of the other to which the agent ought to attend, since they always count in regarding him as having human dignity. They specify the basic content of "well-being." Some go on to correlate certain characteristics shared by everyone with certain agapeistic treatments. Entire fields of action are defined by reference to acknowledging or enhancing characteristics valued equally in each case. Here is one of the clearest points at which religious beliefs may have effects on the content of the principle. I said earlier that beliefs may intelligibly modify what it means to love the neighbor. Descriptive and evaluative elements are frequently built in as constitutive features specifying who he is and how he should be treated.

Anything said here will necessarily seem cryptic, for the answers given will once more reflect to some extent comprehensive doctrines about God and human nature. But three characteristics may be cited because they appear so often. The first is quite straightforwardly the God-relation. That men are equally related to God and that this state of affairs is equally valuable is not in dispute. Kierkegaard's statement on equality before God was quoted in chapter 6. So far as a correlated agapeistic treatment is concerned, I have also had occasion to note Barth's stress on witness. The concern is, then, with conscious life in relation to God. It has been argued often enough, of course, that this is what distinguishes agape most clearly. "That burning love of souls is what charity means; charity is not, as people often think nowadays, a fatuous amiability towards every vagary of misconduct and misbelief." [5]

4. See Bernard Williams, "The Idea of Equality," *Philosophy, Politics and Society,* pp. 110–31.
5. Geach, *God and the Soul,* pp. 115–16.

The second characteristic has to do with the neighbor's status as a creature, his "psycho-physical existence." Here the assumption is that each man has interests which may be injured or enhanced. They may have little or nothing to do with moral merit. The agent may see himself as called to conform to God's creative activity which sends rain on the just and unjust. Jesus' own behavior likewise is seen as paradigmatic, when for instance he does not dismiss his hearers without feeding them first (Mk. 8:3).[6] And many of his teachings stress the urgent importance of meeting mundane needs (apart from merit). So in Mt. 25:35 ff., the needs include food, drink, shelter, clothing, health, and liberty. Perhaps one may generalize by grouping such interests under physical survival, acquirement of skill and knowledge, and so on, with "welfare" as a possible blanket heading. This characteristic is also sometimes linked to a psychological assumption that each man desires affection and self-respect. Each man is capable of feeling pain and loss, not only from physical causes of an immediate kind, but also from deprivation of human affection and support.[7] This in turn connects with frequent references in the literature to the neighbor's alleged "need for love." Consider the following statements.

The need which *Agape* goes out to meet is always in the end the need for love and for nothing else.[8]

The fundamental human craving is to belong, to count in the community of being, to have one's freedom in and with the response of others, to enjoy God as one who makes us members of one society. . . . The root anxiety is that of 'not-belonging', of not counting.[9]

6. Häring, *Law of Christ*, 1:389–91.

7. Note, for example, the assumption sometimes held to be operative in psychotherapy: "The deprivation originally suffered by the patient is a deprivation of mothering, a deprivation of primal, absolute, and unconditional loving" (Paul Halmos, *The Faith of the Counsellors* [London: Constable, 1965], p. 50).

8. Burnaby, *Amor Dei*, p. 310; see also Thomas, *Christian Ethics and Moral Philosophy*, p. 446.

9. Williams, *Spirit and the Forms of Love*, p. 146.

Such a need includes but is not always restricted to one-to-one relations of reciprocity in kind. It often refers in addition to a more primitive and loose amalgam of things, e.g., the need to be "heard," to be allowed to communicate with others, to count in the social community, and the like. In other words, it often seems nearly synonymous with the general characteristic I have noted: the need of the neighbor to have his basic interests considered and his welfare accounted as valuable as another's.

A final characteristic is more difficult to isolate even roughly and far more controversial. One may call it the characteristic of "freedom," waiving most of the well-known difficulties with that concept. This includes "not only conscious choices and deliberate decisions but also those subtler modulations and more spontaneous expressions of individual preference which could scarcely be called 'choices' or 'decisions' without some forcing of language." [10] Many believe, of course, that to refer to freedom is to skate onto thin theological (to say nothing of philosophical) ice. But clearly there are schemes that hold that whatever God in His grace does for men, He does not take their own initiative and action from them. So one may speak, as Kierkegaard seems to do, of some generic accountability to God, independent of differences in talent and achievement, in relation to which no special advantages, privileges, or short-cuts obtain. The energy with which one loves may affect, again, how but not whether one is loved, nor whether all men are in an equal condition of accountability.

Tillich also distinguishes whether from how one loves, and connects the latter to honoring creaturely freedom. He does so in the context of an attempt to make forgiveness and judgment compatible. For him, "judgment is an act of love which surrenders that which resists love to self-destruction." [11] When out of love God condemns, this is "not the negation of love but the negation of the negation of love." [12] Tillich calls this condemnation love's "strange work" and claims that without it there would be "chaotic surrender" to the

10. Vlastos, "Justice and Equality," p. 49.
11. Tillich, *Systematic Theology,* 1:283.
12. Ibid., cf. pp. 284–87.

forces of disintegration. It is always held together with the "proper work" of forgiveness. How are these two works united?

> They are one because love does not enforce salvation. If it did it would commit a double injustice. It would disregard the claim of every person to be treated not as a thing but as a centered, deciding, free, and responsible self. Since God is love and His love is one with His power, He has not the power to force somebody into His salvation. He would contradict Himself. And this God cannot do. At the same time such an act would disregard the strange work of love, namely the destruction of what destroys love. It would violate the unconditional character of love and with it the divine majesty. Love must destroy what is against love, but not him who is the bearer of that which is against love. . . . But the unity of his will is destroyed, he is thrown into a conflict with himself, the name of which is despair. . . . The hell of despair is the strange work that love does within us in order to open us up for its own work. . . . But even despair does not make us into a mechanism. It is a test of our freedom and personal dignity, even in relation to God.[13]

Tillich thus distinguishes between a legitimate wrath and an illegitimate hate. Hate connotes ultimate exclusion; wrath is the reaction of love against those attitudes and actions opposed to it.[14]

This sort of account is often seen to be directly relevant for agapeistic treatments. If the human agent is to conform to grace, then whatever he does for others he ought not to take their own initiative and ability to act from them. And if God in His incessant action on every human creature does not enforce or coerce, then surely between these same finite creatures qualitatively greater restrictions govern what they may do for each other. Finally, attention to the characteristic of freedom is normally held to link with reverence for the other's moral capacities.

13. Tillich, *Love, Power and Justice*, pp. 114–15.

14. Paul Tillich, "Being and Love," *Moral Principles of Action*, ed. Ruth Nanda Anshen (New York: Harper and Brothers, 1952), pp. 665–66.

We must have regard not simply to their *ends,* but also to their *efforts.* Were happiness their sole interest there would, I think, be no objection of principle (though there might well be one of a tactical order) to treating them as simply our 'patient' beneficiaries. But in relation to the pursuit of ends under the idea of value this will not do. Here it is of the essence of proper respect that we encourage others to be co-agents, and accept and welcome them as such, as co-operating with ourselves in a common enterprise: and we are, each of us, to engage in this enterprise only in ways that are consistent with this attitude.[15]

Such a statement seems indisputable. What is often not precisely considered in the literature are the complex interrelations between these three characteristics, and whether and in what ways they relate and may conflict in practice. A major reason why people disagree about what is the most loving action in a given situation is that they often attach different priorities to, for instance, welfare or freedom. Thus if I stress the latter, I may come close to holding that to be loving is synonymous with "doing one's own thing." Loving the neighbor *means* fostering his subjective identity and integrity. The conditions which avoid exterior constraints and impositions and enhance personal freedom are *eo ipso* what love requires. In short, I may espouse a kind of permissive anti-authoritarianism. Agape is then often connected with wider assumptions about what is good for another; and specifically, about whether this can be assessed objectively in part by the agent, or whether the recipient himself determines most of what should count as his relevant interests to be considered. Moreover, there may be different kinds of correlations between characteristics and treatments. Equality of welfare may include agapeistic treatments common to everyone and equality of freedom may lead to unequal treatments. Efforts toward physical survival may be indiscriminate, but indiscriminate praise would be self-defeating.

Many other characteristic issues arise in connection with what has

15. Maclagan, "Respect for Persons as a Moral Principle — II," p. 294.

been said about equal regard.[16] I shall, however, discuss only one other. It seems to me too often neglected in the literature, and while what I say here will have to be only introductory, at least it should be identified.

The distinction already emphasized between the sameness of human dignity and the differences based on preference and merit might lead one to conclude (as Kierkegaard apparently does, for example) that no positive material connection exists between agape and *any* special relation. That is, on the basis of agape can anything be said beyond what applies in any human relation? Do the same general restraints and positive injunctions set the boundaries, as it were, within which special relations come into their own? It would be premature to accept this conclusion if only because one class of special relations has so often been assumed to connect more directly with agape. This class includes persons to whom one stands in a special *moral* relation. We often talk about special moral obligations and particular considerations due, e.g., spouses, children, friends, colleagues, perhaps co-religionists, perhaps fellow-countrymen. In the literature I think some positive connection between agape and these obligations is assumed far more often than it is elucidated explicitly.

16. For instance, there is the question about who qualifies as a neighbor: are there limits below which a living being no longer possesses the necessary characteristics to warrant assigning equal value to his well-being? Surprisingly, little explicit attention is given to this question in the literature, despite its obvious importance. Virtually everyone would agree that responsibility is not a necessary condition in that infants and the merely immature obviously qualify. Furthermore, certain characteristics are taken to be clearly irrelevant in deciding whether someone is to be counted as a neighbor or not, e.g., racial differences. The most difficult cases include mental defectives. Such cases may give trouble especially to those who tie irreducible value to rationality or potential rationality. The loss of such potentiality may signify attenuation of regard. Religious belief may often make an enormous difference here in backing a policy of neither disqualification nor refusal actively to help. For to disqualify altogether from regard is a step seen as little short of assuming omniscience (see, e.g., Earl E. Harris, "Respect for Persons," *Ethics and Society,* pp. 127–28). And to help actively is one natural outcome of believing they are related to God. This may be one of the points which is not so obvious an outcome from the principle of utility. At least it would seem that the often painstaking help required has great dis-utility value.

And when examined the assumption may be open to question. For
agape enjoins one to attribute to everyone alike an irreducible worth
and dignity, to rule out comparisons at the most basic level, to refuse
to defer to the particular social and ethnic groups to which individuals
happen to belong. What, then, does agape imply for special moral
relations, if — as is so often assumed — *no other principles intervene?* Is agape irrelevant beyond a certain point, or relevant in ways
which are misleadingly indiscriminate? Shall I, for example, marry
the first woman I find who will have me and whom I can make
happy? And is there backing only for as much social egalitarianism as
possible? [17] These last two questions of course involve us in too
many unexamined leaps, but that they come rather naturally to mind
suggests in a crude way the nature of the issue.

More precisely it is this. Only one sort of restriction in scope seems
permitted by the concept of agape as equal regard. It is limited
solely by what one may call the conditions of finitude. To avail myself
again of a common distinction, insofar as the agent is bound to inter-
act with a limited number of human beings, and sometimes in quite
superficial ways, the most that can be required is equal consideration
but not identical treatment (again, beyond what may apply in any
human relation). For the agent simply is incapable of enhancing the
welfare of every neighbor with whom he has to do in the same way
or to the same extent. Moreover, the possibility of conflict between

17. At this point there is an important similarity in a range of characteristic
problems between agape and utilitarianism. Note the following early criticism of
the latter: " 'Everybody to count for one, nobody for more than one.' Does this
mean that, in respect of whatever is proportioned out, each is to have the same
share whatever his character, whatever his conduct? Shall he if passive have as
much as if active? Shall he if useless have as much as if virtuous? Shall he if
criminal have as much as if virtuous? If the distribution is to be made without
reference to the natures and deeds of the recipients, then it must be shown
that a system which equalizes, as far as it can, the treatment of good and bad,
will be beneficial. If the distribution is not to be indiscriminate, then the formula
disappears. The something distributed must be apportioned otherwise than by
equal division. There must be adjustment of amounts to deserts; and we are left
in the dark as to the mode of adjustment — we have to find other guidance"
(Herbert Spencer, *The Data of Ethics* [London: Williams and Norgate, 1907],
pp. 191–92. Cf. Rescher, *Distributive Justice,* pp. 42–43).

the various wants of various neighbors means that whereas he may consider them all, he cannot possibly satisfy them all. Such a restriction is incontestable. Yet in itself it seems to provide no criteria for choosing initially between those who may come equally within the range of the agent's help. The question then is whether the restriction of finitude alone is adequate to the purpose, i.e., whether the obligations of special moral relations can be founded directly upon it. For the restriction allows that close personal relations, for instance, must be confined to a few because they are so time-consuming, but not because they require special qualifications, such as openness, shared interests, sensitivity, and so on.

One reason for saying these obligations cannot be so founded is that they often reflect the *differences* as well as the sameness between human beings. This is a hackneyed observation, but crucial nonetheless.

> Human beings are the same in respect of being featherless bipeds, of being sentient agents, perhaps rational ones, perhaps children of God. They are not the same in respect of height, age, sex, intellectual ability, strength of character. These latter differences may be irrelevant, as the egalitarians assert: but they are not proved not to be differences by the fact that in other respects men are similar.[18]

Again, agape may set aside as many differences as possible which are judged to be irrelevant, e.g., racial differences. But not all differences can thus be set aside and some legitimately remaining form an integral part of many special relations. These differences may be divided roughly and with many overlaps into three classes: obvious physical differences such as age, sex, intellectual endowments, and beauty; differences in particular interests, tastes, and values, many of which may not be the appropriate subject for moral praise and blame; meritarian differences, reflecting the possessor's use of his talents and opportunities. It is this final class that gives particular trouble for agape.

Why not then conclude that the urgencies of particular obligations

18. J. R. Lucas, "Against Equality," *Philosophy* 40 (October, 1965):297.

cannot be directly founded upon agape, that the latter simply sets the boundaries within which special relations come into their own? Let me first examine this conclusion in slightly more detail. The importance of the boundaries should not of course in any way be minimized. And while agape remains logically distinct, it may still provide a kind of powerful indirect support for the success of the particular objectives within various special relations. In the case of marriage, for instance, one finds the argument that the relation itself depends on more than specific human differences and preferential judgments which nonetheless set it apart.[19] It is excessively vulnerable, if you like, when governed only by preferential criteria. It requires a deliberate vow, which once made does not accommodate changes in external circumstances and temperamental harmony. Resolution more than taste may effectively buttress the objective of permanence. The concepts of independence from change, fidelity, and so on obviously begin to range on the concept of agape itself. While they all remain independent of one another, there is once more overlap in this case. It is as if once the vow is made (and the element of preference may be legitimately determinative in leading up to it), with one person identified for whose welfare the agent is particularly responsible, the principle of agape may then furnish powerful, perhaps virtually indispensable support.

It is also important to recognize, I think, that there may be differences in the degree to which agape is directly supportive, due to the different kinds of special relations. One might distinguish at least: the obligations deriving from the voluntary acceptance of a particular role, office, or position, e.g., husband or teacher; the obligations deriving from relations not voluntarily established, e.g., being a son; specific promises of undertakings. All of these are to be distinguished from obligations in any human relation. The point is, varying ratios of unqualified care, preference, and merit may be involved. Thus for example, in deciding to marry, I may weigh beauty, intellectual ability, strength of character, and so on; but when my wife becomes pregnant, I may hope for a boy or girl but I shall take home and help to raise whichever she delivers at the hospital. Or

19. As we saw in the case of de Rougemont, *Love in the Western World*.

again, as a teacher I may have to fail a student because he did not do the work, even when I know he may then be expelled from school, drafted, and possibly killed in combat in Vietnam. I can indeed express my personal concern to him about the consequences of my action, but I cannot alter the roles we both have voluntarily assumed and the fact that the university is among other things an institution based on achievement. Yet because I do not admire or approve of what my son has done, I do not thereby cease to have affection for him nor do I make his performance a condition for giving him as happy a home life as possible.

Why does indirect support of this kind leave many vaguely dissatisfied? One reason comes immediately to mind. There is a characteristic unease with the restrictedness of special relations. For obligations pertaining to them may become the effective center of gravity, so urgent and really ultimate that they swamp universal human dignity as such. The latter retreats to a vague, residual status of "common humanity." Consider the following account of the views of "common-sense" which arrive at a kind of "self-referential altruism."

> The altruism of common-sense is always limited in scope. It does not hold that any of us has an equally strong obligation to benefit everyone whom he can affect by his actions. According to it, each of us has specially strong obligations to benefit certain persons and groups of persons who stand in certain special relations to *himself*. And these special relations to himself are the ultimate and sufficient ground of these specially urgent obligations. Each person may be regarded as a centre of a number of concentric circles. The persons and the groups to whom he has the most urgent obligations may be regarded as forming the innermost circle. Then comes a circle of persons and groups to whom his obligations are moderately urgent. Finally there is the outermost circle of persons (and animals) to whom he has only the obligation of "common humanity". This is what I mean by saying that the altruism which common-sense accepts is "self-referential." [20]

20. Broad, "Certain Features in Moore's Ethical Doctrines," pp. 54–55.

The agapist may well see this as a case of misplaced emphasis at least, perhaps going beyond any conceivable restriction of finitude. His cause for wariness can be indicated by an example. A man sits in his living room and watches the evening news on television. There is the daily report on casualties in the Vietnam war. He listens with indifference or mild satisfaction to euphemisms about the "body-count" of enemy soldiers. The tendency to apathy about the fate of those beyond the range of his special obligations, or outside the groups with which he identifies, needs no historical documentation. Talk about common humanity may retreat into the mists of pious irrelevance. Thus self-referential altruism cannot be regarded with equanimity, however accurate de facto and however important a gain over simply unimaginative and more deliberate forms of egoism. The tendency then for patriots to become uncritical, for parents to become doting, and so on, must be guarded against. The agapist prefers to begin at the other end, with the negative restraints and positive injunctions applicable in any human relation. And in addition to the sensitivity this may afford for the lot of those beyond the range of his special obligations, it may also produce different reasons for action in cases of forced choice between conflicting interests. His judgment about an armed conflict, for instance, may be based on his concern to protect innocent third parties but not merely on a limited identification with his own group threatening always to end in the assumption of "my country right or wrong." However subtle and difficult, his own criteria must be retained, if an ethics of protection is not to lapse into an uncritical nationalism.

Such a reason is hardly decisive however, since it really reverts back to the factors obtaining in any human relation. It only underscores the moral dangers in special relations against which agape safeguards. How might the agapist proceed if he undertook to found particular obligations and rights in special relations directly upon agape? He might begin by holding that the respective urgencies of particular obligations would involve an estimation of the comparative efficiency and long-term importance of various kinds of service open to the agent. For example, he might note that he has a better chance of securing substantial benefits for others if he does not confine himself solely to the widest possible distribution of his energies.

For such confinement necessarily restricts attention to more or less minimal wants impersonally satisfied. He might in addition, though never instead, serve a more complex range of psychological as well as physical and social needs by attending to those to whom he stands in intimate relation. Thus, he might contribute to the permanent psychological security of his children and thereby maximize their chances for personal happiness as well as social prosperity. (Moreover, he might argue that it is more likely in the long run that everyone's children will be well taken care of if each parent restricts primary attention to his own.) If this latter example sounds intolerably "unreal," as if agape simply casts around for receptacles, it might be replied that we are at the moment concerned only with conceptual elucidation. For all I have said, in actual life the pervasiveness of feelings of special attachment and devotion, simply natural and spontaneous, may remain, stabilized and integrated by agape perhaps, but not abolished by it.

This is not the place to pursue such a program. Generally I am inclined to think that it would prove impossible to execute in every case and that — formally — a preferable alternative would be to hold that at the very least special obligations ought to presuppose and never require less than agape requires. Agape is the guardian in rather than the direct inspiration of every special relation. It sets the boundaries within which the power of romantic eros, for example, may be allowed distinctive expression. Insofar as many such particular obligations and bonds legitimately involve preference and the like, their respective urgencies cannot all, exhaustively and without remainder, be simply derived from or founded directly upon agape.

I shall try to say a little more about this difficult question when I consider friendship and justice. And it is time to revisit some of the other features.

Self-Sacrifice

At this point I shall examine more specifically how equal regard is related to the other features considered in chapter 1 and to self-love and justice. Following the earlier order, I shall begin with self-sacrifice.

Serious difficulties arise when one follows out the implications of treating self-sacrifice as the quintessence of agape in Niebuhrian fashion. Such difficulties are illustrated by the question about the blank check. The feature of self-sacrifice in itself would appear to provide no way of distinguishing between attention to another's needs and submission to his exploitation and no warrant for resisting the latter. Consider for example what has been called the "inversion" of the golden rule. "Do unto others as you would have them do unto you" is inverted to "Do unto others as *they* would have you do unto them." The following are some implications of such an inversion.

> Let us suppose that we should do unto others as they would have us do unto them. What sort of conduct would this require of us? Well, for one thing, if you want me to assign to you all of my property, then this rule implies that I should do so, for it requires me to do unto you as you would have me do unto you, and in this case you would have me sign over to you all of my property. If your demands should be increased, and you want me to be your slave for life and do your every bidding, the rule would require me to do this. Such requirements are absurd, and the rule that leads to them can be no better. Under such a rule, no woman's "virtue" would be safe from the desires of any importuning male. Indeed, rape would be morally impossible, since no one would have a right to resist. This reasoning leads irresistibly to the conclusion that this "rule" leads to consequences that are absurd and morally wrong.[21]

It is not as if in the name of self-sacrifice we can resist exploitation (or at least have some warrant for doing so) as well as attend to needs. In order to resist at all and in any sense it appears that we must have recourse to some additional principle, such as justice; which, however, ranks below sacrificial love in Niebuhr's hierarchy.

Moreover, once again insufficient attention is accorded the distinction between the treatment of someone else in relation to myself and the treatment of someone else in relation to still another (or

21. M. G. Singer, "The Golden Rule," p. 296.

others) than myself. It is obvious that self-sacrifice has significantly less relevance (and what little it has may be patently unhelpful) to the dilemmas peculiar to the latter, which nonetheless occasion a great number of our moral decisions. That Niebuhr is aware of this at least to a degree is indicated in the following passage, which suggests how peculiarly difficult the matter is for him, given his attempt to hold together sacrificial love and a viable social ethic.

> It is not even right to insist that every action of the Christian must conform to *agape*, rather than to the norms of relative justice and mutual love by which life is maintained and conflicting interests are arbitrated in history. For as soon as the life and interest of others than the agent are involved in an action or policy, the sacrifice of those interests ceases to be "self-sacrifice." It may actually become an unjust betrayal of their interests. Failure to understand this simple fact and this paradoxical relation between individual and collective action has resulted in the unholy alliance between Christian perfectionism and cowardly counsels of political expediency in dealing with tyrants in our own day.[22]

Finally, the feature of self-sacrifice cannot be intelligibly applied to the several parties in a given transaction. A question some philosophers ask about any normative principle is whether it would be self-frustrating if everyone acted on it.[23] Their contention is that an ethical principle can be meant for everyone only if it has a point which is not dependent on a great number of persons acting on an opposite principle. Its meaning must not thus be "parasitic." If one subjects self-sacrifice to such a test, it is not at all clear that it fares very well. I have already observed how its meaning and point relate necessarily to that with which it is compared and usually contrasted: what decisively identifies self-sacrifice for Niebuhr is not so much its promotion of other-regarding attitudes and actions but

22. Niebuhr, *Nature and Destiny of Man,* 2:88.
23. See, e.g., Baier, *The Moral Point of View,* pp. 196–97.

simply the process of non-accommodation to self-interest. And suppose everyone did act self-sacrificially, would the consequences not be self-frustrating? Consider a passage from the earliest Halachic Midrash, the *Sifra,* which has been much discussed in Rabbinic literature.[24] "If two men are traveling on a journey and one has a pitcher of water, if both drink they will both die, but if only one drinks, he will reach civilization." Is it better that both should drink and die rather than that one should witness his companion's death? Or should the one holding the water drink it? Both alternatives have been commended, and interesting points have been made on each side, with related cases also discussed.[25] My concern is only with two points that emerge from the discussion. (1) A strict obligation for one man to hand the water to the other would in effect be self-defeating, since the recipient would be under the same obligation to hand it back again, and so on. (2) To say that it is contradictory to exhort *everyone* to act self-sacrificially all of the time is not to forbid *anyone* from giving another the preference on certain occasions. It is assumed in the case in question that both desire to drink. The issue is whether it is wrong for both to die, if one can live. But if we suppose that one freely gives the water to the other who drinks it and survives, the gift could surely be characterized as morally laudable and perhaps supererogatory (a subject to be considered later). Ample room may still be allowed for a fictional Sidney Carton or a factual Captain Oates.

If one agrees that the implications of treating self-sacrifice as invariably the preferred or purest expression of agape are approximately what has been suggested above, then a consideration of modifications is in order. I think the difficulties are largely avoided when equal regard remains as the center of gravity. For then one has certain reasons at his disposal for distinguishing between attention to needs and

24. Louis Jacobs, "Greater Love Hath No Man . . . The Jewish Point of View of Self-Sacrifice," *Judaism* 6 (Winter, 1957):41–47. See also his "Disinterestedness," *Judaism* 6 (Summer, 1957):202–09.

25. For example, while the rabbis disagree on whether the agent should sacrifice his life to save another's, they agree that he ought not to sacrifice another's life to save his own (Jacobs, "Greater Love Hath No Man," p. 44).

submission to exploitation. These reasons were enumerated in chapter 1. In self-other relations, for instance, some distinction is allowed between what is good for a man and what he may happen to want, however perplexing it often is to apply this distinction in practice. One can also allow for the furtherance of interests of some third parties even when the agent benefits as well, without having to say each time that his actions no longer conform to agape. In this way one's supreme ethical principle need not be supplemented so quickly, so often, and yet always by less laudable principles. Finally, equal regard can be intelligibly applied to the several parties in a given transaction. It would not be self-frustrating if everyone acted on it. Whatever other problems might obtain, a world in which each man's interests were weighed prior to his doing anything in particular is a world in which each could consistently adhere to this same principle. For equal regard is contingently related to the process of non-accommodation to self-interest; its point and meaning are not tied necessarily to any such process. As I noted earlier, at a minimum many self-benefitting actions may be morally right because they do further other peoples' interests. One need not assume even in this life that neighbor-regard and self-sacrifice are automatically correlative. Sometimes then Niebuhr appears to confuse the position that self-interest is unreflectively strong and quickly excessive, so that the bulk of imposing moral considerations must always be other-regarding ones, with the position that in every instance where one is regarding the interests of others he must *eo ipso* be sacrificing his own. Actually one might hold the first but deny the second; they are clearly not equivalent.

How should self-sacrifice be assessed? If one conceives of it as an often appropriate exemplification of neighbor-regard, subordinate to such regard rather than the quintessence of it, no such self-frustrating conclusions follow. Generally therefore I am inclined to think that instead of appraising self-sacrifice as the purest and most perfect manifestation of agape, the difficulties I have considered are avoided if one allows it only *instrumental* warrant. Self-sacrifice must always be purposive in promoting the welfare of others and never simply expressive of something resident in the agent. It is simply one possible exemplification and by-product of devotion to others for their own sakes.[26]

While he objectifies self-sacrifice, perhaps Niebuhr might grant, if pressed, that he never intended to concentrate the self's attention on its own state, on non-accommodation to self-seeking. And he might question whether it is a valid criterion always to ask if a normative principle would be self-frustrating should everyone act on it. He might try to distinguish between the validity of sacrificial love and its practical realizability. That is, he might simply argue for a universal recommendation to act in certain ways together with an awareness that these actions will never be forthcoming from all quarters. The recommendation is typically linked to efforts to remedy the patent immorality of many. He is not interested in any view that a principle embodies, or ought to be realizable in, an ideal situation. One must be careful in any case to distinguish the logical objections to self-sacrifice from other parts of Niebuhr's program, most of which, for all I have said, might still be retained in modified form. It would still be open to someone to hold, for example, that neighbor-regard carries no guarantee of "historical success" in Niebuhr's sense, that suffering may be alleviated but not always eliminated, that conflicts between genuine goods and choices in favor of the lesser of two evils are sometimes unavoidable. Again, ample room may be allowed for sacrificial actions which benefit others. One's entire theological scheme will usually affect decisions on these further questions.

Mutuality

In introducing the general feature of mutuality, I said that some of its defenders have maintained that apart from it, the criterion for

---

26. Paul Ramsey appears to have something of this sort in mind in his proposal to "de-adjectify" neighbor-love. "Love is simply love, the genuine article; and it intends the good of the beloved one and not the response of mutuality; it intends the good of the other and not its own actual self-sacrifice or suffering. It is the *neighbor,* and not mutuality or heedlessness or sacrifice or suffering, who stands ever before the eyes of love" (*Nine Modern Moralists,* p. 146. Cf. Thomas, *Christian Ethics and Moral Philosophy,* p. 519).

agapeistic actions appears to be only what exemplifies or expresses
something resident in the agent. It seems to me that such a conclusion does not follow, at least concerning equal regard. Perhaps
Kierkegaard comes uncomfortably close at times to such a conclusion.
He does insist rather stridently on the complete indifference to any
kind of response.[27] The case of the enemy is really convenient because it indicates with superior clarity whether the regard is thus
indifferent. One might conclude then that the neighbor is little more
than an *occasion* for disclosing the state of the agent. But whether
this conclusion applies to most of his treatment of neighbor-love can,
I think, be legitimately questioned. In any case, the conclusion need
not follow concerning equal regard taken in itself. For one should
distinguish between the independence of the existence of regard from
a response and regard manifested in a concern about states of others
independent of concern about reciprocity. So far as I can see, there
is nothing to preclude an acceptance of the latter. Indeed, any serious regard for others would seem invariably to result in actions whose
aim is to establish, continue, or alter certain states in other men,
and whose collateral effects are largely confined to others. (Of course
there is the busybody possibility, but that is another matter.) One
might even go on to allow, without substantial concession, for one
sense in which serious regard about the states of others includes a
concern about reciprocity, without being exhausted by such concern or dependent upon reciprocity for its existence. For example, an
agent may be concerned, as we have seen, about another's conscious
relationship to God. But this itself may include concern about how
that relationship is manifested in the recipient's relationships with
other men, and more specifically in concern about the recipient's
own agapeic disposition. Genuine regard for the neighbor's well-
being involves concern that he should regard *his* neighbor. One test
of such regard is how the other reciprocates concern shown to him.
While not a complete test, it may nonetheless be revealing. A grate-

27. The classic illustration is his discussion of "the work of love in remem-
bering one dead." "One who is dead is not an actual object; he is only the
occasion which continually reveals what resides in the one loving who relates
himself to him or which helps to make clear how it is with one living who does
not relate himself to him" (*Works of Love,* p. 319).

ful son or daughter will not necessarily make a good parent, but an ungrateful one is less likely to, barring a change of heart. The recipient's willingness to respond to the agent's concern is one gauge of the other's personal well-being, and in this sense reciprocation may be the object of unselfish regard. Thus the only alternatives are not, as is often supposed by the disputants, either an interest in a response which is actually an interest in self-aggrandizement, or a confinement to the agent's inner states so that, for example, a recluse may love as fully and appropriately as a parent or statesman.

If one takes agape to require an active concern about states of others, something more should be added about the connection between equal regard and what was discussed earlier under both personal and social relations.

When the exigencies of personal relations were considered in chapter 1, I said that claims often vary because they revolve around different conceptions of friendship. Among those who ascribe supreme and overriding value to personal and reciprocal relations, where friendship in particular is an (or the) intrinsic good, there is a selective emphasis on the affinities between equal regard and such relations. Similarly, those who contrast equal regard and friendship are inclined to ignore such affinities in their effort to isolate an essential difference. It may be that here we really do have a case where the relation is more complex than either side acknowledges.

The affinities include at least the following.[28] First, a friend is cared about for his own sake: he counts in himself. While he is doubtless a member of various groups, he himself remains always somewhat unclassifiable. One could never say that he was indifferently interchangeable with someone else in his same station or with approximately his abilities. Beneath or behind the relative worth he may have in comparison with others, he has an incomparable worth in himself. And it is just this uniqueness which marks a relation like friendship. Second, any persistent calculation of mutual advantages

---

28. In addition to the treatments considered in chapter 1, see Maclagan, "Respect for Persons as a Moral Principle — I," pp. 201–04, on both affinities and differences.

does seem out of place. One does not indeed measure out the giving and taking very carefully.

Yet this is often as far as the conception of friendship explicitly extends for a D'Arcy, Burnaby, or Johann. And for a Kierkegaard, such a conception misses an essential difference, at least as friendship is commonly understood. Whether one agrees with Kierkegaard here does not strictly depend on whether one agrees with his own denial of any affinities. The essential difference is simply this. Equal regard is unalterable; to abandon it would never be appropriate. Alternately, friendship may fluctuate; it depends at least in part on mutual liking, and usually on admiration and esteem as well. In short, it depends on a combination of "suchness" with "thatness." Thus I may have to resign myself to certain changes in my relation to my friend, changes which eat away at the special bond between us. It is not that I can ever sweepingly just "give up on him" or cease to care at all, for agape itself prohibits that. But I cannot honestly deny that I feel differently than I did. The reasons may be due to failures on my part or his which bring suffering and perhaps a sense of precariousness and transiency in most personal sharing. But the reasons may simply involve changes in the spheres of our interests, in the things we count as important or what we believe we have to do.

It is of course not only Kierkegaard who insists on a distinction between agape and friendship. We saw how Barth does so as well, though unlike Kierkegaard he refuses to say they must be opposed. Most of the historic discussions of friendship have certainly characterized it as subject to change and with special conditions attached.[29] It lacks the permanent stability of agape. On the other hand, friendships may grow so ardent as effectively to involve rejection of those outside. Some have consequently held than an agapeistic attitude is required to safeguard friendship or philia from degenerating into elitism.[30] While conscious preference may be inevitable, it can result

29. See, e.g., the eighth and ninth books of Aristotle's *Nichomachean Ethics*; and Part II, *The Doctrine of Virtue*, of Kant's *The Metaphysic of Morals*. On the last, see also H. J. Paton, "Kant on Friendship," *Proceedings of the British Academy* 42 (London: Oxford University Press, 1956), pp. 45–66.

30. E.g., Tillich, *Love, Power, and Justice*, p. 119.

in aristocratic isolation which is a corruption of philia and must be guarded against. One might say then that the presence of agape is a necessary but not a sufficient condition for philia, and that the presence of philia is a sufficient but not a necessary condition for agape.

Even if one agrees that there are conceptual differences as well as important areas of overlap, I think one can and ought still to take note how often actual cases avoid any strict discontinuities. For example, even when changes do occur, they rarely efface a relation altogether. The relation as it once was may give any present actions toward the other part of their intelligibility and significance. One rather lengthy illustration may help to make the point. A society which perhaps prized friendship more than most was that of nineteenth-century England, or at least certain segments of it. One such segment included the Tractarian movement, centered largely around John Henry Newman. Among many who shared a friendship with Newman was his one-time pupil, Mark Pattison, who later (as Rector of Lincoln College, Oxford) was influential in the development of the modern University.[31] For the six or seven years after he was elected to a fellowship at Lincoln (1839), Pattison devoted himself heart and soul to Tractarianism. He worked closely with Newman on several scholarly projects. A genuine friendship developed which was never entirely dissolved. Yet as the years passed Pattison's religious views changed enormously. There was a steady erosion of his former beliefs. The most he could say of theology in his mature years was that it was "a perplexing but not altogether profitless inquiry."[32] He came to regard Newman's own views as utterly untenable, though he never questioned his intellectual integrity or sincerity. Only once or twice in later years did the two men encounter each other. Relations were friendly but now lacked all intimacy. In 1884 however, when Pattison was seriously ill and obviously soon to die, Newman, in his eighty-third year, came down unexpectedly to Oxford from Birmingham to call. Pattison was shaken and touched.

31. The summary here is based on V. H. H. Green, *Oxford Common Room: A Study of Lincoln College and Mark Pattison* (London: Edward Arnold Ltd., 1957).
32. Ibid., p. 224.

He stayed nearly three hours. It was not like Pattison to allow
any visitor completely disinterested motives. "It was not all
personal regard, but the hope, however slight, that I might
still be got over in my last moments." But he was "dreadfully
agitated, distressed even" at such "proof of affection." What
they discussed is narrated in the ill man's own words: "The
conversation at first turned on old times and recollections. It
gradually slid into religious discourse, when I found as I expected that he had not realized the enormous distance at which
I had left behind the standpoint of 1845. . . . I was in great
embarrassment as to how to express myself. Newman did not
of course attempt the vulgar arts of conversion, nor was there
anything like clerical cant, or affectation of unction like a par-
son's talk by a death-bed. He dwelt upon his own personal
experiences since he had been reconciled to the Church, the
secret comfort and support which had been given him in the way
of supernatural grace under many great trials, that he had never
been deserted by such help for a moment, that his soul had
found sweet peace and rest in the bosom of the Church. Then we
got for a moment, but only for a moment, on more controversial
matter. Here he had nothing to say, but the old argument of the
Apologia. . . . We very soon changed the conversation." [33]

Of course it is impossible to ascertain Newman's motives definitely.
Nevertheless, the conceptual differences I have considered would be
extremely difficult to isolate with any precision. Part of the kindness
of his action derives from the special relation once shared which
consisted of friendship, connected roles, and common interests and
commitments. Likewise, some of the regard expressed would apply
in any relation. The significance of the action requires incorporation
of all such features.

As soon as one assumes that equal regard includes an active concern
about states of others, clearly it does apply to social as well as to
personal relations. As I noted earlier, if the neighbor includes anyone

33. Ibid., p. 322.

affected by my actions, then the welfare of many whom I may never meet directly will still have to be weighed and may be overriding. It seems also apparent that equal regard leads to attempts to minimize conflict and to foster cooperativeness and community. Thus there is compatibility and overlap between such regard and social cooperativeness.

Yet certain advantages accrue, I think, if equal regard rather than social cooperativeness remains as the most central feature of agape. To begin with, equal regard has built into it more substantive moves typically held to be part of agape than does social cooperativeness. For example, there is a radically equalitarian element in agape which the proponents of cooperativeness often doubtless assume but which does not so self-evidently follow from the principle considered in itself. At least it would seem that members of a community may cooperate in a variety of ways without strictly requiring the affirmation that one member's well-being is as valuable as another's. Moreover, the permanent stability usually taken to characterize agape, even in the face of conflict and perhaps the lack of any reciprocity, is caught more obviously by equal regard. There is, for instance, the persistence of regard despite obstacles, and an unwillingness to break a relation entirely even at the cost of, for example, forgiveness in a situation of injury. Once again, no necessary incompatibility or disagreement in fact need obtain. The issue is one of conceptual adequacy to the most recurrent usage.

Self-Love

The value judgments of self-love distinguished in chapter 2 may now be examined further, and compared more specifically with agape as other-regard.

To a great extent, disputes center on the strength and permanence of natural self-assertion. Theologians such as Nygren who offer an account which looks like a version of psychological egoism rarely if ever consider the extensive discussion of that doctrine by philosophers. This is regrettable, because certain stock objections have seemed to many of them conclusive. I shall not rehearse all of these objections now, but suggest the general line often taken. "The question is not whether egoism is strong in human nature but whether we ever have any concern or desire for the welfare of others except as a means to our own, any concern for or interest in their welfare for its own sake, which is not derived from our concern for our own welfare." [34] Clearly many people believe that their acts of service and sacrifice and similar acts of others are not solely and always for the sake of their own private ends. The burden of proof is on the proponent of psychological egoism to explain how all of these people are mistaken all of the time. In so doing, he need not claim that people always *behave* acquisitively, but only that no matter how other-regarding their behavior, the controlling *desire* remains acquisitive. In the face of the many counterexamples of other-regard predictably cited, this claim has generally retreated into an unverifiable and a priori characterization of human motives.

Consider the following counterexample. A man is walking home late at night. As he crosses a bridge he hears someone below him in the water call for help. There is no one else nearby and he is a strong swimmer. He jumps in, rescues the person, performs artificial respiration, tries to bandage some cuts, and manages to secure professional medical aid. He learns with satisfaction that the person will live. It may be that he is predominantly concerned about the recognition he will get from the person rescued or the community, or about some other private aim. But surely it seems that some people in such a situation would be predominantly concerned about the welfare of the other person for his own sake.

Even a single case such as this suggests two of the points most frequently made against psychological egoism. First, one must not confuse the object of the man's desire with the satisfaction he gets when the object is realized. His governing aim is the other person's life and not his own satisfaction. He may be so constituted that satisfaction follows, but that is another matter. Second, that men do sometimes wish each other well and act cooperatively toward one another is indicated by our having concepts like healing and instructing. One may question whether the concepts would be there if people did not often have the aims and actually follow them.

34. Frankena, *Ethics*, p. 19.

Such points have convinced many that the case for psychological egoism is less than compelling on general experiential grounds. Distinctively theological points have also been introduced both for and against. For example, to say with Barth that the "secret of humanity" is the primordial bond between men, receiving and rendering assistance, and so on, involves a different view of "unchangeable human nature" than that of the psychological egoist. Acquisitive eros effectively governs all of the actions of particular men but not all of the actions of all men. It is a matter of personal history and not of a property of human nature.

Suppose one agrees that for a variety of reasons the case for psychological egoism seems less than compelling. I think that another claim is sometimes confused with psychological egoism and that this second claim, when identified in its own right, is much more often found in the literature and supportable by more unambiguous psychological evidence. The claim is that in any love-relation some self-love is *unavoidable* as a matter of psychological fact. The claim is to be distinguished from psychological egoism as follows. It is one thing to say that some self-love is unavoidable, another that it alone is always determinative. It is one thing to say that the agent is unable to love others without loving himself, another that loving them is simply a way of loving himself.[35]

In considering mutual love relations earlier, I noted that one condition was each person's regard for his own integrity, his endeavor to maintain his own considered insights and commitments. The unavoidable element of self-love I now have in mind is sometimes not identified with such a clear and reflective consciousness of one's total identity. It has minimally to do with a certain unreflective and vital energy which the agent brings. It might be called sexual eros or epithymia. Tillich calls it "the normal drive towards vital self-fulfilment."[36] He contends that it is inevitably present in every love-relation and that "Puritans" are wrong in being incurably suspicious of it. One might formally regard it as part of the spontaneous self-love which is not blameworthy but not particularly praiseworthy,

35. Cf. Irving Singer, *Nature of Love*, pp. 91–114.
36. Tillich, *Love, Power, and Justice*, p. 30.

taking care, however, not to miss the positive importance attached to it by those like Tillich. It is pervasive in the sense that it contributes to the "timbre" of all love-relations.[37] Tillich does admit that it easily falls under the sway of the "pleasure principle" where the other person is used as a means to self-fulfilment. Natural vitality easily becomes inordinate and destructive. Agape ought to remain the controlling criterion for epithymia, so as to guard the integrity of the other person against violation and abuse. Nevertheless, no love-relation is ever devoid of epithymia: love would be impoverished without it.

Sometimes in addition the claim does involve a clear consciousness and affirmation of one's total identity. Here one approaches the condition of self-regard in *mutual* love relations. But the stress now is more on the natural, psychological capacity for entering into any love-relation, requited or otherwise. It is simply the case, some have argued, that in order to be able to love the neighbor for his own sake, the agent must attain and maintain a certain level of self-love. The psychological egoist wrongly assumes that the more one loves himself for his own sake the less he can love others for theirs. But he fails to perceive the de facto conjunction between the two. Those who actually love their neighbors will be found on examination always to love themselves as well.[38] This kind of self-love is expansive, rather than restrictive. Whether anything like enough empirical evidence can be marshalled to support this claim is a question I cannot consider here. The claim is very like the position of coincidence previously discussed — as Johann says, "a man must apprehend and be present to himself in his uniqueness if he is to cherish another."[39] This statement, however, does not clarify the sense in which self-love is said to be unavoidable. Sometimes the coincidence

---

37. See also Maclagan, "Respect for Persons as a Moral Principle — I," p. 213.

38. "Love of others and love of ourselves are not alternatives. On the contrary, an attitude of love toward themselves will be found in all those who are capable of loving others. *Love, in principle, is indivisible as far as the connection between 'objects' and one's own self is concerned*" (Erich Fromm, *The Art of Loving* [New York: Harper and Row, 1962], p. 59. See also Fromm, *Man for Himself* [New York: Rinehart and Company, 1947], pp. 119–41).

39. Johann, *The Meaning of Love*, pp. 31–32.

is left at that. A man is unable to love others unless he loves himself; but also and of equal importance, a man pursues a trivial and self-defeating policy when he remains in solitude. At other times the coincidence contains only one kind of internal sequence: in order to love another, a man must *first* love himself. Self-love is then unavoidable in that neighbor-love is really derivative from it. In any event, the claim I have considered should be kept separate from the debate about psychological egoism, except perhaps as a cogent alternative. And unlike psychological egoism, it is an alternative which the agapist could accept without inconsistency.

In chapter 2 I turned to another value-judgment of self-love, where a man first loves himself. But this state of affairs is not very positively valued. In Barth's words, "God will never think of blowing on this fire, which is bright enough already." The most one should say is that self-love properly serves as the paradigm of the wishes of others in the sense of the golden rule. And it is the connection between the golden rule and neighbor love that I want especially to explore. But I shall defer doing so until I have considered further the relation of love and justice. As was pointed out in chapter 3, one wide conception of justice is virtually equated with the formal requirement of reason, and frequently linked to golden rule arguments and the requirement of universalizability.

A final way of relating self-love and neighbor-love is that which I previously termed coincidence. Here self-love is a manifest obligation, yet its enlightened pursuit is never an alternative to neighbor-love, being rather correlative with it. This is the case in terms of a temporal long run. The possibility of basic conflicts of interests appears simply to be ruled out, perhaps by definitional fiat — a plausible supposition, considering that some of the most apparent cases of conflict of interests (which might throw doubt on any assumption of an operative harmony finally universal) are usually ignored. What shall one say, for example, of those who decide that seeking the welfare of others must involve them in courses of action which could end in martyrdom? Do the Martin Luther Kings always have it both ways? Are the forces of evil, if you like, that quiescent in this life? And what of the countless less conspicuous cases such as the woman who quietly suppresses many of her own private aspirations for the sake of holding her family together? To agree that she may be sacrificing too much is not to deny that legitimate interests sometimes unavoidably clash and cannot always be harmonized away. She may simply endure because to realize her own aspirations as fully as she would like would involve too much suffering on the part of those who depend upon her.

Moreover, the claim that self-regard and other-regard are not alternative options may be understood in at least two different senses. The first and perhaps most common is that the agent's own private interests will be realized after all if he pursues a life of other-regard. These interests are usually understood as healthy self-integration, personal identity and centeredness, and similar versions of self-realization. A second sense involves the belief that the objectives of a life of agape here and now are never altogether frustrated or rendered wholly pointless. Here the possibility of unavoidable clashes of interests in a wide number of cases need not be formally denied. But even the potential martyr may argue that whatever may happen to him, the objectives of agape (for instance, an increasingly nonviolent community) may still be furthered. The religious believer often holds that the tides of human history will not prove finally unsupportive of the life of agape, for such a life is congruent with the character of providential action. And that for him is enough. He does not look for private benefits in addition. He may even hold that the life of love defines what should count as personal benefits. One does not characterize these benefits by virtue of some prospective state established as desirable by independent or non-agapeistic criteria. Whatever the effect on or response from others, or the extent of material loss and personal cost to the agent, the life of love will come to be experienced by its exemplars as its own reward.

There is I think a third sense in which self-regard and other-regard may be held not to be alternative options. It is consistent with the views of D'Arcy and others, though he would not think of it in these terms. It has to do with reasons for valuing the self which are identical with those for valuing others. It is largely independent of the question concerning the prospect of coincidence when based on a temporal long run. While there may be conflicts of interest in many circumstances, valuing the self as well as others remains a manifest obligation. One might adopt as a formal contention the utilitarian formula that each person ought to count himself as one but no more than one and ought never to accord himself a privileged position. In any event, reasons include a psychological estimate of the strength and permanence of natural self-assertion. As I noted, D'Arcy and others maintain that there are roughly equivalent dangers of excessive self-giving and self-assertion.[40] Another reason is more strictly theological. Here, as we have seen, even Kierkegaard and Barth may be of several minds, depending on the context. At least the agent ought to value providential guidance in his own life, and not allow idiosyncratic achievements and failures to deter him, or be taken as a condition for receiving grace. This valuation may appropriately dispose him to value his own history as one for which there is no identical replacement. And in chapter 1, as a third possible reason against the issuing of a blank check, I cited the contention that just as the neighbor ought to be regarded as a human being prior to a particular human being, so the agent ought to value himself in the same way. The agent's basic self-regard, then, ought not to be simply dependent on the number of his achievements or the extent to which he is found likeable, but on his being as well a man of flesh and blood and a creature of God, a person who is more than a means to some other end.

Agape and a Wide Conception of Justice

In chapter 3 I argued that many discussions of "love and justice" would be more illuminating if greater pains were taken to distinguish

---

40. The possible corruptions of ostensible unselfishness, for instance, are stressed by D'Arcy. Note also the following passage from F. M. Forster's *The Longest Journey*:

"I never knew a woman who was so unselfish and yet had such capacities for life."

"Does one generally exclude the other?" asked Rickie.

"Unselfish people, as a rule, are deathly dull. They have no colour. They think of other people because it is easier. They give money because they are too stupid or too idle to spend it properly on themselves. That was the beauty of your mother — she gave away, but she also spent on herself, or tried to."

some of the various senses of justice as well as of love. One could then proceed to consider the different sorts of possible relations, as I did briefly at the end of that chapter. I propose now to discuss in more detail two possible relations: that between agape and a wide conception of justice; and, among narrower conceptions of justice, that between agape and that egalitarian notion with which there is the largest material overlap.

I shall first consider a wide conception of justice frequently linked to golden rule arguments and the requirement of universalizability.[41] In chapter 4 I said that universalizability requires that in a particular situation of moral choice one logically commits himself or someone else to making the same judgment in any other situation which is similar in the morally relevant respects. The agent must be willing to apply the same general standard of treatment to others as he wishes to see applied to himself, and regardless of whether he is on the giving or the receiving end of such treatment (the condition sometimes called reversibility). Moral judgments must have "general application" or at least must be capable of being made generally applicable. That is, one must be able to disregard any reference to particular individuals and leave intact the substance of the moral judgment. One's answer to the question, "Why do you think that action is right?" can never be, "Just because *I* do it" or "Just because *he* does it." One must be willing to see any normative principle adopted applied to anyone who performs or benefits from an action falling under it. General application requires coherence and consistency.

While the issues relating to universalizability are complex and ones on which by and large I do not wish to pronounce, one may identify two senses in which agape is often taken to differ from a wide conception of justice linked to golden rule arguments and universalizability. First, as often interpreted, such a wide conception of justice may provide logical room for principles of substance other

41. Justice is also often taken as the traditional name for the following dictum: what is right for one person must be right for any similar person in similar circumstances. See Marcus George Singer, *Generalization in Ethics* (New York: Alfred A. Knopf, 1961), e.g., p. 46; Alan Gewirth, "The Generalization Principle," *The Philosophical Review* 73 (April, 1964):229–42.

than agape and not easily reconcilable with it. Some have argued
that the quasi-Nietzschean principle roughly analogous to survival-of-
the-fittest, for example, may conform to the golden rule.

An obvious example of an alternative to the principle of benevolence is the attitude of one who believes, in a quasi-Nietzschean
manner, in the effectiveness of competition and strife in producing
the more valuable human qualities, which he takes to consist in
strength, independence and the like. If this man concedes that
the excellence of others is of equal importance with his own,
and is prepared to allow that others may do to him what he
believes he may do to them, then his outlook is a moral outlook,
conforms to the golden rule, and is an alternative to the principle of benevolence. For he may well not at all concede that
it is his business actively to concern himself either with gratifying
the desires or even with furthering the excellence of others.[42]

If this is correct, then the universalizability test is no guarantee that
other peoples' interests ought to be actively promoted, their needs
assessed with care and met with diligence, regard for them upheld
despite obstacles. The positive furtherance of other peoples' interests
enjoined by agape exceeds what a quasi-Nietzschean would suppose
himself constrained to undertake. Yet even if one agrees with the
above, it still must be stressed that the golden rule, as commonly
understood, and agape have a very large field in common. For the
position of the quasi-Nietzschean is sometimes held to be logically
acceptable but practically unacceptable. The quasi-Nietzschean finds
in practice that the golden rule requires him to attend to the
interests of others in ways which restrict his freedom to maneuver
considerably. Universalizability effectively narrows the range of morally permitted disagreements, and in an other-regarding direction.
An egoistic, "anything goes" policy is held not to be a moral policy.
Agreements can perhaps be reached of a basic, minimal kind.

A second, further way of locating a difference concerns what

---

42. I. M. Crombie, "Moral Principles," *Christian Ethics and Contemporary
Philosophy*, pp. 241–42. Cf. Warnock, *Contemporary Moral Philosophy*, p. 45.

might be called agent-stringency. I just alluded to the basic and
minimal agreements which golden rule arguments are often said to
generate. Sometimes these arguments are identified as "the rock-
bottom duties that are duties for all and from every point of view,
and to which anyone may call attention." [43] They refer to duties such
as truth-telling and promise-keeping, the non-performance of which
is a fit subject of reproach from others; they often have to do with
what people owe one another, or what is calculated to be mutually
advantageous, or what makes community life tolerable. A distinction
is traditionally drawn between duties of this kind and actions called
works of supererogation. The non-performance of the latter sort of
action is not a fit subject for reproach from others, but the performance may nonetheless be judged by others to be extremely
laudable. Consider the case of a soldier who falls on a live hand
grenade in order to protect his comrades with his own body.[44]
Clearly most people would judge this to be a laudable action. But it
would be odd to reproach someone who did not fall on the hand
grenade for having failed in his duty, or for a superior to order
him to fall on it.

For many, to live the agapeistic way of life is to go the second
mile in respect to supererogation as well as the first mile in respect
to duties. And two things should be especially noticed here. First,
the agent need not apply the distinction to his own actions. Indeed,
he has authority for saying that he should regard himself as an
unprofitable servant after going the second mile as well as the first.
And he may find references to "stringency" or "higher duty" ill-suited
to convey his devotion to the other for the other's own sake. He
may also sense that he is led to such actions by grace and not by
his own resolve; his operations may appear spontaneous and joyous.

43. J. O. Urmson, "Saints and Heroes," *Essays in Moral Philosophy,* ed.
A. I. Melden (Seattle: University of Washington Press, 1958), p. 204. Cf. Joel
Feinberg, "Supererogation and Rules," *International Journal of Ethics* 71 (1961):
276–88; Roderick M. Chisholm, "Supererogation and Offence: A Conceptual
Scheme for Ethics," *Ratio* 5 (1963):1–14. These last two articles are reprinted
in Judith J. Thomson and Gerald Dworkin, eds., *Ethics* (New York: Harper and
Row, 1968), pp. 391–429, and subsequent references will be to that volume.
44. Urmson, "Saints and Heroes," pp. 202–03.

Yet in various instances a distinction may still be drawn along roughly the following lines.[45]

While he may *exhort* others to go the second mile, he cannot *reproach* them for not attempting it as he can when they do not go the first. This is a point at which agape is genuinely radical so far as the agent is concerned. He is exhorted to be devoted to others in ways approaching supererogation and not only in ways involving duties. If one wishes generally to assign works of supererogation to the realm of optional "ideals," which by definition do not necessarily affect other peoples' interests, then there may be something slightly paradoxical in the agapeistic ideal. For if the essence of any ideal involves expressing one's own vision of human excellence, to realize the agapeistic ideal one must be the sort of person who furthers the interests of others. A man may be intelligibly harder on himself than on his neighbors when in so doing he positively contributes to their welfare. In any event, in performing actions which go beyond what the agent may properly require of others and yet which benefit them, the actions in question need not contradict the golden rule as commonly understood, but instead may add to it. For the golden rule primarily condemns those actions which involve the agent's claiming some special privilege without good reason.[46] But in the case of agape, the standards applicable to everyone, including the agent, are accepted, and then are supplemented by a more rigorous standard for himself.

Second, it can be argued that such supplementation is one thing which clearly sets apart agape as neighbor-love. Then one must be clear about what is being compared or contrasted with it. And at this point some of the literature tends to conflate (1) the unexacting standard of perhaps the conventional man, where the letter (if that) rather than the spirit of justice is maintained, where duty is never far removed from advantage, giving and getting has to be propor-

---

45. One need not insist that the distinction between supererogation and duties is always clear or easily applied. For example, an action such as the one discussed earlier where a man jumps in to save someone who is drowning, with no one else nearby and the rescuer a strong swimmer, might fall somewhere between supererogation and duty.

46. M. G. Singer, "The Golden Rule," p. 303.

tional, backs mutually scratched, etc., and (2) in-principled psychological egoism.[47] When Jesus asks about the goodness of loving only those who love you, it seems clear that he regards (1) as inadequate, but not that he necessarily asserts (2). At least (2) is a second step not self-evidently following from (1). For in the case of (1), there may be some willingness to act cooperatively, some limited capacity for fellow-feeling, and so on, but where actions benefitting others are always hedged about by conditions for returns, and there are only safe bets and small risks. Agape then differs in degree and severity.

I have proceeded rapidly over some difficult territory. I propose to return to examine several points further, while admitting beforehand that all I can do here is signal them. I do not claim to offer extensively argued resolutions of the issues I shall identify. But the issues are important in themselves and too often neglected.

Within historical theological treatments, the distinction between duties and works of supererogation appears often to arise in two principal contexts. The first concerns a definition of supererogation as any act which goes beyond what God commands for salvation and which confers extra merit on the performer. When such desert is tied to a doctrine of indulgences, one sometimes finds the claim that various superabundant merits of Christ and the saints constitute a kind of spiritual treasury which may be dispensed to those who lack what is minimally required for salvation. Various well-known objections have been lodged against this concept of supererogation by parties both inside and outside Roman Catholicism. To imply that works of supererogation can be oversubscriptions of basic human worth by some which compensate for undersubscriptions by others seems to many bizarre and misleading.[48] Whether such objections reflect a correct interpretation of the doctrine (or at least certain constructions of it) is a question which may be bypassed now. A second context has to do with the Catholic distinction between commands which bind and counsels which invite. Duty is the object of a command; fulfillment is an *opus debitum* and nonfulfillment

---

47. Kierkegaard, for example, seems to run these together: *Works of Love,* pp. 65–66.
48. See for example Feinberg, "Supererogation and Rules," pp. 407–09.

is a sin. To invite or suggest rather than to oblige distinguishes counsel from command. Fulfillment is a work of supererogation and nonfulfillment a "positive imperfection." Presumably, for our purposes, an agent *may* will his own disadvantage, though he need not — he may without fault fail to go the extra mile. The decision rests with the one exhorted. Some Roman Catholics have recently expressed dissatisfaction with the distinction between command and counsel, particularly with reference to the evangelical counsels such as poverty, chastity, and obedience which define religious orders within the visible church. Questions have been raised, for example, about the scriptural justification for such counsels.[49]

Whatever criticisms may be brought specifically to bear within either of these contexts, discussions of the distinction between duty and supererogation in theological literature have served to instill or at least to foster the concept in our ordinary thinking. And the distinction helps to make intelligible what I have called agent-stringency. One need not conceive of supererogation as always a kind of oversubscription, especially not in a crude sense of accumulating extra bonuses to compensate for moral slackness or spiritual deficiency in oneself or others. But the concept of supererogation can allow for certain complexities in the moral life which the typical notion of duty fails to include. For a variety of laudable attitudes and actions seem not strictly to be duties, i.e., are not what is normally involved when one adheres to contracts, complies with job-specifications and role-definitions, and fulfills special promises. Sometimes one may wish to say that a given action is permitted rather than required. One regards a rebuke for its non-performance as inappropriate. Yet its performance is far from being morally indifferent when it enhances significantly the welfare of others. Such an action may be spontaneous and uncoerced; it goes beyond or is simply other than behavior dictated by obligatory formulas and authoritative sanctions.

49. See for instance John W. Glaser, S.J., "Commands-Counsels: Pauline Teaching?" *Theological Studies* 31 (June, 1970):275–87. For an incisive discussion of the religious orders, see Karl Rahner, S.J., "The Theology of the Religious Life," *Religious Orders in the Modern World* (London: Geoffrey Chapman, 1965), pp. 41–75.

Are supererogation (in the general sense above) and agent-stringency always allowed by a wide conception of justice? Suppose one agrees that justice also makes logical room for alternative normative principles which are less risky and (so far as agape is concerned) less laudable. Is it still wholly adequate to say that the agapist can in every case accept the standards applicable to everyone and go on to supplement these by a more rigorous other-regarding standard for himself? Are there instances where justice is not only supplemented but contravened? I shall consider two possible replies. In the first, the standards of justice include impartiality and being able to adopt a third party point of view or spectator-stance. Here certain upper limits may be set to agent-stringency, or else justice is not only supplemented but may in some cases be contravened. In the second, justice requires simple consistency, and allows for impersonally specified differences between agent and spectator. Here no upper limits may be set, though perhaps at the price of making the notion of justice seem almost vacuous.

In some versions of justice a consistent and thoroughgoing impartiality is enjoined. In the following statement by John Stuart Mill the golden rule and the second great commandment are closely linked to support the requirement that, in weighing his concern for his own welfare against his concern for that of others, the agent is required to be as strictly impartial as a disinterested and benevolent spectator.

> I must again repeat what the assailants of utilitarianism seldom have the justice to acknowledge, that the happiness which forms the utilitarian standard of what is right in conduct is not the agent's own happiness but that of all concerned. As between his own happiness and that of others, utilitarianism requires him to be as strictly impartial as a disinterested and benevolent spectator. In the golden rule of Jesus of Nazareth, we read the complete spirit of the ethics of utility. To do as you would be done by, and to love your neighbor as yourself, constitute the ideal perfection of utilitarian morality.[50]

50. John Stuart Mill, *Utilitarianism*, in *Mill's Ethical Writings*, ed. J. B. Schneewind (New York: Collier Books, 1965), pp. 291–92.

To adopt an impartial spectator-standpoint seemed to Mill and others to involve a denial that one was directly obliged to promote the happiness of other persons *as such* or the happiness of oneself *as such*. What one was obliged to do was to maximize the happiness of all, consistently and impartially. Hence a cardinal feature of utilitarianism has traditionally been that each man should be valued no more — but also no less — than any other, so that the agent is morally entitled to take his own interests into account. This obviously does not mean that in situation X the agent ought to weigh his own interests as equal to the sum total of the interests of everyone else affected. Rather, one may state the obligation in terms of a different interpretation of the second great commandment from the one considered earlier. "You shall love your neighbor as yourself" does not mean "You shall love him as you *now* love yourself," but instead, you ought to count yourself as one but no more than one, and never accord yourself a privileged position.

Utilitarianism is something of an umbrella term nowadays, and some of its well-known problems may be passed over here, e.g., whether happiness can ever be an entirely empirical concept, whether the egoistic theory of human motivation of at least part of classical utilitarianism is compatible with being an impartial spectator as between the agent's own happiness and that of others, or whether the rightness or wrongness of an action can be determined *solely* by its consequences. The question of whether the agent is morally entitled to take his own interests into account may be distinguished from these problems, and bears on a requirement that moral judgments must allow the agent to adopt an impartial third-person point of view, applicable to everyone's actions, including his own. In estimating how the balance of advantage is likely to go, the agent cannot arbitrarily exclude himself. He must count each person involved as one, including himself.

Clearly the demand for impartiality will pose a problem for someone who arbitrarily prefers his own interests to those of others, who is unwilling to apply the same standard to an action, regardless of whether he or someone else performs it. And this is perfectly cogent, especially if one assumes that without special prodding each man generally is more inclined to pursue his own interests than the interests of others. To this extent, the concepts of impartiality and neighbor-love do not diverge. But impartiality might likewise cut the other way. Suppose that the agent has to decide between an appreciable sacrifice of his own (legitimate) interests and a much more marginal though still genuine sacrifice of the interests of another, and further, that taking into account the multilateral interests of affected third parties does not decisively alter the character of the choice. What should one say then? Suppose further that if the agent were to assess another case of this sort between two other parties, he would judge that the lesser sacrifice of interests is preferable. The only difference in the former case is that he, as a particular individual, is involved. And this difference is precisely what is disallowed.

It would still be open to someone who agreed with this application of impartiality to hold that other-regard is the soundest and most urgent *practical counsel* because people are typically inclined to neglect it. One might contend, in Aristotelian fashion, that the mean of moral virtue should be sought by "leaning against" the defect or excess to which men are particularly disposed. The sting in the commandment remains directed against an uncritical intensification of natural self-assertion. In general a varying ratio obtains between the extent to which self-regard is taken to be spontaneous, and quickly excessive, and the extent to which it is a subject of moral concern. Moreover, anyone who takes at all seriously the historic doctrines concerning sin and moral evil will always treat with skepticism the agent's ability to be an impartial and benevolent spectator in cases where his own interests are at stake. Hence he may be legitimately disposed to give another the preference in situations where interests appear to him roughly balanced, to lean against his extraordinary resourcefulness at self-deception on his own behalf.

Such a policy of practical attrition against the application of impartiality to self-benefitting actions might be justifiably extended to a considerable degree. In the case of the woman tied to a demanding parent, one might urge her to break away only if one could plausibly contend that the weight of advantage *for all* is likely to be greater if she does than if she does not. So she might argue, for example, that finally it is good to teach parents not to be indifferent to the happiness of their children; and it is good for her to go her own way. In order then for her self-benefitting action to be morally right she ought to be able to appeal to other-regarding considerations and take her own welfare into account insofar as it is part of the general welfare. Despite all such practical attrition, however, she is prevented from saying that other-regarding considerations must be *exhaustive,* that her conclusions do not apply to her own case. For when she disregards the fact that it is she or Sarah or Joan who breaks away, she concludes that *anyone* ought to break away in these circumstances. Then if she makes an exception in her own case she is arbitrarily excluding herself in estimating how the balance of advantage is likely to go, something which impartiality forbids her to do.[51]

The reply then comes to this. To supplement the standards applicable to everyone with a more rigorous standard for the agent cannot mean that the agent is at liberty to disregard his own interests altogether. Whatever other-regarding actions are enjoined must not prevent his adoption of a spectator-standpoint. Otherwise the agent in effect cannot adhere to the standards applicable to everyone. In this way justice may have a limiting effect on agape qua radical other-regard. Justice may not only rule out the familiar move to the side of one's own interests. It may also rule out the less familiar move too far to the side of another's interests. Both involve a claim to arbitrary privilege and a failure to count each individual as one and no more than one. A consistent and thoroughgoing impartiality sets a limit in either direction for the sake of maximizing benefits to all. Such maximization is the criterion for any moral justification for provisional or tactical discrepancies.

For some versions of agapism, the above would not of course constitute an objection at all, but a clarification of what agape enjoins.

51. To say that an agent is entitled to take account of his own interests in this way is not of course to say that he must be strictly impartial concerning the actions received and given. That is, impartiality does not commit him to a kind of *lex talionis* doctrine of an eye for an eye and a tooth for a tooth. For example, it could hardly be to the advantage of all for the agent or anyone else attacked by a would-be killer to repay his assailant in kind, if a less violent and harmful means of defense were available.

One such version I mentioned at the end of a discussion of the position I have called coincidence. There may be reasons, both psychological and theological, for valuing the self which are identical with those for valuing others. Some agent-stringency could still supplement justice where justice is seen to allow the unexacting standards of perhaps the conventional man, who insists that giving and getting have to be proportional and duty never far removed from personal advantage. To urge the second mile may often constitute practical counsel toward equalizing the advantage for all in a world overburdened by moral blandness and patent immorality.

However, it may be possible to devise a reply to the objection on behalf of that version of agapism which holds that self-benefitting actions have to be justified in their entirety by derivation from other-regard. Whether or not one finds this reply convincing in every respect, it will indicate further the complexity of the considerations at stake.

A second reply, then, might contend generally for some relevant differences between agent and spectator. Such differences may all be impersonally specified in that they refer to any agent or any spectator; in this minimal sense, at least, to acknowledge them does not prevent one from adopting a third party standpoint or passing the universalizability test. The differences may be linked to the distinction between those ordinary duties which someone may blame others for not performing, and those actions the non-performance of which does not warrant such reproach, though their performance may be extremely laudable.

In the first place, so the reply might go, one must distinguish between generalization in the sense of legislation for *everyone* and universalizability in the sense of *anyone* so circumstanced. In some instances, as perhaps in the case of self-sacrifice, it seems legitimate to query a principle because the conclusions to which it leads are unacceptable and absurd if everyone followed it on all occasions. Yet as I noted in chapter 4, moral judgments can be universalizable without always requiring the agent to ask: what would happen if *everyone* did this? There can be personal and non-societal (though still universalizable) as well as societal rules. In some instances the agent ought consciously to refrain from legislating for everyone.

To press for the blanket adoption of certain personal judgments may sometimes seem a form of moral arrogance. No arbitrariness need be involved, if one assumes that the basic state of affairs holds for any agent. One might then go on to argue that there are morally relevant differences between the judgment the agent makes about two other parties, where impartiality is in place, and the judgment he makes in his private capacity on an issue affecting his own interests and another's. The differences may sometimes be a matter of knowledge. In his private capacity the agent may be struck by morally relevant features in certain situations so unusual that in his experience they seem repeatable largely in principle. Consequently he may think it hazardous or even presumptuous to prescribe his course of action to others. But, a more germane consideration at the moment, these differences also reflect the right of each agent qua agent to participate voluntarily and purposively in a range of alternatives exceeding what he can appropriately require of others, or blame others for not performing. This same right ought to be honored in the case of each agent. An agent may for example reproach himself for not forgiving another in certain terms that differ from those he would use in demanding that another party forgive a third. One way, then, in which agape goes beyond a wide conception of justice is that the agent may reproach others for not acting justly but may not so reproach them for not acting agapeistically.

Let us return to the woman tied to a demanding parent. Suppose we say that she has to decide between an appreciable sacrifice of her own legitimate interests and a more marginal though still legitimate sacrifice of the interests of her parent. Suppose too that if she were to assess another case of this sort between two other parties, she would judge that the lesser sacrifice of interests is preferable. We need not conclude from this, someone making this reply might argue, that the only difference between the two cases is that she, as a particular individual, is involved, a difference which in itself can be admittedly disallowed. In assessing the case between the two other parties, she may assume, as with the two men who desire to drink the water and reach civilization, that both are pressing to have their own interests fully respected. At least she may not see herself as entitled to reproach them when they exert such pressure. She may still hold that to adhere to radical other-regard in her case requires her to stay with her parent. If so, it seems plausible to maintain that one may disregard the fact that it is she as a particular individual who goes the second mile. Anyone who holds the beliefs and ideals she does should in certain circumstances act in a way that ordinary canons of justice cannot be strictly required of everyone. Naturally her application of radical other-regard might be disputed. Again, if she broke away to become a medical doctor, one could appeal to the likely multilateral interests of affected third parties which might override explicit commitments to others, especially to a single other. But to disagree in this way about application is not necessarily to deny that the moral principle appealed to is an exclusively other-regarding one.

Someone who offered such a reply, and argued that self-benefitting actions are morally justified only when derived from other-regard, would maintain that his position does not contravene justice in the sense of universalizability. He might argue that it is a moral decision rather than a logical conclusion to say that the agent has an obligation, independent of the possibility of benefit to others, to take his own interests into account.

Which of these two replies (or any others) one takes to be decisive depends then in part on one's view of what constitutes a wide conception of justice. I think in any case that the substantive psychological and theological grounds adduced earlier for valuing the self are very compelling, and that self-benefitting actions need not be exhaustively (even if principally) justified from other-regard. This is a question which I cannot pursue further here. I wish finally to underscore one major reason which I think accounts for the traditional distinction between duties and works of supererogation. In certain moral schemes, of course, no room is provided for counsels which suggest as well as obligations which bind. Some strict utilitarians, for instance, seem to hold that *any* action is either obligatory or forbidden, depending on whether the action in question contributes to the greatest happiness of the greatest number.[52] But where the distinction appears, it seems often to be tied to an assumption about morally relevant differences between the agent's relation to himself

52. Chisholm, "Supererogation and Offence . . . ," p. 427.

and to anyone else. Those differences again make agent-stringency more intelligible, even if one agrees that certain upper limits must be set to it.

In the theological literature before us, consider for example the misgivings which sometimes exist about the very phrase "self-love." Tillich, like Barth, thinks that "within the unity of self-consciousness there is no real separation, comparable to the self-separation of a self-centered being from all other beings." [53] One consequence is that I may hold myself responsible for what I do in a way which differs from what I can fittingly do for another. I cannot always seek to do for others what I can and ought to do for myself. I ought to further my neighbor's happiness, but I ought not to choose his way of life for him. [54] Yet I do regard my way of life as meaningfully *mine*, something for which I am directly accountable. This is so even when the believer sees his particular way of life as a calling from God and not his arbitrary creation. For however indebted he may be to other persons, or they to him, obedience or disobedience remains finally his alone.

I shall try now to summarize why the agent may fittingly on various occasions be more latitudinarian with others than with himself. There are, first of all, epistemological grounds. In his own case

53. Tillich, *Love, Power, and Justice*, p. 33. Cf. Ross, *The Right and the Good*, p. 168: "The desire to produce an indifferent pleasure for another is good, and the desire to produce it for oneself is indifferent. That this is what we really think seems perfectly clear. And it is not really paradoxical. For though the pleasure will be similar whether it is enjoyed by the agent or another, the desire for pleasure for oneself is quite a different thing from the desire to produce it for another, since one's relation to oneself is entirely different from one's relation to any other person."

54. "It is contradictory to say that I make another person's *perfection* my end and consider myself obligated to promote this. For the *perfection* of another man, as a person, consists precisely in *his own* power to adopt his end in accordance with his own concept of duty; and it is self-contradictory to demand that I do (make it my duty to do) what only the other person himself can do" (Immanuel Kant, *The Doctrine of Virtue* [Part II of *The Metaphysic of Morals*], trans. Mary J. Gregor [New York: Harper and Row, 1964], pp. 44–45). Whether this passage contradicts Kant's moral philosophy as a whole is a disputed point, however. Cf. Allen W. Wood, *Kant's Moral Religion* (Ithaca, N.Y.; Cornell University Press, 1970), pp. 74–78.

the agent has a wealth of information which is private. He may refuse to intervene in another's case beyond a certain point even when the case seems parallel to his own in the relevant respects. For he is liable to err, and may rightly fear presumption. His counsel will often be restricted in his own mind to the status of advice and exhortation; he will not see the other as obliged to take it. Second, there are considerations of social tactics. Discretion and conventional civility are of course corruptible. But so too the censorious man who insists on always reminding others of their obligations may sometimes offend to no good effect. Explicit rebukes may on occasion create far more disharmony than is warranted by the issues at stake. Third, and most disputably, the agent may think that loving another includes attending to the characteristic of freedom as part of the well-being of each person valued equally. The judgment someone makes about two other parties may be distinguished from his own role in effecting the judgment or enabling it to be carried out. I mentioned earlier that sometimes such attention is taken to mean that one ought to revere the other's moral capacities, to allow for his efforts as well as his ends. To suggest rather than require seems not infrequently an appropriate testimony to the importance of such efforts. Alternatively, the agent reveres his own moral capacities by direct exertion. In a theological context, the believer may also wish to allow for the mystery of personal decision in relation to providential guidance. Epistemologically, the guidance may be concrete and particular for this other man in this time and place, experienceable only to him. And at whatever inner recesses of motivation, each man is himself accountable for any refusal of such guidance.

A final sort of objection to agent-stringency is this. Attention to the agent may neglect the community of faith of which (let us assume) he is a part. Hence it would be preferable to speak of *community-stringency*. Here is perhaps a point at which Barth's insistence on a faith-love correlation might persuasively apply. The distinction between duties and works of supererogation is maintained in the sense that all men may be reproached for the non-performance of duties; but those in the community of believers may be intelligibly harder on themselves and so reproach one another for not going the second mile as well.

This objection is important, but a digressive reference to it will have to suffice here. Certain duties, to which anyone might call attention, were defined as binding for all and from every point of view. Now the way of life which agape enjoins, as I have said, exceeds what a so-called conventional man would urge on the basis of rather unexacting standards, or see himself bound by, or wish to call attention to. Further, the agapist may not only be guided by a more risky normative standard, but may also justify an agapeistic way of life by appealing to distinctive beliefs and special authorities, such as the life and teaching of Jesus, as the moral paradigm. It may make sense for those who locate themselves in a discernible community founded on such belief and authority to exhort and reproach one another concerning the requirements which transcend one's fundamental duties from every point of view. "Anyone so circumstanced" may apply only to them: each agent legislates more stringently for himself and for other agapists. Anyone who lives in accordance with agape ought to behave in a way that ordinary canons of justice cannot strictly require of everyone, and specifically those who do not share the belief or accept the authority involved. But those in the community may think it appropriate to press on one another the claims some of which serve to set the community apart.

The requirements in question can be taken in a broad sense to apply to all members of the community. They need not be confined, that is, to such specific ways of life as the acceptance of poverty, chastity, and obedience.

In addition to such broad community requirements, there may be skepticism about the scope of universal moral agreements; doubts that there *are* very many duties which everyone will accept as binding from any point of view. The community may then be doubly disposed to stress agreements in relation to its own moral vision. Such a scheme furnishes the context in which certain moral conclusions are intelligible and where various actions are subject to distinctive appraisal. So a convert to Roman Catholicism may suddenly find himself under distinctive constraints held to be binding on the entire community. To love God and to love others as himself is now his final action-guide. Yet the community has also applied this action-guide to specific classes of conduct and expressed moral conclusions about them. He ought not to murder; and this prohibition is held to rule out the direct and intentional killing of noncombatants in wartime. Much traditional Roman Catholicism would deny of course that the murder prohibition and related classes of conduct fell outside the scope of plausibly universal moral agreements. But it is arguable that both the first and second mile requirements binding on the faithful, and certain moral conclusions about specific classes of conduct, are most intelligible to those inside the community. Moreover, when human activities such as corporate worship, prayer, and ascetic discipline are defined as part of normative ethics (as noted in chapter 1), then the life of the community involves additional action-guidance which sets it apart. To be a practicing Catholic, a practicing Jew, and so on, includes behavioral particularism not required of everyone, and yet uniformly required of those in the community. Finally, to hold that believers may be harder on one another because they have entered into or elected to stay with a community which accepts certain injunctions may avoid any implication that there can be two classes of the faithful. The dangers of complacency are thereby confronted.

Those who are wary of community-stringency might reply that such a step risks the removal of morally relevant distinctions between the agent's relation to himself and to anyone else. If each believer may be as hard on others as he is on himself, then any area for agent-freedom seems effectively to disappear. Furthermore, perhaps a theological objection might be lodged against the very attempt to locate persons along an "inner-outer" spectrum. Those within the community are neither more nor less accountable than those outside. All men are equally accountable, just as grace is equally accessible to all. Practicing believers are consciously aware that this is the case. They come together to confess the reliance of all men on grace. But they ought not to risk the dangers of superficial moralizing by reproaching some for failure to behave in certain ways. Let the duties required for a tolerable society be defended on publically intelligible grounds, applicable to believer and nonbeliever alike. But let each person within the community exhort others to go the second mile, without reproaching anyone other than himself, inside or outside, for failure.

A decision about community-stringency will likely reflect a range of interlocking beliefs about grace and personal agency, ecclesiology, and the general relation held to obtain between ethical principles like love and justice and religious beliefs and secular morality.

Agape and Equalitarian Justice

It was maintained in chapter 3 that the closer one approaches equalitarian notions of justice, the greater the material overlap with agape. Such notions, in general, include references to what is due men as men apart from, and subject only to subsequent modification by, particular conduct (sometimes employing the language of "natural rights"); and allow for unequal rights only on the same grounds as those which warrant equal rights of other kinds.[55] The latter case would pertain roughly to inequalities such as those mentioned earlier in considering the characteristic of freedom and its differential exercise. I also observed earlier that the agapist is formally at liberty to distinguish between needs and preferences. He may contend that both count in regarding the neighbor's well-being. The point of crucial overlap is that in the case of agape and these notions of justice, one reasons solely from equalitarian premises. If one distinguishes between the neighbor's generic characteristics, one values each of them equally in comparison to the same characteristics in others. Appropriate treatments for a particular recipient may nonetheless differ, depending on the characteristic in question. Equality of welfare may include agapeistic treatments common to everyone, and equality of freedom may lead to unequal treatment.

To contend that agape and equalitarian justice are deeply conjoined in at least part of their extension is not to say that they are interchangeable. Agape is normally taken as a more inclusive standard in that it applies in situations where justice has far less direct relevance. In intimate personal relations like friendship and

55. Vlastos, "Justice and Equality," p. 40.

parenthood the giving and taking need not be measured out very carefully. A nicely calculated more and less is not the dominant criterion. Alternatively, it was observed that the several conceptions of justice are usually understood to be confined to the sort of moral situation in which the parties all regard themselves as representatives of interests which deserve to be considered and are actively pressing them. Agape also refers more directly to the agent's basic loyalties. I mentioned in chapter 1 how many have identified a common self-giving element in devotion to God and the fellow-man for which no word seems quite as suitable as love. But most people would find it far less appropriate to talk of being just toward God.

Without viewing these concepts as interchangeable, then, I will turn now to the deep conjunction between them. To reason solely from equalitarian premises raises common difficulties and exerts common pressures. I shall illustrate the difficulties and pressures in turn.

The nature of the difficulties has already been anticipated. The process of distinguishing between generic characteristics requires that both equal and unequal distribution be justified on equalitarian premises, and allows that there may be conflict in practice. One must contend that under the characteristics of welfare or need, for example, resources are sometimes to be distributed unequally when needs are unequal in order to equalize benefits. And under the characteristic of freedom, one may disperse praise unequally because one of the wants persons share equally is proportionate recognition of acquired ex-cellences. They are at liberty to live and develop in a distinctive way which constitutes part of the well-being to be equally weighed and variously assessed. Further, there is no formal contradiction between diverse attention to different characteristics: "It would be sheer confusion to think that there would be any incompatibility between deciding to distribute praise according to merit and economic goods according to need." [56]

Yet there surely are conflicts in practice. To cite again an earlier case: one may stress the importance of another's need for psycholog-ical stability and security and withhold certain truths from him when one has good reason to suppose they might seriously threaten such

56. Ibid., p. 88.

security. Or alternatively, one may think the other's dignity as a responsible agent involves a policy of non-deception, and it is preferable to risk an unwanted diminution in security (for at least the matter will not be decided for him) than be condescendingly protective. Attention to different characteristics may therefore produce discordant indications. Conflicts may also extend to considerations falling under the same characteristic. When one looks closely at the notion of merit or desert based on freedom, for instance, one may be forced to weigh prize versus reward, gratitude versus recognition, compensation versus reparation.[57]

No theoretical formula, of course, will provide an easy resolution to the perplexities of actual decision-making. And one cannot avoid bringing to bear the wider assumptions about human nature and human good discussed earlier. I have also located certain pressures which agape characteristically exerts.

I said that agape enjoins one to identify with the neighbor's point of view, to try imaginatively to see what it is for him to live the life he does, to occupy the position he holds. Clearly the other's right to assume a point of view different from one's own is also affirmed. And the agent honors his own freedom by not confusing identification with a compulsion to adopt the other's stance, to share his particular likes and dislikes. Such identification is taken nonetheless to imply that some minimal consideration is due each person which is never to be set aside for the sake of personal gratification or long-range social benefits. He is never *merely* a means or instrument. To ignore him completely or treat him as a pure social functionary, for example, is not permitted on any grounds. A further inference often drawn is that, in one's behavior toward another, one should be influenced more by the immediate and reasonably foreseen effects on him than by the more remote and grandiose goals of the society at large. If through no fault of his own an individual ceases to be a public asset, he should still receive equal consideration. And those who believe that his nature and destiny exceeds any political or secular definition

57. See illustrations of these conflicts in the case of a C. P. Snow-like contest between two leading candidates for the mastership of a Cambridge college: Joel Feinberg, *Doing and Deserving* (Princeton: Princeton University Press, 1970), esp. pp. 78–79.

of it — that a political or secular account cannot say all there is to
say, or indeed even the most essential thing — will have especially
powerful reasons to resist a social productiveness criterion of human
worth. One is enjoined to honor from first to last the space he
occupies and the time he has.

Index